EPISTEMOLOGY OF THE CLOSET

Eve Kosofsky Sedgwick

HARVESTER WHEATSHEAF

New York   London   Toronto   Sydney   Tokyo   Singapore

Chapter 4, "The Beast in the Closet," first appeared in
Ruth Bernard Yeazell, ed., *Sex, Politics, and Science in the
Nineteenth-Century Novel*, Selected Papers from the English
Institute. 1983–84. The Johns Hopkins University Press,
Baltimore/London, 1986, pp. 148–86. Reprinted by
permission of the publisher.

First published 1991 by
Harvester Wheatsheaf
66 Wood Lane End, Hemel Hempstead
Hertfordshire HP2 4RG
A division of
Simon & Schuster International Group

British Library Cataloguing in Publication Data

Sedgwick, Eve Kosofsky
  Epistemology of the closet.
  1. Fiction in European languages.   Special subjects: Male homosexuality
  Critical studies
  I. Title
  809.39353

  ISBN 0-7450-0990-5

Printed in the United States of America
1 2 3 4 5 6 7 8 9

The paper used in this publication meets the minimum
requirements of American National Standard for Information
Sciences—Permanence of Paper for Printed Library Materials,
ANSI Z39.48-1984. ∞

Contents

Acknowledgments

I've depended in this writing on gifts of intimacy, interrogation, ideas, and narrative from many people, among them Henry Abelove, Madeline Casey, Cynthia Chase, Robert Dawidoff, Maud Ellmann, Joseph Gordon, Timothy Gould, Neil Hertz, Marsha Hill, Jonathan Kamholtz, Sally Kamholtz, David Kosofsky, Leon Kosofsky, Rita Kosofsky, Doris Sommer, Deborah Swedberg, Nancy Waring, Barry Weller, Carolyn Williams, Joshua Wilner, and Patricia Yaeger. Andrew Parker lavished on the project his wealth of support, provocation, and learning; Mary Russo and he performed the Dickinsonian magic of making the Connecticut River Valley seem the center of the universe. The first excitation to writing this book came in 1984 from reading an essay by D. A. Miller, "Secret Subjects, Open Secrets," whose author was the first addressee and first reader of most of these chapters. Cindy Patton's conversation and work have personified for me a certain ideal, implicit in this book, of transitivity: across discourses, institutions, genders, and sexualities, and between activism and theory. Michèle Aina Barale, Paula Bennett, Joseph Allen Boone, Philip Brett, Jack Cameron, Jonathan Dollimore, Lee Edelman, Kent Gerard, Jonathan Goldberg, George Haggerty, Janet Halley, Wayne Koestenbaum, Joseph Litvak, Donald Mager, Jeffrey Nunokawa, Elizabeth Potter, Bruce Russell, and Robert Schwartzwald shared with me research, critique, ideas, and a sense of purpose. Hal Sedgwick made me happy. Students like Rafael Campo, Nelson Fernandez, Gary Fisher, Hali Hammer, Sean Holland, Leslie Katz, and Eric Peterson were generous with warmth, criticism, stories, ideas, and talents. Michael Moon came late to the scene of this writing and substantially transformed it, fulfilling our foray.

The greatest gift from all these people has been encouragement: not only in the sense of narcissistic supply, though there's no substitute for that, but in the root sense — they gave courage. On the whole there isn't a vast amount of courage available to those who feel they want it, in the fairly protected (though notionally left-leaning) academic milieux in which scholars have today, when we're lucky, the privilege of doing sustained intellectual work. I've been able to turn again and again to one powerful upwelling of courage: that of gay female and male scholars who have chosen, during these frightening years, to be open in a particular sexuality, often in the struggle for very survival as well as for dignity, pleasure, and thought. I learn from Michael Lynch that courage of even the most spectacular nature isn't after all a spectacle, an arena with fixed sightlines, but instead a kind of floating permeable rialto of common lending, borrowing, extravagant indebtedness, and exchange.

◆   ◆   ◆

Money—that is, invaluable time—for the writing of much of *Epistemology of the Closet* came from the John Simon Guggenheim Memorial Foundation. The Mrs. William Beckman Lectureship at the University of California, Berkeley, provided the time for work on two chapters, and indeed each chapter of the book reflects the abundant stimulus of lecture occasions and audiences. The MLA awarded "The Beast in the Closet" a Crompton-Noll Prize in gay and lesbian criticism. And both Amherst College and Duke University offered important material support.

Credits

Several parts of this book have been previously published. Versions of Chapters 1 and 5 appeared as "Epistemology of the Closet (I and II)" in *Raritan* 7, no. 4 (Spring 1988) and 8, no. 1 (Summer 1988). A version of Chapter 4 appeared, under its own title, in Ruth Bernard Yeazell, ed., *Sex, Politics, and Science in the Nineteenth-Century Novel*, Selected Papers from the English Institute, 1983–84 (Baltimore: Johns Hopkins University Press, 1986). A version of Axiom 6, from the Introduction, appeared under the title "Pedagogy in the Context of an Antihomophobic Project," in *South Atlantic Quarterly* 89, no. 1 (Winter 1990). I am grateful for permission to reprint these sections.

Introduction: Axiomatic

Epistemology of the Closet proposes that many of the major nodes of thought and knowledge in twentieth-century Western culture as a whole are structured—indeed, fractured—by a chronic, now endemic crisis of homo/heterosexual definition, indicatively male, dating from the end of the nineteenth century. The book will argue that an understanding of virtually any aspect of modern Western culture must be, not merely incomplete, but damaged in its central substance to the degree that it does not incorporate a critical analysis of modern homo/heterosexual definition; and it will assume that the appropriate place for that critical analysis to begin is from the relatively decentered perspective of modern gay and antihomophobic theory.

The passage of time, the bestowal of thought and necessary political struggle since the turn of the century have only spread and deepened the long crisis of modern sexual definition, dramatizing, often violently, the internal incoherence and mutual contradiction of each of the forms of discursive and institutional "common sense" on this subject inherited from the architects of our present culture. The contradictions I will be discussing are not in the first place those between prohomosexual and antihomosexual people or ideologies, although the book's strongest motivation is indeed the gay-affirmative one. Rather, the contradictions that seem most active are the ones internal to all the important twentieth-century understandings of homo/heterosexual definition, both heterosexist and antihomophobic. Their outlines and something of their history are sketched in Chapter 1. Briefly, they are two. The first is the contradiction between seeing homo/heterosexual definition on the one hand as an issue of active importance primarily for a small, distinct, relatively fixed homosexual minority (what I refer to as a minoritizing view), and seeing it on the other hand as an issue of continuing, determinative importance in the lives of people across the spectrum of sexualities (what I refer to as a universalizing view). The second is the contradiction between seeing same-sex object choice on the one hand as a matter of liminality or transitivity between genders, and seeing it on the other hand as reflecting an impulse of separatism—though by no means necessarily political separatism—within each gender. The purpose of this book is not to adjudicate between the two poles of either of these contradictions, for, if its argument is right, no epistemological grounding now exists from which to do so. Instead, I am trying to make the strongest possible introductory case for a hypothesis about the centrality of this nominally marginal, conceptually intractable set of definitional issues to the important knowledges and understandings of twentieth-century Western culture as a whole.

The word "homosexual" entered Euro-American discourse during the last third of the nineteenth century—its popularization preceding, as it happens, even that of the word "heterosexual."[1] It seems clear that the sexual behaviors, and even for some people the conscious identities, denoted by the new term "homosexual" and its contemporary variants already had a long, rich history. So, indeed, did a wide range of other sexual behaviors and behavioral clusters. What *was* new from the turn of the century was the world-mapping by which every given person, just as he or she was necessarily assignable to a male or a female gender, was now considered necessarily assignable as well to a homo- or a hetero-sexuality, a binarized identity that was full of implications, however confusing, for even the ostensibly least sexual aspects of personal existence. It was this new development that left no space in the culture exempt from the potent incoherences of homo/heterosexual definition.

New, institutionalized taxonomic discourses—medical, legal, literary, psychological—centering on homo/heterosexual definition proliferated and crystallized with exceptional rapidity in the decades around the turn of the century, decades in which so many of the other critical nodes of the culture were being, if less suddenly and newly, nonetheless also definitively reshaped. Both the power relations between the genders and the relations of nationalism and imperialism, for instance, were in highly visible crisis. For this reason, and because the structuring of same-sex bonds can't, in any historical situation marked by inequality and contest *between* genders, fail to be a site of intensive regulation that intersects

---

1. On this, see Jonathan Katz, *Gay/Lesbian Almanac: A New Documentary* (New York: Harper & Row, 1983), pp. 147–50; for more discussion, David M. Halperin, *One Hundred Years of Homosexuality* (New York: Routledge, 1989), p. 155*n*.1 and pp. 158–59*n*.17.

virtually every issue of power and gender,[2] lines can never be drawn to circumscribe within some proper domain of sexuality (whatever that might be) the consequences of a shift in sexual discourse. Furthermore, in accord with Foucault's demonstration, whose results I will take to be axiomatic, that modern Western culture has placed what it calls sexuality in a more and more distinctively privileged relation to our most prized constructs of individual identity, truth, and knowledge, it becomes truer and truer that the language of sexuality not only intersects with but transforms the other languages and relations by which we know.

Accordingly, one characteristic of the readings in this book is to attend to performative aspects of texts, and to what are often blandly called their "reader relations," as sites of definitional creation, violence, and rupture in relation to particular readers, particular institutional circumstances. An assumption underlying the book is that the relations of the closet—the relations of the known and the unknown, the explicit and the inexplicit around homo/heterosexual definition—have the potential for being peculiarly revealing, in fact, about speech acts more generally. It has felt throughout this work as though the density of their social meaning lends any speech act concerning these issues—and the outlines of that "concern," it turns out, are broad indeed—the exaggerated propulsiveness of wearing flippers in a swimming pool: the force of various rhetorical effects has seemed uniquely difficult to calibrate.

But, in the vicinity of the closet, even what *counts* as a speech act is problematized on a perfectly routine basis. As Foucault says: "there is no binary division to be made between what one says and what one does not say; we must try to determine the different ways of not saying such things. . . . There is not one but many silences, and they are an integral part of the strategies that underlie and permeate discourses."[3] "Closetedness" itself is a performance initiated as such by the speech act of a silence—not a particular silence, but a silence that accrues particularity by fits and starts, in relation to the discourse that surrounds and differentially constitutes it. The speech acts that coming out, in turn, can comprise are as strangely specific. And they may have nothing to do with the acquisition of new information. I think of a man and a woman I know,

2. This is an argument of my *Between Men: English Literature and Male Homosocial Desire* (New York: Columbia University Press, 1985).

3. Michel Foucault, *The History of Sexuality*. Volume I: *An Introduction*, trans. Robert Hurley (New York: Pantheon, 1978), p. 27.

best friends, who for years canvassed freely the emotional complications of each other's erotic lives—the man's eroticism happening to focus exclusively on men. But it was only after one particular conversational moment, fully a decade into this relationship, that it seemed to either of these friends that permission had been given to the woman to refer to the man, in their conversation together, as *a gay man.* Discussing it much later, both agreed they had felt at the time that this one moment had constituted a clear-cut act of coming out, even in the context of years and years beforehand of exchange predicated on the man's *being* gay. What was said to make this difference? Not a version of "I am gay," which could only have been bathetic between them. What constituted coming out for this man, in this situation, was to use about himself the phrase "coming out"—to mention, as if casually, having come out to someone else. (Similarly, a T-shirt that ACT UP sells in New York bearing the text, "I am out, therefore I am," is meant to do for the wearer, not the constative work of reporting that s/he *is* out, but the performative work of coming out in the first place.) And as Chapter 1 will discuss, the fact that silence is rendered as pointed and performative as speech, in relations around the closet, depends on and highlights more broadly the fact that ignorance is as potent and as multiple a thing there as is knowledge.

Knowledge, after all, is not itself power, although it is the magnetic field of power. Ignorance and opacity collude or compete with knowledge in mobilizing the flows of energy, desire, goods, meanings, persons. If M. Mitterrand knows English but Mr. Reagan lacks—as he did lack—French, it is the urbane M. Mitterrand who must negotiate in an acquired tongue, the ignorant Mr. Reagan who may dilate in his native one. Or in the interactive speech model by which, as Sally McConnell-Ginet puts it, "the standard . . . meaning can be thought of as what is recognizable solely on the basis of interlocutors' mutual knowledge of established practices of interpretation," it is the interlocutor who has or pretends to have the *less* broadly knowledgeable understanding of interpretive practice who will define the terms of the exchange. So, for instance, because "men, with superior extralinguistic resources and privileged discourse positions, are often less likely to treat perspectives different from their own as mutually available for communication," their attitudes are "thus more likely to leave a lasting imprint on the common semantic stock than women's."[4]

---

4. Sally McConnell-Ginet, "The Sexual (Re)Production of Meaning: A Discourse-Based Theory," manuscript, pp. 387–88, quoted in Cheris Kramarae and Paula A. Treichler, *A Feminist Dictionary* (Boston: Pandora Press, 1985), p. 264; emphasis added.

Such ignorance effects can be harnessed, licensed, and regulated on a mass scale for striking enforcements—perhaps especially around sexuality, in modern Western culture the most meaning-intensive of human activities. The epistemological asymmetry of the laws that govern rape, for instance, privileges at the same time men and ignorance, inasmuch as it matters not at all what the raped woman perceives or wants just so long as the man raping her can claim not to have noticed (ignorance in which male sexuality receives careful education).[5] And the rape machinery that is organized by this epistemological privilege of unknowing in turn keeps disproportionately under discipline, of course, women's larger ambitions to take more control over the terms of our own circulation.[6] Or, again, in an ingenious and patiently instructive orchestration of ignorance, the U.S. Justice Department ruled in June, 1986, that an employer may freely fire persons with AIDS exactly so long as the employer can claim to be ignorant of the medical fact, *quoted in the ruling*, that there is no known health danger in the workplace from the disease.[7] Again, it is clear in political context that the effect aimed at—in this case, it is hard to help feeling, aimed at with some care—is the ostentatious declaration, for the private sector, of an organized open season on gay men.[8]

5. Catherine A. MacKinnon makes this point more fully in "Feminism, Marxism, Method, and the State: An Agenda for Theory," *Signs* 7, no. 3 (Spring 1982): 515–44.

6. Susan Brownmiller made the most forceful and influential presentation of this case in *Against Our Will: Men, Women, and Rape* (New York: Simon & Schuster, 1975).

7. Robert Pear, "Rights Laws Offer Only Limited Help on AIDS, U.S. Rules," *New York Times*, June 23, 1986. That the ruling was calculated to offer, provoke, and legitimate harm and insult is clear from the language quoted in Pear's article: "A person," the ruling says, for instance, "cannot be regarded as handicapped [and hence subject to federal protection] simply because others shun his company. Otherwise, a host of personal traits, from ill temper to poor personal hygiene, would constitute handicaps."

8. Not that gay men were intended to be the only victims of this ruling. In even the most conscientious discourse concerning AIDS in the United States so far there has been the problem, to which this essay does not pretend to offer any solution, of doing justice at once to the relative (and increasing) heterogeneity of those who actually have AIDS and to the specificity with which AIDS discourse at every level has until very recently focused on male homosexuality. In its worldwide epidemiology, of course, AIDS has no distinctive association with gay men, nor is it likely to for long here either. The acknowledgment/management of this fact was the preoccupation of a strikingly sudden media-wide discursive shift in the winter and early spring of 1987. If the obsessively homophobic focus of AIDS phobia up to that moment scapegoated gay men by (among other things) subjecting their sexual practice and lifestyles to a glaring and effectually punitive visibility, however, it worked in an opposite way to expunge the claims by expunging the visibility of most of the disease's other victims. So far, here, these victims have been among groups already the most vulnerable—intravenous drug users, sex workers, wives and girlfriends of closeted men—on whom invisibility, or a public subsumption under the incongruous heading of gay men, can have no protective effect. (It has been notable, for instance, that media coverage of prostitutes with AIDS has shown no interest in the health of the women themselves, but only in their potential for infecting men. Again, the campaign to provide

Although the simple, stubborn fact or pretense of ignorance (one meaning, the Capital one, of the word "stonewall") can sometimes be enough to enforce discursive power, a far more complex drama of ignorance and knowledge is the more usual carrier of political struggle. Such a drama was enacted when, only a few days after the Justice Department's private-sector decision, the U.S. Supreme Court correspondingly opened the public-sector bashing season by legitimating state antisodomy laws in *Bowers v. Hardwick*.[9] In a virulent ruling whose language made from beginning to end an insolent display of legal illogic—of what Justice Blackmun in dissent called "the most willful blindness"[10]—a single, apparently incidental word used in Justice White's majority opinion became for many gay or antihomophobic readers a focus around which the inflammatory force of the decision seemed to pullulate with peculiar density.[11] In White's opinion,

> to claim that a right to engage in sodomy is "deeply rooted in this nation's history and tradition" or "implicit in the concept of ordered liberty" is, at best, facetious.[12]

What lends the word "facetious" in this sentence such an unusual power to offend, even in the context of a larger legal offense whose damage will be

---

drug users with free needles had not until early 1987 received even the exiguous state support given to safer-sex education for gay men.) The damages of homophobia on the one hand, of classism / racism / sexism on the other; of intensive regulatory visibility on the one hand, of discursive erasure on the other: these pairings are not only incommensurable (and why measure them against each other rather than against the more liberating possibilities they foreclose?) but very hard to interleave with each other conceptually. The effect has been perhaps most dizzying when the incommensurable damages are condensed upon a single person, e.g., a nonwhite gay man. The focus of this book is on the specific damages of homophobia; but to the extent that it is impelled by (a desire to resist) the public pressures of AIDS phobia, I must at least make clear how much that is important even to its own ambitions is nonetheless excluded from its potential for responsiveness.

9. Graphic encapsulation of this event on the front page of the *Times*: at the bottom of the three-column lead story on the ruling, a photo ostensibly about the influx of various navies into a welcoming New York for "the Liberty celebration" shows two worried but extremely good-looking sailors in alluring whites, "asking directions of a police officer" (*New York Times*, July 1, 1986).

10. "The Supreme Court Opinion. Michael J. Bowers, Attorney General of Georgia, Petition v. Michael Hardwick and John and Mary Doe, Respondents," text in *New York Native*, no. 169 (July 14, 1986): 15.

11. The word is quoted, for instance, in isolation, in the sixth sentence of the *Times*'s lead article announcing the decision (July 1, 1986). The *Times* editorial decrying the decision (July 2, 1986) remarks on the crudity of this word before outlining the substantive offensiveness of the ruling. The *New York Native* and the gay leaders it quoted also gave the word a lot of play in the immediate aftermath of the ruling (e.g., no. 169 [July 14, 1986]: 8, 11).

12. *New York Native*, no. 169 (July 14, 1986): 13.

much more indelible, has to be the economical way it functions here as switchpoint for the cyclonic epistemological undertows that encompass power in general and issues of homosexual desire in particular.

One considers: (1) *prima facie*, nobody could, of course, actually for an instant mistake the intent of the gay advocates as facetious. (2) *Secunda facie*, it is thus the court itself that is pleased to be facetious. Trading on the assertion's very (3) transparent stupidity (not just the contemptuous demonstration that powerful people don't have to be acute or right, but even more, the contemptuous demonstration — this is palpable throughout the majority opinions, but only in this word does it bubble up with active pleasure — of how obtuseness itself arms the powerful against their enemies), the court's joke here (in the wake of the mock-ignorant mock-jocose threat implicit in "at best") is (4) the clownish claim to be able at will to "read" — i.e., project into — the minds of the gay advocates. This being not only (5) a parody of, but (6) more intimately a kind of aggressive jamming technique against, (7) the truth/paranoid fantasy that it is gay people who can read, or project their own desires into, the minds of "straight" people.

Inarguably, there is a satisfaction in dwelling on the degree to which the power of our enemies over us is implicated, not in their command of knowledge, but precisely in their ignorance. The effect is a real one, but it carries dangers with it as well. The chief of these dangers is the scornful, fearful, or patheticizing reification of "ignorance"; it goes with the unexamined Enlightenment assumptions by which the labeling of a particular force as "ignorance" seems to place it unappealably in a demonized space on a never quite explicit ethical schema. (It is also dangerously close in structure to the more palpably sentimental privileging of ignorance as an originary, passive innocence.) The angles of view from which it can look as though a political fight is a fight against ignorance are invigorating and maybe revelatory ones but dangerous places for dwelling. The writings of, among others, Foucault, Derrida, Thomas Kuhn, and Thomas Szasz have given contemporary readers a lot of practice in questioning both the ethical/political disengagement and, beyond that, the ethical/political simplicity of the category of "knowledge," so that a writer who appeals too directly to the redemptive potential of simply upping the cognitive wattage on any question of power seems, now, naive. The corollary problems still adhere to the category of "ignorance," as well, but so do some additional ones: there are psychological operations of shame, denial, projection around "ignorance" that make it an especially galvanizing category for the individual reader, even as they give it a rhetorical potency that it would be hard for writers to forswear and foolhardy for them to embrace.

Rather than sacrifice the notion of "ignorance," then, I would be more interested at this point in trying, as we are getting used to trying with "knowledge," to pluralize and specify it. That is, I would like to be able to make use in sexual-political thinking of the deconstructive understanding that particular insights generate, are lined with, and at the same time are themselves structured by particular opacities. If ignorance is not—as it evidently is not—a single Manichaean, aboriginal maw of darkness from which the heroics of human cognition can occasionally wrestle facts, insights, freedoms, progress, perhaps there exists instead a plethora of *ignorances*, and we may begin to ask questions about the labor, erotics, and economics of their human production and distribution. Insofar as ignorance is ignorance *of* a knowledge—a knowledge that may itself, it goes without saying, be seen as either true or false under some other regime of truth—these ignorances, far from being pieces of the originary dark, are produced by and correspond to particular knowledges and circulate as part of particular regimes of truth. We should not assume that their doubletting with knowledges means, however, that they obey identical laws identically or follow the same circulatory paths at the same pace.[13]

Historically, the framing of *Epistemology of the Closet* begins with a puzzle. It is a rather amazing fact that, of the very many dimensions along which the genital activity of one person can be differentiated from that of another (dimensions that include preference for certain acts, certain zones or sensations, certain physical types, a certain frequency, certain symbolic investments, certain relations of age or power, a certain species, a certain number of participants, etc. etc. etc.), precisely one, the gender of object choice, emerged from the turn of the century, and has remained, as *the* dimension denoted by the now ubiquitous category of "sexual orientation." This is not a development that would have been foreseen from the viewpoint of the fin de siècle itself, where a rich stew of male algolagnia, child-love, and autoeroticism, to mention no more of its components, seemed to have as indicative a relation as did homosexuality

13. For an essay that makes these points more fully, see my "Privilege of Unknowing," *Genders*, no. 1 (Spring 1988): 102–24, a reading of Diderot's *La Religieuse*, from which the preceding six paragraphs are taken.

to the whole, obsessively entertained problematic of sexual "perversion" or, more broadly, "decadence." Foucault, for instance, mentions the hysterical woman and the masturbating child, along with "entomologized" sexological categories such as zoophiles, zooerasts, auto-monosexualists, and gynecomasts, as typifying the new sexual taxonomies, the *"specification of individuals"* that facilitated the modern freighting of sexual definition with epistemological and power relations.[14] True as his notation is, it suggests without beginning to answer the further question: why the category of "the masturbator," to choose only one example, should by now have entirely lost its diacritical potential for specifying a particular kind of person, an identity, at the same time as it continues to be true — becomes increasingly true — that, for a crucial strain of Western discourse, in Foucault's words "the homosexual was now a species."[15] So, as a result, is the heterosexual, and between *these* species the human species has come more and more to be divided. *Epistemology of the Closet* does not have an explanation to offer for this sudden, radical condensation of sexual categories; instead of speculating on its causes, the book explores its unpredictably varied and acute implications and consequences.

At the same time that this process of sexual specification or species-formation was going on, the book will argue, less stable and identity-bound understandings of sexual choice also persisted and developed, often among the same people or interwoven in the same systems of thought. Again, the book will not suggest (nor do I believe there currently exists) any standpoint of thought from which the rival claims of these minoritizing and universalizing understandings of sexual definition could be decisively arbitrated as to their "truth." Instead, the performative effects of the self-contradictory discursive field of force created by their overlap will be my subject. And, of course, it makes every difference that these impactions of homo/heterosexual definition took place in a setting, not of spacious emotional or analytic impartiality, but rather of urgent homophobic pressure to devalue one of the two nominally symmetrical forms of choice.

As several of the formulations above would suggest, one main strand of argument in this book is deconstructive, in a fairly specific sense. The analytic move it makes is to demonstrate that categories presented in a culture as symmetrical binary oppositions — heterosexual/homosexual,

---

14. Foucault, *History of Sexuality*, pp. 105, 43.
15. Foucault, *History of Sexuality*, p. 43.

in this case—actually subsist in a more unsettled and dynamic tacit relation according to which, first, term B is not symmetrical with but subordinated to term A; but, second, the ontologically valorized term A actually depends for its meaning on the simultaneous subsumption and exclusion of term B; hence, third, the question of priority between the supposed central and the supposed marginal category of each dyad is irresolvably unstable, an instability caused by the fact that term B is constituted as at once internal and external to term A. Harold Beaver, for instance, in an influential 1981 essay sketched the outlines of such a deconstructive strategy:

> The aim must be to reverse the rhetorical opposition of what is "transparent" or "natural" and what is "derivative" or "contrived" by demonstrating that the qualities predicated of "homosexuality" (as a dependent term) are in fact a condition of "heterosexuality"; that "heterosexuality," far from possessing a privileged status, must itself be treated as a dependent term.[16]

To understand these conceptual relations as irresolvably unstable is not, however, to understand them as inefficacious or innocuous. It is at least premature when Roland Barthes prophesies that "once the paradigm is blurred, utopia begins: meaning and sex become the objects of free play, at the heart of which the (polysemant) forms and the (sensual) practices, liberated from the binary prison, will achieve a state of infinite expansion."[17] To the contrary, a deconstructive understanding of these binarisms makes it possible to identify them as sites that are *peculiarly* densely charged with lasting potentials for powerful manipulation—through precisely the mechanisms of self-contradictory definition or, more succinctly, the double bind. Nor is a deconstructive analysis of such definitional knots, however necessary, at all sufficient to disable them. Quite the opposite: I would suggest that an understanding of their irresolvable instability has been continually available, and has continually lent discursive authority, to antigay as well as to gay cultural forces of this century. Beaver makes an optimistic prediction that "by disqualifying the autonomy of what was deemed spontaneously immanent, the whole sexual system is fundamentally decentred and exposed."[18] But there is reason to

---

16. Harold Beaver, "Homosexual Signs," *Critical Inquiry* 8 (Autumn 1981): 115.
17. *Roland Barthes by Roland Barthes*, trans. Richard Howard (New York: Hill and Wang, 1977), p. 133.
18. Beaver, "Homosexual Signs," pp. 115–16.

believe that the oppressive sexual system of the past hundred years was if anything born and bred (if I may rely on the pith of a fable whose value doesn't, I must hope, stand or fall with its history of racist uses) in the briar patch of the most notorious and repeated decenterings and exposures.

These deconstructive contestations can occur, moreover, only in the context of an entire cultural network of normative definitions, definitions themselves equally unstable but responding to different sets of contiguities and often at a different rate. The master terms of a particular historical moment will be those that are so situated as to entangle most inextricably and at the same time most differentially the filaments of other important definitional nexuses. In arguing that homo/heterosexual definition has been a presiding master term of the past century, one that has the same, primary importance for all modern Western identity and social organization (and not merely for homosexual identity and culture) as do the more traditionally visible cruxes of gender, class, and race, I'll argue that the now chronic modern crisis of homo/heterosexual definition has affected our culture through its ineffaceable marking particularly of the categories secrecy/disclosure, knowledge/ignorance, private/public, masculine/feminine, majority/minority, innocence/initiation, natural/artificial, new/old, discipline/terrorism, canonic/noncanonic, wholeness/decadence, urbane/provincial, domestic/foreign, health/illness, same/different, active/passive, in/out, cognition/paranoia, art/kitsch, utopia/apocalypse, sincerity/sentimentality, and voluntarity/addiction.[19] And rather than embrace an idealist faith in the necessarily, immanently self-corrosive efficacy of the contradictions inherent to these definitional binarisms, I will suggest instead that contests for discursive power can be specified as competitions for the material or rhetorical leverage required to set the terms of, and to profit in some way from, the operations of such an incoherence of definition.

Perhaps I should say something about the project of hypothesizing that certain binarisms that structure meaning in a culture may be "ineffaceably marked" by association with this one particular problematic — inefface-

---

19. My casting of all these definitional nodes in the form of binarisms, I should make explicit, has to do not with a mystical faith in the number two but, rather, with the felt need to schematize in some consistent way the treatment of social vectors so exceedingly various. The kind of falsification necessarily performed on each by this reduction cannot, unfortunately, itself be consistent. But the scope of the kind of hypothesis I want to pose does seem to require a drastic reductiveness, at least in its initial formulations.

ably even when invisibly. Hypothesizing is easier than proving, but indeed I cannot imagine the protocol by which such hypotheses might be *tested*; they must be deepened and broadened — not the work of one book — and used, rather than proved or disproved by a few examples. The collecting of instances of each binarism that would appear to "common sense" to be unmarked by issues of homo/heterosexual definition, though an inexhaustibly stimulating heuristic, is not, I believe, a good test of such a hypothesis. After all, the particular kinds of skill that might be required to produce the most telling interpretations have hardly been a valued part of the "common sense" of this epistemologically cloven culture. If a painstaking process of accumulative reading and historical de- and recontextualization does not render these homologies resonant and productive, that is the only test they can directly fail, the only one they need to pass.

The structure of the present book has been markedly affected by this intuition — by a sense that the cultural interrogations it aims to make imperative will be trivialized or evacuated, at this early stage, to the degree that their procedures seem to partake of the a priori. I've wanted the book to be inviting (as well as imperative) but resolutely non-algorithmic. A point of the book is *not to know* how far its insights and projects are generalizable, not to be able to say in advance where the semantic specificity of these issues gives over to (or: itself structures?) the syntax of a "broader" or more abstractable critical project. In particular, the book aims to resist in every way it can the deadening pretended knowingness by which the chisel of modern homo/heterosexual definitional crisis tends, in public discourse, to be hammered most fatally home.

Perhaps to counter that, it seems now that the book not only has but constitutes an extended introduction. It is organized, not as a chronological narrative, but as a series of essays linked closely by their shared project and recurrent topics. The Introduction, situating this project in the larger context of gay/lesbian and antihomophobic theory, and Chapter 1, outlining its basic terms, are the only parts that do not comprise extended readings. Chapter 2 (on *Billy Budd*) and Chapter 3 (on Wilde and Nietzsche), which were originally conceived as a single unit, offer a different kind of introduction: an assay, through the specificity of these texts and authors, of most of the bravely showy list of binarized cultural nexuses about which the book makes, at other places, more generalized assertions. Chapter 4 discusses at length, through a reading of James's "The Beast in the Jungle," the elsewhere recurrent topos of male homosexual panic. And Chapter 5, on Proust, focuses more sharply on the book's preoccupation with the speech-act relations around the closet.

In consonance with my emphasis on the performative relations of double and conflicted definition, the theorized prescription for a *practical* politics implicit in these readings is for a multi-pronged movement whose idealist and materialist impulses, whose minority-model and universalist-model strategies, and for that matter whose gender-separatist and gender-integrative analyses would likewise proceed in parallel without any high premium placed on ideological rationalization between them. In effect this is how the gay movements of this century have actually been structured, if not how they have often been perceived or evaluated. The breadth and fullness of the political gestalt of gay-affirmative struggle give a powerful resonance to the voice of each of its constituencies. The cost in ideological rigor, though high indeed, is very simply inevitable: this is not a conceptual landscape in which ideological rigor across levels, across constituencies is at all possible, be it ever so desirable.

Something similar is true at the level of scholarship. Over and over I have felt in writing the book that, however my own identifications, intuitions, circumstances, limitations, and talents may have led its interpretations to privilege constructivist over essentialist, universalizing over minoritizing, and gender-transitive over gender-separatist understandings of sexual choice, nevertheless the space of permission for this work and the depth of the intellectual landscape in which it might have a contribution to make owe everything to the wealth of essentialist, minoritizing, and separatist gay thought and struggle also in progress. There are similar points to be made about the book's limitation to what may sound, in the current climate of exciting interstitial explorations among literature, social history, and "cultural studies," like unreconstructedly literary readings of essentially canonical texts. I must hope that, as the taken-for-grantedness of what constitutes a literary text, a literary reading, a worthwhile interpretive intervention, becomes more and more unstable under such pressures, the force of anyone's perseveration in this specialized practice (I use "specialized" here not with the connotation of the "expert's" technique, but with the connotation of the wasteful, value-making partiality of the sexual perversion) could look less like a rearguard defense than like something newly interrogable and interrogatory. Even more is this true of the book's specification of male, and of Euro-American male, sexual definition as its subject. Any critical book makes endless choices of focus and methodology, and it is very difficult for these choices to be interpreted in any other light than that of the categorical imperative: the fact that they are made in a certain way here seems a priori to assert that they would be best made in the same way everywhere. I would ask that, however sweeping the claims made by this book may seem to be, it not be read as making that particular claim. Quite the opposite: a real measure of the success of such an analysis would lie in its ability, in the hands of an inquirer with different needs, talents, or positionings, to clarify the distinctive kinds of resistance offered to it from different spaces on the social map, even though such a project might require revisions or rupturings of the analysis as first proffered. The only imperative that the book means to treat as categorical is the very broad one of pursuing an antihomophobic inquiry. If the book were able to fulfill its most expansive ambitions, it would make certain specific kinds of readings and interrogations, perhaps new, available in a heuristically powerful, productive, and significant form for other readers to perform on literary and social texts with, ideally, other results. The meaning, the legitimacy, and in many ways even the possibility for good faith of the positings this book makes depend radically on the production, by other antihomophobic readers who may be very differently situated, of the widest possible range of other and even contradictory availabilities.

This seems, perhaps, especially true of the historical periodization implied by the structure of this book, and its consequences. To hypothesize the usefulness of taking the century from the 1880s to the 1980s as a single period in the history of male homo/heterosexual definition is necessarily to risk subordinating the importance of other fulcrum points. One thinks, for instance, of the events collectively known as Stonewall — the New York City riots of June, 1969, protesting police harassment of patrons of a gay bar, from which the modern gay liberation movement dates its inauguration. A certain idealist bias built into a book about *definition* makes it too easy to level out, as from a spuriously bird's-eye view, the incalculable impact — including the cognitive impact — of political movements per se. Yet even the phrase "the closet" as a publicly intelligible signifier for gay-related epistemological issues is made available, obviously, only by the difference made by the post-Stonewall gay politics oriented around coming *out* of the closet. More generally, the centrality in this book's argument of a whole range of valuations and political perspectives that are unmistakably post-Stonewall will be, I hope, perfectly obvious. It is only in that context that the hypothesis of a certain alternative, overarching periodization of definitional issues can be appropriately entertained.

The book that preceded this one, *Between Men: English Literature and Male Homosocial Desire*, attempted to demonstrate the immanence of men's same-sex bonds, and their prohibitive structuration, to male-female bonds in nineteenth-century English literature. The relation of this book to its predecessor is defined most simply by the later time span that it treats. This has also involved, however, a different negotiation between feminist and antihomophobic motives in the two studies. *Between Men* ends with a coda pointing toward "the gaping and unbridgeable rift in the male homosocial spectrum" at the end of the nineteenth century, after which "a discussion of male homosocial desire as a whole really gives way to a discussion of male homosexuality and homophobia as we know them."[20] (For more on that facile "as we know them," see Axiom 5 below.) *Epistemology of the Closet*, which depends analytically on the conclusions reached in *Between Men*, takes up the story at exactly that point, and in that sense can more accurately be said to be primarily an antihomophobic book in its subject matter and perspective. That is to say, in terms that I will explain more fully in Axiom 2 below, the book's first focus is on sexuality rather than (sometimes, even, as opposed to) gender. *Between Men* focused on the oppressive effects on women and men of a cultural system in which male-male desire became widely intelligible primarily by being routed through triangular relations involving a woman. The inflictions of this system, far from disappearing since the turn of the century, have only become adapted and subtilized. But certainly the pressingly immediate fusion of feminist with gay male preoccupations and interrogations that *Between Men* sought to perform has seemed less available, analytically, for a twentieth-century culture in which at least some versions of a same-sex desire unmediated through heterosexual performance have become widely articulated.

Epistemology of the Closet is a feminist book mainly in the sense that its analyses were produced by someone whose thought has been macro- and microscopically infused with feminism over a long period. At the many intersections where a distinctively feminist (i.e., gender-centered) and a distinctively antihomophobic (i.e., sexuality-centered) inquiry have

20. Sedgwick, *Between Men*, pp. 201, 202.

seemed to diverge, however, this book has tried consistently to press on in the latter direction. I have made this choice largely because I see feminist analysis as being considerably more developed than gay male or anti-homophobic analysis at present—theoretically, politically, and institutionally. There are more people doing feminist analysis, it has been being done longer, it is less precarious and dangerous (still precarious and dangerous enough), and there is by now a much more broadly usable set of tools available for its furtherance. This is true notwithstanding the extraordinary recent efflorescence of gay and lesbian studies, without which, as I've suggested, the present book would have been impossible; that flowering is young, fragile, under extreme threat from both within and outside academic institutions, and still necessarily dependent on a limited pool of paradigms and readings. The viability, by now solidly established, of a persuasive feminist project of interpreting gender arrangements, oppressions, and resistances in Euro-American modernism and modernity from the turn of the century has been a condition of the possibility of this book but has also been taken as a permission or imperative to pursue a very different path in it. And, indeed, when another kind of intersection has loomed—the choice between risking a premature and therefore foreclosing reintegration between feminist and gay (male) terms of analysis, on the one hand, and on the other hand keeping their relation open a little longer by deferring yet again the moment of their accountability to one another—I have followed the latter path. This is bound to seem retardataire to some readers, but I hope they are willing to see it as a genuine deferral, in the interests of making space for a gay male–oriented analysis that would have its own claims to make for an illuminating centrality, rather than as a refusal. Ultimately, I do feel, a great deal depends—for all women, for lesbians, for gay men, and possibly for all men—on the fostering of our ability to arrive at understandings of sexuality that will respect a certain irreducibility in it to the terms and relations of gender.

A note on terminology. There is, I believe, no satisfactory rule for choosing between the usages "homosexual" and "gay," outside of a post-Stonewall context where "gay" must be preferable since it is the explicit choice of a large number of the people to whom it refers. Until recently it seemed that "homosexual," though it severely risked anachronism in any application before the late nineteenth century, was still somehow less temporally circumscribed than "gay," perhaps because it sounded more official, not to say diagnostic. That aura of timelessness about the word

has, however, faded rapidly—less because of the word's manifest inade-
quacy to the cognitive and behavioral maps of the centuries *before* its
coining, than because the sources of its authority for the century *after* have
seemed increasingly tendentious and dated. Thus "homosexual" and
"gay" seem more and more to be terms applicable to distinct, nonoverlap-
ping periods in the history of a phenomenon for which there then remains
no overarching label. Accordingly I have tried to use each of the terms
appropriately in contexts where historical differentiation between the
earlier and later parts of the century seemed important. But to designate
"the" phenomenon (problematical notion) as it stretches across a larger
reach of history, I have used one or the other interchangeably, most often
in contrast to the immediately relevant historical usage. (E.g., "gay" in a
turn-of-the-century context or "homosexual" in a 1980s context would
each be meant to suggest a categorization broad enough to include at least
the other period as well.) I have not followed a convention, used by some
scholars, of differentiating between "gay" and "homosexual" on the basis
of whether a given text or person was perceived as embodying (respec-
tively) gay affirmation or internalized homophobia; an unproblematical
ease in distinguishing between these two things is not an assumption of
this study. The main additional constraint on the usage of these terms in
this book is a preference against employing the noun "gayness," or "gay"
itself as a noun. I think what underlies this preference is a sense that the
association of same-sex desire with the traditional, exciting meanings of
the adjective "gay" is still a powerfully assertive act, perhaps not one to be
lightly routinized by grammatical adaptations.

Gender has increasingly become a problem for this area of terminology, and one to which I have, again, no consistent solution. "Homosexual" was a relatively gender-neutral term and I use it as such, though it
has always seemed to have at least some male bias—whether because of
the pun on Latin *homo* = man latent in its etymological macaronic, or
simply because of the greater attention to men in the discourse surrounding it (as in so many others). "Gay" is more complicated since it makes a
claim to refer to both genders but is routinely yoked with "lesbian" in
actual usage, as if it did not—as increasingly it does not—itself refer to
women. As I suggest in Axiom 3, this terminological complication is
closely responsive to real ambiguities and struggles of gay/lesbian politics
and identities: e.g., there are women-loving women who think of themselves as lesbians but not as gay, and others who think of themselves as gay
women but not as lesbians. Since the premises of this study make it

impossible to presuppose either the unity or the distinctness of women's and men's changing, and indeed synchronically various, homosexual identities, and since its primary though not exclusive focus is in fact on male identities, I sometimes use "gay and lesbian" but more often simply "gay," the latter in the oddly precise sense of a phenomenon of same-sex desire that is being treated as indicatively but not exclusively male. When I mean to suggest a more fully, equitably two-sexed phenomenon I refer to "gay men and women," or "lesbians and gay men"; when a more exclusive one, to "gay men."

Finally, I feel painfully how different may be a given writer's and reader's senses of how best to articulate an argument that may for both seem a matter of urgency. I have tried to be as clear as I can about the book's moves, motives, and assumptions throughout; but even aside from the intrinsic difficulty of its subject and texts, it seems inevitable that the style of its writing will not conform to everyone's ideal of the pellucid. The fact that—if the book is right—the most significant stakes for the culture are involved in precisely the volatile, fractured, dangerous relations of visibility and articulation around homosexual possibility makes the prospect of its being misread especially fraught; to the predictable egoistic fear of its having no impact or a risible one there is added the dread of its operating destructively.

Let me give an example. There is reason to believe that gay-bashing is the most common and most rapidly increasing among what are becoming legally known as bias-related or hate-related crimes in the United States. There is no question that the threat of this violent, degrading, and often fatal extrajudicial sanction works even more powerfully than, and in intimately enforcing concert with, more respectably institutionalized sanctions against gay choice, expression, and being. The endemic intimacy of the link between extrajudicial and judicial punishment of homosexuality is clear, for instance, from the argument of legislators who, in state after state, have fought to exclude antigay violence from coverage under bills that would specifically criminalize bias-related crime—on the grounds that to specify a condemnation of *individual* violence against persons perceived as gay would vitiate the *state's* condemnation of homosexuality. These arguments have so far been successful in most of the states where the question has arisen; in fact, in some states (such as New York) where coverage of antigay violence was not dropped from hate-crimes bills, apparently solid racial/ethnic coalitions have fractured so badly over the issue that otherwise overwhelmingly popular bills have been repeatedly defeated. The state's treatment of nonstate antigay violence, then, is an increasingly contested definitional interface of terms that impact critically but nonexclusively on gay people.

In this highly charged context, the treatment of gay-bashers who do wind up in court is also very likely to involve a plunge into a thicket of difficult and contested definitions. One of the thorniest of these has to do with "homosexual panic," a defense strategy that is commonly used to prevent conviction or to lighten sentencing of gay-bashers — a term, as well, that names a key analytic tool in the present study. Judicially, a "homosexual panic" defense for a person (typically a man) accused of antigay violence implies that his responsibility for the crime was diminished by a pathological psychological condition, perhaps brought on by an unwanted sexual advance from the man whom he then attacked. In addition to the unwarranted assumptions that all gay men may plausibly be accused of making sexual advances to strangers and, worse, that violence, often to the point of homicide, is a legitimate response to any sexual advance whether welcome or not, the "homosexual panic" defense rests on the falsely individualizing and pathologizing assumption that hatred of homosexuals is so private and so atypical a phenomenon in this culture as to be classifiable as an accountability-reducing illness. The widespread acceptance of this defense really seems to show, to the contrary, that hatred of homosexuals is even more public, more typical, hence harder to find any leverage against than hatred of other disadvantaged groups. "Race panic" or "gender panic," for instance, is not accepted as a defense for violence against people of color or against women; as for "heterosexual panic," David Wertheimer, executive director of the New York City Gay and Lesbian Anti-Violence Project, remarks, "If every heterosexual woman who had a sexual advance made to her by a male had the right to murder the man, the streets of this city would be littered with the bodies of heterosexual men."[21] A lawyer for the National Gay Rights Advocates makes explicit the contrast with legal treatment of other bias-related crimes: "There is no factual or legal justification for the use of this [homosexual panic] defense. Just as our society will not allow a defendant to use racial or gender-based prejudices as an excuse for his violent acts, a defendant's homophobia is no defense to a violent crime."[22]

21. Peter Freiberg, "Blaming the Victim: New Life for the 'Gay Panic' Defense," *The Advocate*, May 24, 1988, p. 12. For a more thorough discussion of the homosexual panic defense, see "Burdens on Gay Litigants and Bias in the Court System: Homosexual Panic, Child Custody, and Anonymous Parties," *Harvard Civil Rights–Civil Liberties Law Review* 19 (1984): 498–515.

22. Quoted from Joyce Norcini, in "NGRA Discredits 'Homosexual Panic' Defense," *New York Native*, no. 322 (June 19, 1989): 12.

Thus, a lot of the popularity of the "homosexual panic" defense seems to come simply from its ability to permit and "place," by pathologizing, the enactment of a socially sanctioned prejudice against one stigmatized minority, a particularly demeaned one among many. Its special plausibility, however, seems also to depend on a difference between antigay crime and other bias-related antiminority crime: the difference of how much less clear, perhaps finally how impossible, is the boundary circumscription of a minoritizing gay identity. After all, the reason why this defense borrows the name of the (formerly rather obscure and little-diagnosed) psychiatric classification "*homosexual* panic" is that it refers to the supposed uncertainty about his own sexual identity of the perpetrator of the antigay violence. That this should be the typifying scenario of defenses of gay-bashers (as uncertainty about one's own race, religion, ethnicity, or gender is not in other cases of bias-related violence) shows once again how the overlapping aegises of minoritizing and universalizing understandings of male homo/heterosexual definition can tend to redouble the victimization of gay people. In effect, the homosexual panic defense performs a double act of minoritizing taxonomy: there is, it asserts, one distinct minority of gay people, and a second minority, equally distinguishable from the population at large, of "latent homosexuals" whose "insecurity about their own masculinity" is so anomalous as to permit a plea based on diminution of normal moral responsibility. At the same time, the efficacy of the plea depends on its universalizing force, on whether, as Wertheimer says, it can "create a climate in which the jurors are able to identify with the perpetrator by saying, 'My goodness, maybe *I* would have reacted the same way.'"[23] The reliance of the homosexual panic plea on the fact that this male definitional crisis is systemic and endemic is enabled only, and precisely, by its denial of the same fact.

When in my work on *Between Men*, knowing nothing about this judicial use of "homosexual panic" (at that time a less common and publicized defense), I needed a name for "a structural residue of terrorist potential, of *blackmailability*, of Western maleness through the leverage of homophobia," I found myself attracted to just the same phrase, borrowed from the same relatively rare psychiatric diagnosis. Through a linguistic theft whose violence I trusted would be legible in every usage of the phrase, I tried to turn what had been a taxonomic, minoritizing medical

---

23. Freiberg, "Blaming the Victim," p. 11.

category into a structural principle applicable to the definitional work of an entire gender, hence of an entire culture. I used it to denominate "the most private, psychologized form in which many twentieth-century Western men experience their vulnerability to the social pressure of homophobic blackmail" — as, specifically, "only one path of control, complementary to public sanctions through the institutions described by Foucault and others as defining and regulating the amorphous territory of 'the sexual.'"[24]

The forensic use of the "homosexual panic" defense for gay-bashers depends on the medically mediated ability of the phrase to obscure an overlap between individual pathology and systemic function. The reason I found the phrase attractive for my purposes was quite the opposite: I thought it could dramatize, render visible, even render scandalous the same space of overlap. The set of perceptions condensed in that usage of "male homosexual panic" proved, I think, a productive feature of *Between Men* for other critics, especially those doing gay theory, and I have continued my explorations of the same phrase, used in the same sense, in *Epistemology of the Closet*. Yet I feel, as well, with increasing dismay, in the increasingly homophobic atmosphere of public discourse since 1985, that work done to accentuate and clarify the explanatory power of this difficult nexus may not be able to be reliably insulated from uses that ought to be diametrically opposed to it. For instance, it would not require a willfully homophobic reader to understand these discussions of the centrality and power of male homosexual panic as actually contributing to the credibility of the pathologizing "homosexual panic" legal defense of gay-bashers. All it would require would be a failure or refusal to understand how necessarily the discussions are embedded within their context — the context, that is, of an analysis based on systemwide skepticism about the positivist taxonomic neutrality of psychiatry, about the classificatory coherence (e.g., concerning "individual responsibility") of the law. If, foreseeing the possibility of this particular misuse, I have, as I hope, been able to take the explanatory measures necessary to guard against it, still there may be too many others unforeseen.

Of course, silence on these issues performs the enforcing work of the status quo more predictably and inexorably than any attempt at analysis. Yet the tensions and pleasures that, even ideally, make it possible for a

24. Sedgwick, *Between Men*, p. 89.

writer to invest such a project with her best thought may be so different from those that might enable a given reader to.

◆   ◆   ◆

In the remainder of this Introduction I will be trying to articulate some of the otherwise implicit methodological, definitional, and axiomatic groundings of the book's project and explaining, as well, something of my view of its position within broader projects of understanding sexuality and gender.

Anyone working in gay and lesbian studies, in a culture where same-sex desire is still structured by its distinctive public/private status, at once marginal and central, as *the* open secret, discovers that the line between straining at truths that prove to be imbecilically self-evident, on the one hand, and on the other hand tossing off commonplaces that turn out to retain their power to galvanize and divide, is weirdly unpredictable. In dealing with an open-secret structure, it's only by being shameless about risking the obvious that we happen into the vicinity of the transformative. In this Introduction I shall have methodically to sweep into one little heap some of the otherwise unarticulated assumptions and conclusions from a long-term project of antihomophobic analysis. These nails, these scraps of wiring: will they bore or will they shock?

Under the rule that most privileges the most obvious:

Axiom 1: People are different from each other.

It is astonishing how few respectable conceptual tools we have for dealing with this self-evident fact. A tiny number of inconceivably coarse axes of categorization have been painstakingly inscribed in current critical and political thought: gender, race, class, nationality, sexual orientation are pretty much the available distinctions. They, with the associated demonstrations of the mechanisms by which they are constructed and reproduced, are indispensable, and they may indeed override all or some other forms of difference and similarity. But the sister or brother, the best friend, the classmate, the parent, the child, the lover, the ex-: our families, loves, and enmities alike, not to mention the strange relations of our work, play, and activism, prove that even people who share all or most of our own positionings along these crude axes may still be different enough from us, and from each other, to seem like all but different species.

Everybody has learned this, I assume, and probably everybody who survives at all has reasonably rich, unsystematic resources of nonce taxonomy for mapping out the possibilities, dangers, and stimulations of their human social landscape. It is probably people with the experience of oppression or subordination who have most *need* to know it; and I take the precious, devalued arts of gossip, immemorially associated in European thought with servants, with effeminate and gay men, with all women, to have to do not even so much with the transmission of necessary news as with the refinement of necessary skills for making, testing, and using unrationalized and provisional hypotheses about what *kinds of people* there are to be found in one's world.[25] The writing of a Proust or a James would be exemplary here: projects precisely of *nonce* taxonomy, of the making and unmaking and *re*making and redissolution of hundreds of old and new categorical imaginings concerning all the kinds it may take to make up a world.

I don't assume that all gay men or all women are very skilled at the nonce-taxonomic work represented by gossip, but it does make sense to suppose that our distinctive needs are peculiarly disserved by its devaluation. For some people, the sustained, foregrounded pressure of loss in the AIDS years may be making such needs clearer: as one anticipates or tries to deal with the absence of people one loves, it seems absurdly impoverishing to surrender to theoretical trivialization or to "the sentimental" one's descriptive requirements that the piercing bouquet of a given friend's particularity be done some justice. What is more dramatic is that—in spite of every promise to the contrary—every single theoretically or politically interesting project of postwar thought has finally had the effect of delegitimating our space for asking or thinking in detail about the multiple, unstable ways in which people may be like or different from each other. This project is not rendered otiose by any demonstration of how fully people may differ also from themselves. Deconstruction, founded as a very science of *différ(e/a)nce*, has both so fetishized the idea of difference and so vaporized its possible embodiments that its most thoroughgoing practitioners are the last people to whom one would now look for help in thinking about particular differences. The same thing seems likely to prove true of theorists of postmodernism. Psychoanalytic theory, if only through the almost astrologically lush plurality of its overlapping taxonomies of physical zones, developmental stages, repre-

25. On this, see Patricia Meyer Spacks, *Gossip* (New York: Alfred A. Knopf, 1985).

sentational mechanisms, and levels of consciousness, seemed to promise to introduce a certain becoming amplitude into discussions of what different people are like—only to turn, in its streamlined trajectory across so many institutional boundaries, into the sveltest of metatheoretical disciplines, sleeked down to such elegant operational entities as *the* mother, *the* father, *the* preoedipal, *the* oedipal, *the* other or Other. Within the less theorized institutional confines of intrapsychoanalytic discourse, meanwhile, a narrowly and severely normative, difference-eradicating ethical program has long sheltered under developmental narratives and a metaphorics of health and pathology.[26] In more familiar ways, Marxist, feminist, postcolonial, and other engagé critical projects have deepened understandings of a few crucial axes of difference, perhaps necessarily at the expense of more ephemeral or less global impulses of differential grouping. In each of these inquiries, so much has been gained by the different ways we have learned to deconstruct the category of *the individual* that it is easy for us now to read, say, Proust as the most expert operator of our modern technologies for dismantling taxonomies of the person. For the emergence and persistence of the vitalizing worldly taxonomic energies on which Proust also depends, however, we have no theoretical support to offer. And these defalcations in our indispensable antihumanist discourses have apparently ceded the potentially forceful ground of profound, complex variation to humanist liberal "tolerance" or repressively trivializing celebration at best, to reactionary suppression at worst.[27]

This is among other things a way of saying that there is a large family of things *we know* and need to know about ourselves and each other with which we have, as far as I can see, so far created for ourselves almost no theoretical room to deal. The shifting interfacial resistance of "literature itself" to "theory" may mark, along with its other denotations, the surface tension of this reservoir of unrationalized nonce-taxonomic energies; but, while distinctively representational, these energies are in no sense peculiarly literary.

In the particular area of sexuality, for instance, I assume that most of us

26. For a good discussion of this, see Henry Abelove, "Freud, Male Homosexuality, and the Americans," *Dissent* 33 (Winter 1986): 59–69.

27. Gayle Rubin discusses a related problem, that of the foreclosed space for acknowledging "benign sexual variation," in her "Thinking Sex: Notes for a Radical Theory of the Politics of Sexuality," in Carole S. Vance, ed., *Pleasure and Danger: Exploring Female Sexuality* (Boston: Routledge & Kegan Paul, 1984), p. 283.

know the following things that can differentiate even people of identical gender, race, nationality, class, and "sexual orientation"—each one of which, however, if taken seriously as pure *difference*, retains the unaccounted-for potential to disrupt many forms of the available thinking about sexuality.

• Even identical genital acts mean very different things to different people.

• To some people, the nimbus of "the sexual" seems scarcely to extend beyond the boundaries of discrete genital acts; to others, it enfolds them loosely or floats virtually free of them.

• Sexuality makes up a large share of the self-perceived identity of some people, a small share of others'.

• Some people spend a lot of time thinking about sex, others little.

• Some people like to have a lot of sex, others little or none.

• Many people have their richest mental/emotional involvement with sexual acts that they don't do, or even don't *want* to do.

• For some people, it is important that sex be embedded in contexts resonant with meaning, narrative, and connectedness with other aspects of their life; for other people, it is important that they not be; to others it doesn't occur that they might be.

• For some people, the preference for a certain sexual object, act, role, zone, or scenario is so immemorial and durable that it can only be experienced as innate; for others, it appears to come late or to feel aleatory or discretionary.

• For some people, the possibility of bad sex is aversive enough that their lives are strongly marked by its avoidance; for others, it isn't.

• For some people, sexuality provides a needed space of heightened discovery and cognitive hyperstimulation. For others, sexuality provides a needed space of routinized habituation and cognitive hiatus.

• Some people like spontaneous sexual scenes, others like highly scripted ones, others like spontaneous-sounding ones that are nonetheless totally predictable.

• Some people's sexual orientation is intensely marked by autoerotic pleasures and histories—sometimes more so than by any aspect of alloerotic object choice. For others the autoerotic possibility seems secondary or fragile, if it exists at all.

• Some people, homo-, hetero-, and bisexual, experience their sexuality as deeply embedded in a matrix of gender meanings and gender differentials. Others of each sexuality do not.

The list of individual differences could easily be extended. That many of them could differentiate one from another period of the same person's life as well as one person's totality from another's, or that many of them record differentia that can circulate from one person to another, does not, I believe, lessen their authority to demarcate; they demarcate at more than one site and on more than one scale. The impact of such a list may seem to depend radically on a trust in the self-perception, self-knowledge, or self-report of individuals, in an area that is if anything notoriously resistant to the claims of common sense and introspection: where would the whole, astonishing and metamorphic Western romance tradition (I include psychoanalysis) be if people's sexual desire, of all things, were even momentarily assumed to be transparent to themselves? Yet I am even more impressed by the leap of presumptuousness necessary to dismiss such a list of differences than by the leap of faith necessary to entertain it. To alienate conclusively, *definitionally*, from anyone on any theoretical ground the authority to describe and name their own sexual desire is a terribly consequential seizure. In this century, in which sexuality has been made expressive of the essence of both identity and knowledge, it may represent the most intimate violence possible. It is also an act replete with the most disempowering mundane institutional effects and potentials. It is, of course, central to the modern history of homophobic oppression.

The safer proceeding would seem to be to give as much credence as one finds it conceivable to give to self-reports of sexual difference — weighting one's credence, when it is necessary to weight it at all, in favor of the less normative and therefore riskier, costlier self-reports. To follow this proceeding is to enclose protectively large areas of, not mere agnosticism, but more active potential pluralism on the heavily contested maps of sexual definition. If, for instance, many people who self-identify as gay experience the gender of sexual object-choice, or some other proto-form of individual gay identity, as the most immutable and immemorial component of individual being, I can see no grounds for either subordinating this perception to or privileging it over that of other self-identified gay people whose experience of identity or object-choice has seemed to themselves to come relatively late or even to be discretionary. In so homophobic a culture, anyone's dangerous decision to self-identify as gay ought to command at least that entailment of *bona fides* and propriodescriptive authority. While there are certainly rhetorical and political grounds on which it may make sense to choose at a given moment between articulating, for instance, essentialist and constructivist (or minoritizing and universalizing) accounts of gay identity, there are, with equal certainty, rhetorical and political grounds for underwriting continuously the legitimacy of both accounts. And beyond these, there are crucial reasons of respect. I have felt that for this study to work most incisively would require framing its questions in such a way as to perform the least possible delegitimation of felt and reported differences and to impose the lightest possible burden of platonic definitional stress. Repeatedly to ask how certain categorizations work, what enactments they are performing and what relations they are creating, rather than what they essentially *mean*, has been my principal strategy.

> *Axiom 2: The study of sexuality is not coextensive with the study of gender; correspondingly, antihomophobic inquiry is not coextensive with feminist inquiry. But we can't know in advance how they will be different.*

Sex, gender, sexuality: three terms whose usage relations and analytical relations are almost irremediably slippery. The charting of a space between something called "sex" and something called "gender" has been one of the most influential and successful undertakings of feminist thought. For the purposes of that undertaking, "sex" has had the meaning of a certain group of irreducible, biological differentiations between members of the species Homo sapiens who have XX and those who have XY chromosomes. These include (or are ordinarily thought to include) more or less marked dimorphisms of genital formation, hair growth (in populations that have body hair), fat distribution, hormonal function, and reproductive capacity. "Sex" in this sense — what I'll demarcate as "chromosomal sex" — is seen as the relatively minimal raw material on which is then based the social construction of *gender*. Gender, then, is the far more elaborated, more fully and rigidly dichotomized social production and reproduction of male and female identities and behaviors — of male and female *persons* — in a cultural system for which "male/female" functions as a primary and perhaps model binarism affecting the structure and meaning of many, many other binarisms whose apparent connection to chromosomal sex will often be exiguous or nonexistent. Compared to chromosomal sex, which is seen (by these definitions) as tending to be immutable, immanent in the individual, and biologically based, the meaning of gender is seen as culturally mutable and variable, highly relational (in the sense that each of the binarized genders is defined primarily by its relation to the other), and inextricable from a history of power differentials between genders. This feminist charting of what Gayle Rubin refers to as a "sex/gender system,"[28] the system by which chromosomal sex is turned into, and processed as, cultural gender, has tended to minimize the attribution of people's various behaviors and identities to chromosomal sex and to maximize their attribution to socialized gender constructs. The purpose of that strategy has been to gain analytic and critical leverage on the female-disadvantaging social arrangements that prevail at a given time in a given society, by throwing into question their legitimative ideological grounding in biologically based narratives of the "natural."

"Sex" is, however, a term that extends indefinitely beyond chromosomal sex. That its history of usage often overlaps with what might, now, more properly be called "gender" is only one problem. ("I can only love someone of my own sex." Shouldn't "sex" be "gender" in such a sentence? "M. saw that the person who approached was of the opposite sex." Genders—insofar as there are two and they are defined in contradistinction to one another—may be said to be opposite; but in what sense is XX the opposite of XY?) Beyond chromosomes, however, the association of "sex," precisely through the physical body, with reproduction and with genital activity and sensation keeps offering new challenges to the conceptual clarity or even possibility of sex/gender differentiation. There is a powerful argument to be made that a primary (or *the* primary) issue in gender differentiation and gender struggle is the question of who is to have control of women's (biologically) distinctive reproductive capability. Indeed, the intimacy of the association between several of the most signal forms of gender oppression and "the facts" of women's bodies and women's reproductive activity has led some radical feminists to question, more or less explicitly, the usefulness of insisting on a sex/gender distinc-

28. Gayle Rubin, "The Traffic in Women: Notes on the 'Political Economy' of Sex," in Rayna R. Reiter, ed., *Toward an Anthropology of Women* (New York: Monthly Review Press, 1975), pp. 157–210.

tion. For these reasons, even usages involving the "sex/gender system" within feminist theory are able to use "sex/gender" only to delineate a problematical *space* rather than a crisp distinction. My own loose usage in this book will be to denominate that problematized space of the sex/ gender system, the whole package of physical and cultural distinctions between women and men, more simply under the rubric "gender." I do this in order to reduce the likelihood of confusion between "sex" in the sense of "the space of differences between male and female" (what I'll be grouping under "gender") and "sex" in the sense of sexuality.

For meanwhile the whole realm of what modern culture refers to as "sexuality" and *also* calls "sex"—the array of acts, expectations, narratives, pleasures, identity-formations, and knowledges, in both women and men, that tends to cluster most densely around certain genital sensations but is not adequately defined by them—that realm is virtually impossible to situate on a map delimited by the feminist-defined sex/ gender distinction. To the degree that it has a center or starting point in certain physical sites, acts, and rhythms associated (however contingently) with procreation or the potential for it, "sexuality" in this sense may seem to be of a piece with "chromosomal sex": biologically necessary to species survival, tending toward the individually immanent, the socially immutable, the given. But to the extent that, as Freud argued and Foucault assumed, the distinctively sexual nature of human sexuality has to do precisely with its excess over or potential difference from the bare choreographies of procreation, "sexuality" might be the very opposite of what we originally referred to as (chromosomal-based) sex: it could occupy, instead, even more than "gender" the polar position of the relational, the social/symbolic, the constructed, the variable, the representational (see Figure 1). To note that, according to these different findings, *something* legitimately called sex or sexuality is all over the experiential and conceptual map is to record a problem less resolvable than a necessary choice of analytic paradigms or a determinate slippage of semantic meaning; it is rather, I would say, true to quite a range of contemporary worldviews and intuitions to find that sex/sexuality *does* tend to represent the full spectrum of positions between the most intimate and the most social, the most predetermined and the most aleatory, the most physically rooted and the most symbolically infused, the most innate and the most learned, the most autonomous and the most relational traits of being.

If all this is true of the definitional nexus between sex and sexuality, how much less simple, even, must be that between sexuality and gender. It will

Biological		Cultural
Essential		Constructed
Individually immanent		Relational

Constructivist Feminist Analysis

chromosomal sex ──────────────────── gender
gender inequality

Radical Feminist Analysis

chromosomal sex
reproductive relations ──────────────── reproductive relations
sexual inequality   sexual inequality

Foucault-influenced Analysis

chromosomal sex ──────── reproduction ──────── sexuality

Figure 1.   Some Mappings of Sex, Gender, and Sexuality

be an assumption of this study that there is always at least the potential for an analytic distance between gender and sexuality, even if particular manifestations or features of particular sexualities are among the things that plunge women and men most ineluctably into the discursive, institutional, and bodily enmeshments of gender definition, gender relation, and gender inequality. This, too, has been posed by Gayle Rubin:

> I want to challenge the assumption that feminism is or should be the privileged site of a theory of sexuality. Feminism is the theory of gender oppression. . . . Gender affects the operation of the sexual system, and the sexual system has had gender-specific manifestations. But although sex and gender are related, they are not the same thing.[29]

This book will hypothesize, with Rubin, that the question of gender and the question of sexuality, inextricable from one another though they are in that each can be expressed only in the terms of the other, are nonetheless not the same question, that in twentieth-century Western culture gender and sexuality represent two analytic axes that may productively be imagined as being as distinct from one another as, say, gender and class, or class and race. Distinct, that is to say, no more than minimally, but nonetheless usefully.

Under this hypothesis, then, just as one has learned to assume that

29. Rubin, "Thinking Sex," pp. 307–8.

every issue of racial meaning must be embodied through the specificity of a particular class position — and every issue of class, for instance, through the specificity of a particular gender position — so every issue of gender would necessarily be embodied through the specificity of a particular sexuality, and vice versa; but nonetheless there could be use in keeping the analytic axes distinct.

An objection to this analogy might be that gender is *definitionally* built into determinations of sexuality, in a way that neither of them is definitionally intertwined with, for instance, determinations of class or race. It is certainly true that without a concept of gender there could be, quite simply, no concept of homo- or heterosexuality. But many other dimensions of sexual choice (auto- or alloerotic, within or between generations, species, etc.) have no such distinctive, explicit definitional connection with gender; indeed, some dimensions of sexuality might be tied, not to gender, but *instead* to differences or similarities of race or class. The definitional narrowing-down in this century of sexuality as a whole to a binarized calculus of *homo-* or *hetero*sexuality is a weighty fact but an entirely historical one. To use that fait accompli as a reason for analytically conflating sexuality per se with gender would obscure the degree to which the fact itself requires explanation. It would also, I think, risk obscuring yet again the extreme intimacy with which all these available analytic axes do after all mutually constitute one another: to assume the distinctiveness of the *intimacy* between sexuality and gender might well risk assuming too much about the definitional *separability* of either of them from determinations of, say, class or race.

It may be, as well, that a damaging bias toward heterosocial or heterosexist assumptions inheres unavoidably in the very concept of gender. This bias would be built into any gender-based analytic perspective to the extent that gender definition and gender identity are necessarily relational between genders — to the extent, that is, that in any gender system, female identity or definition is constructed by analogy, supplementarity, or contrast to male, or vice versa. Although many gender-based forms of analysis do involve accounts, sometimes fairly rich ones, of intragender behaviors and relations, the ultimate definitional appeal in any gender-based analysis must necessarily be to the diacritical frontier between different genders. This gives heterosocial and heterosexual relations a conceptual privilege of incalculable consequence. Undeniably, residues, markers, tracks, signs referring to that diacritical frontier between genders are everywhere, as well, internal to and determinative of the experience of each gender and its intragender relations; gender-based analysis can never be dispensed with in even the most purely intragender context. Nevertheless it seems predictable that the analytic bite of a purely gender-based account will grow less incisive and direct as the distance of its subject from a social interface between different genders increases. It is unrealistic to expect a close, textured analysis of same-sex relations through an optic calibrated in the first place to the coarser stigmata of gender difference.[30] The development of an alternative analytic axis—call it sexuality—might well be, therefore, a particularly urgent project for gay/lesbian and antihomophobic inquiry.

It would be a natural corollary to Axiom 2 to hypothesize, then, that gay/lesbian and antihomophobic inquiry still has a lot to learn from asking questions that feminist inquiry has learned to ask—but only so long as we don't demand to receive the same answers in both interlocutions. In a comparison of feminist and gay theory as they currently stand, the newness and consequent relative underdevelopment of gay theory are seen most clearly in two manifestations. First, we are by now very used to asking as feminists what we aren't yet used to asking as antihomophobic readers: how a variety of forms of oppression intertwine systemically with each other; and especially how the person who is disabled through one set of oppressions may *by the same positioning* be enabled through others. For instance, the understated demeanor of educated women in our society tends to mark both their deference to educated men and their expectation of deference from women and men of lower class. Again, a woman's use of a married name makes graphic at the same time her subordination as a woman and her privilege as a presumptive heterosexual. Or, again, the distinctive vulnerability to rape of women of all races has become in this country a powerful tool for the racist enforcement by which white people, including women, are privileged at the expense of Black people of both genders. That one is *either* oppressed *or* an oppressor, or that if one happens to be both, the two are not likely to have much to do with each other, still seems to be a common assumption, however, in at any rate

---

30. For valuable related discussions, see Katie King, "The Situation of Lesbianism as Feminism's Magical Sign: Contests for Meaning and the US Women's Movement, 1968–1972," in *Communication* 9 (1986): 65–91. Special issue, "Feminist Critiques of Popular Culture," ed. Paula A. Treichler and Ellen Wartella, 9: 65–91; and Teresa de Lauretis, "Sexual Indifference and Lesbian Representation," *Theatre Journal* 40 (May 1988): 155–77.

male gay writing and activism,[31] as it hasn't for a long time been in careful feminist work.

Indeed, it was the long, painful realization, *not* that all oppressions are congruent, but that they are *differently* structured and so must intersect in complex embodiments that was the first great heuristic breakthrough of socialist-feminist thought and of the thought of women of color.[32] This realization has as its corollary that the comparison of different axes of oppression is a crucial task, not for any purpose of ranking oppressions, but to the contrary because each oppression is likely to be in a uniquely indicative relation to certain distinctive nodes of cultural organization. The *special* centrality of homophobic oppression in the twentieth century, I will be arguing, has resulted from its inextricability from the question of

31. Gay male–centered work that uses more complex models to investigate the intersection of different oppressions includes Gay Left Collective, eds., *Homosexuality: Power and Politics* (London: Allison & Busby, 1980); Paul Hoch, *White Hero Black Beast: Racism, Sexism, and the Mask of Masculinity* (London: Pluto, 1979); Guy Hocquenghem, *Homosexual Desire*, trans. Daniella Dangoor (London: Allison & Busby, 1978); Mario Mieli, *Homosexuality and Liberation: Elements of a Gay Critique*, trans. David Fernbach (London: Gay Men's Press, 1980); D. A. Miller, *The Novel and the Police* (Berkeley and Los Angeles: University of California Press, 1988); Michael Moon, "'The Gentle Boy from the Dangerous Classes': Pederasty, Domesticity, and Capitalism in Horatio Alger," *Representations*, no. 19 (Summer 1987): 87–110; Michael Moon, *Disseminating Whitman* (Cambridge: Harvard University Press, 1990); and Jeffrey Weeks, *Sexuality and its Discontents: Meanings, Myths and Modern Sexualities* (London: Longman, 1980).

32. The influential socialist-feminist investigations have included Michèle Barrett, *Women's Oppression Today: Problems in Marxist Feminist Analysis* (London: Verso, 1980); Zillah Eisenstein, ed., *Capitalist Patriarchy and the Case for Socialist Feminism* (New York: Monthly Review Press, 1979); and Juliet Mitchell, *Women's Estate* (New York: Vintage, 1973). On the intersections of racial with gender and sexual oppressions, see, for example, Elly Bulkin, Barbara Smith, and Minnie Bruce Pratt, *Yours in Struggle: Three Feminist Perspectives on Anti-Semitism and Racism* (New York: Long Haul Press, 1984); Bell Hooks [Gloria Watkins], *Feminist Theory: From Margin to Center* (Boston: South End Press, 1984); Katie King, "Audre Lorde's Lacquered Layerings: The Lesbian Bar as a Site of Literary Production," *Cultural Studies* 2, no. 3 (1988): 321–42; Audre Lorde, *Sister Outsider: Essays and Speeches* (Trumansburg, N.Y.: The Crossing Press, 1984); Cherríe Moraga, *Loving in the War Years: Lo que nunca paso por sus labios* (Boston: South End Press, 1983); Cherríe Moraga and Gloria Anzaldua, eds., *This Bridge Called My Back: Writings by Radical Women of Color* (Watertown: Persephone, 1981; rpt. ed., New York: Kitchen Table: Women of Color Press, 1984); and Barbara Smith, ed., *Home Girls: A Black Feminist Anthology* (New York: Kitchen Table: Women of Color Press, 1983). Good overviews of several of these intersections as they relate to women and in particular to lesbians, can be found in Ann Snitow, Christine Stansell, and Sharon Thompson, eds., *The Powers of Desire: The Politics of Sexuality* (New York: Monthly Review/New Feminist Library, 1983); Vance, *Pleasure and Danger*; and de Lauretis, "Sexual Indifference."

knowledge and the processes of knowing in modern Western culture at large.

The second and perhaps even greater heuristic leap of feminism has been the recognition that categories of gender and, hence, oppressions of gender can have a structuring force for nodes of thought, for axes of cultural discrimination, whose thematic subject isn't explicitly gendered at all. Through a series of developments structured by the deconstructive understandings and procedures sketched above, we have now learned as feminist readers that dichotomies in a given text of culture as opposed to nature, public as opposed to private, mind as opposed to body, activity as opposed to passivity, etc. etc., are, under particular pressures of culture and history, likely places to look for implicit allegories of the relations of men to women; more, that to fail to analyze such nominally ungendered constructs in gender terms can itself be a gravely tendentious move in the gender politics of reading. This has given us ways to ask the question of gender about texts even where the culturally "marked" gender (female) is not present as either author or thematic.

The dichotomy heterosexual/homosexual, as it has emerged through the last century of Western discourse, would seem to lend itself peculiarly neatly to a set of analytic moves learned from this deconstructive moment in feminist theory. In fact, the dichotomy heterosexual/homosexual fits the deconstructive template much more neatly than male/female itself does, and hence, importantly differently. The most dramatic difference between gender and sexual orientation—that virtually all people are publicly and unalterably assigned to one or the other gender, and from birth—seems if anything to mean that it is, rather, sexual orientation, with its far greater potential for rearrangement, ambiguity, and representational doubleness, that would offer the apter deconstructive object. An essentialism of sexual object-choice is far less easy to maintain, far more visibly incoherent, more visibly stressed and challenged at every point in the culture than any essentialism of gender. This is not an argument for any epistemological or ontological privileging of an axis of sexuality over an axis of gender; but it is a powerful argument for their potential distinctness one from the other.

Even given the imperative of constructing an account of sexuality irreducible to gender, however, it should already be clear that there are certain distortions necessarily built into the relation of gay/lesbian and antihomophobic theory to a larger project of conceiving a theory of sexuality as a whole. The two can after all scarcely be coextensive. And this is true not because "gay/lesbian and antihomophobic theory" would fail to cover heterosexual as well as same-sex object-choice (any more than "feminist theory" would fail to cover men as well as women), but rather because, as we have noted, sexuality extends along so many dimensions that aren't well described in terms of the gender of object-choice at all. Some of these dimensions are habitually condensed under the rubrics of object-choice, so that certain discriminations of (for instance) *act* or of (for another instance) *erotic localization* come into play, however implicitly and however incoherently, when categories of object-choice are mobilized. One used, for instance, to hear a lot about a high developmental stage called "heterosexual genitality," as though cross-gender object-choice automatically erased desires attaching to mouth, anus, breasts, feet, etc.; a certain anal-erotic salience of male homosexuality is if anything increasingly strong under the glare of heterosexist AIDS-phobia; and several different historical influences have led to the de-genitalization and bodily diffusion of many popular, and indeed many lesbian, understandings of lesbian sexuality. Other dimensions of sexuality, however, distinguish object-choice quite differently (e.g., human/animal, adult/child, singular/plural, autoerotic/alloerotic) or are not even about object choice (e.g., orgasmic/nonorgasmic, noncommercial/commercial, using bodies only/using manufactured objects, in private/in public, spontaneous/scripted).[33] Some of these other dimensions of sexuality have had high diacritical importance in different historical contexts (e.g., human/animal, autoerotic/alloerotic). Others, like adult/child object choice, visibly do have such importance today, but without being very fully subsumed under the hetero/homosexual binarism. Still others, including a host of them I haven't mentioned or couldn't think of, subsist in this culture as nondiacritical differences, differences that seem to make little difference beyond themselves—except that the hyperintensive structuring of sexuality in our culture sets several of them, for instance, at the exact border between legal and illegal. What I mean at any rate to emphasize is that the implicit condensation of "sexual theory" into "gay/lesbian and antihomophobic theory," which corresponds roughly to our by now unquestioned reading of the phrase "sexual orientation" to mean "gender of object-choice," is at the very least damagingly skewed by the specificity of its historical placement.

33. This list owes something to Rubin, "Thinking Sex," esp. pp. 281–82.

Axiom 3: There can't be an a priori decision about how far it will make sense to conceptualize lesbian and gay male identities together. Or separately.

Although it was clear from the beginning of this book project that its central focus would be on male sexual definition, the theoretical tools for drawing a circumferential boundary around that center have been elusive. They have changed perceptibly even during the period of this writing. In particular, the interpretive frameworks within which lesbian writers, readers, and interlocutors are likely to process male-centered reflections on homo/heterosexual issues are in a phase of destabilizing flux and promise.

The lesbian interpretive framework most readily available at the time this project began was the separatist-feminist one that emerged from the 1970s. According to that framework, there were essentially no valid grounds of commonality between gay male and lesbian experience and identity; to the contrary, women-loving women and men-loving men must be at precisely opposite ends of the gender spectrum. The assumptions at work here were indeed radical ones: most important, as we'll be discussing further in the next chapter, the stunningly efficacious re-visioning, in female terms, of same-sex desire as being at the very definitional center of each gender, rather than as occupying a cross-gender or liminal position between them. Thus, women who loved women were seen as *more* female, men who loved men as quite possibly more male, than those whose desire crossed boundaries of gender. The axis of sexuality, in this view, was not only exactly coextensive with the axis of gender but expressive of its most heightened essence: "Feminism is the theory, lesbianism is the practice." By analogy, male homosexuality could be, and often was, seen as the practice for which male supremacy was the theory.[34] A particular reading of modern gender history was, of course, implicit in and in turn propelled by this gender-separatist framework. In accord with, for instance, Adrienne Rich's understanding of many aspects of women's bonds as constituting a "lesbian continuum," this history, found in its purest form in the work of Lilian Faderman, deemphasized the definitional discontinuities and perturbations between more and less sexualized, more

34. See, among others, Marilyn Frye, *The Politics of Reality: Essays in Feminist Theory* (Trumansburg, N.Y.: The Crossing Press, 1983), and Luce Irigaray, *This Sex Which Is Not One*, trans. Catherine Porter with Carolyn Burke (Ithaca: Cornell University Press, 1985), pp. 170–91.

and less prohibited, and more and less gender-identity-bound forms of female same-sex bonding.[35] Insofar as lesbian object-choice was viewed as epitomizing a specificity of female experience and resistance, insofar as a symmetrically opposite understanding of gay male object-choice also obtained, and insofar also as feminism necessarily posited male and female experiences and interests as different and opposed, the implication was that an understanding of male homo/heterosexual definition could offer little or no affordance or interest for any lesbian theoretical project. Indeed, the powerful impetus of a gender-polarized feminist ethical schema made it possible for a profoundly antihomophobic reading of lesbian desire (as a quintessence of the female) to fuel a correspondingly homophobic reading of gay male desire (as a quintessence of the male).

Since the late 1970s, however, there have emerged a variety of challenges to this understanding of how lesbian and gay male desires and identities might be mapped against each other. Each challenge has led to a refreshed sense that lesbians and gay men may share important though contested aspects of one another's histories, cultures, identities, politics, and destinies. These challenges have emerged from the "sex wars" within feminism over pornography and s/m, which seemed to many pro-sex feminists to expose a devastating continuity between a certain, theretofore privileged feminist understanding of a resistant female identity, on the one hand, and on the other the most repressive nineteenth-century bourgeois constructions of a sphere of pure femininity. Such challenges emerged as well from the reclamation and relegitimation of a courageous history of lesbian trans-gender role-playing and identification.[36] Along with this new historical making-visible of self-defined mannish lesbians came a new salience of the many ways in which male and female homosexual identities had in fact been constructed through and in relation to each other over

35. Adrienne Rich, "Compulsory Heterosexuality and Lesbian Existence," in Catharine R. Stimpson and Ethel Spector Person, eds., *Women, Sex, and Sexuality* (Chicago: University of Chicago Press, 1980), pp. 62–91; Lilian Faderman, *Surpassing the Love of Men* (New York: William Morrow, 1982).

36. See, for instance, Esther Newton, "The Mythic Mannish Lesbian: Radclyffe Hall and the New Woman," in Estelle B. Freedman, Barbara C. Gelpi, Susan L. Johnson, and Kathleen M. Weston, eds., *The Lesbian Issue: Essays from SIGNS* (Chicago: University of Chicago Press, 1985), pp. 7–25; Joan Nestle, "Butch-Fem Relationships," pp. 21–24, and Amber Hollibaugh and Cherríe Moraga, "What We're Rollin' Around in Bed With," pp. 58–62, both in *Heresies* 12, no. 3 (1981); Sue-Ellen Case, "Towards a Butch-Femme Aesthetic," *Discourse: Journal for Theoretical Studies in Media and Culture* 11, no. 1 (Fall–Winter 1988–1989): 55–73; de Lauretis, "Sexual Indifference"; and my "Across Gender, Across Sexuality: Willa Cather and Others," *SAQ* 88, no. 1 (Winter 1989): 53–72.

the last century — by the variously homophobic discourses of professional expertise, but also and just as actively by many lesbians and gay men.[37] The irrepressible, relatively class-nonspecific popular culture in which James Dean has been as numinous an icon for lesbians as Garbo or Dietrich has for gay men seems resistant to a purely feminist theorization.[38] It is in these contexts that calls for a theorized axis of sexuality as distinct from gender have developed. And after the anti-s/m, antipornography liberal-feminist move toward labeling and stigmatizing particular sexualities joined its energies with those of the much longer-established conservative sanctions against all forms of sexual "deviance," it remained only for the terrible accident of the HIV epidemic and the terrifyingly genocidal overdeterminations of AIDS discourse to reconstruct a category of the pervert capacious enough to admit homosexuals of any gender. The newly virulent homophobia of the 1980s, directed alike against women and men even though its medical pretext ought, if anything, logically to give a relative exemptive privilege to lesbians,[39] reminds ungently that it is more to friends than to enemies that gay women and gay men are perceptible as distinct groups. Equally, however, the internal perspective of the gay movements shows women and men increasingly, though far from uncontestingly and far from equally, working together on mutually antihomophobic agendas. The contributions of lesbians to current gay and AIDS activism are weighty, not despite, but because of the intervening lessons of feminism. Feminist perspectives on medicine and health-care issues, on civil disobedience, and on the politics of class and race as well as of sexuality have been centrally enabling for the recent waves of AIDS activism. What this activism returns to the lesbians in-

37. On this see, among others, Judy Grahn, *Another Mother Tongue: Gay Words, Gay Worlds* (Boston: Beacon Press, 1984).

38. On James Dean, see Sue Golding, "James Dean: The Almost-Perfect Lesbian Hermaphrodite," *On Our Backs* (Winter 1988): 18–19, 39–44.

39. This is not, of course, to suggest that lesbians are less likely than persons of any other sexuality to contract HIV infection, when they engage in the (quite common) acts that can transmit the virus, with a person (and there are many, including lesbians) who already carries it. In this particular paradigm-clash between a discourse of sexual *identity* and a discourse of sexual *acts*, the former alternative is uniquely damaging. No one should wish to reinforce the myth that the epidemiology of AIDS is a matter of discrete "risk groups" rather than of particular acts that can call for particular forms of prophylaxis. That myth is dangerous to self-identified or publicly identified gay men and drug users because it scapegoats them, and dangerous to everyone else because it discourages them from protecting themselves and their sex or needle partners. But, for a variety of reasons, the incidence of AIDS among lesbians has indeed been lower than among many other groups.

volved in it may include a more richly pluralized range of imaginings of lines of gender and sexual identification.

Thus, it can no longer make sense, if it ever did, simply to assume that a male-centered analysis of homo/heterosexual definition will have no lesbian relevance or interest. At the same time, there are no algorithms for assuming a priori what its lesbian relevance could be or how far its lesbian interest might extend. It seems inevitable to me that the work of defining the circumferential boundaries, vis-à-vis lesbian experience and identity, of any gay male–centered theoretical articulation can be done only from the point of view of an alternative, feminocentric theoretical space, not from the heart of the male-centered project itself.

However interested I am in understanding those boundaries and their important consequences, therefore, the project of this particular book, just as it will not *assume* their geography, is not the one that can trace them. That limitation seems a damaging one chiefly insofar as it echoes and prolongs an already scandalously extended eclipse: the extent to which women's sexual, and specifically homosexual, experience and definition tend to be subsumed by men's during the turn-of-the-century period most focused on in my discussion, and are liable once again to be subsumed *in* such discussion. If one could demarcate the extent of the subsumption precisely, it would be less destructive, but "subsumption" is not a structure that makes precision easy. The problem is obvious even at the level of nomenclature and affects, of course, that of this book no less than any other; I have discussed above the particular choices of usage made here. Corresponding to those choices, the "gay theory" I have been comparing with feminist theory doesn't mean exclusively gay male theory, but for the purpose of this comparison it includes lesbian theory insofar as that (a) isn't simply coextensive with feminist theory (i.e., doesn't subsume sexuality *fully* under gender) and (b) doesn't a priori deny all theoretical continuity between male homosexuality and lesbianism. But, again, the extent, construction, and meaning, and especially the history of any such theoretical continuity—not to mention its consequences for practical politics—must be open to every interrogation. That gay theory, falling under this definition and centering insistently on lesbian experience, can still include strongly feminist thought would be demonstrated by works as different as those of Gayle Rubin, Audre Lorde, Katie King, and Cherríe Moraga.

Axiom 4: The immemorial, seemingly ritualized debates on nature versus nurture take place against a very unstable background of tacit assumptions and fantasies about both nurture and nature.

If there is one compulsory setpiece for the Introduction to any gay-oriented book written in the late 1980s, it must be the meditation on and attempted adjudication of constructivist versus essentialist views of homosexuality. The present study is hardly the first to demur vigorously from such a task, although I can only wish that its demurral might be vigorous enough to make it one of the last to need to do so. My demurral has two grounds. The first, as I have mentioned and will discuss further in later chapters, is that any such adjudication is impossible to the degree that a conceptual deadlock between the two opposing views has by now been built into the very structure of every theoretical tool we have for undertaking it. The second one is already implicit in a terminological choice I have been making: to refer to "minoritizing" versus "universalizing" rather than to essentialist versus constructivist understandings of homosexuality. I prefer the former terminology because it seems to record and respond to the question, "In whose lives is homo/heterosexual definition an issue of continuing centrality and difficulty?" rather than either of the questions that seem to have gotten conflated in the constructivist/essentialist debate: on the one hand what one might call the question of phylogeny, "How fully are the meaning and experience of sexual activity and identity contingent on their mutual structuring with other, historically and culturally variable aspects of a given society?"; and on the other what one might call that of ontogeny, "What is the cause of homo- [or of hetero-] sexuality in the individual?" I am specifically offering minoritizing/universalizing as an *alternative* (though not an equivalent) to essentialist/constructivist, in the sense that I think it can do some of the same analytic work as the latter binarism, and rather more tellingly. I think it may isolate the areas where the questions of ontogeny and phylogeny most consequentially overlap. I also think, as I suggested in Axiom 1, that it is more respectful of the varied proprioception of many authoritative individuals. But I am additionally eager to promote the obsolescence of "essentialist/constructivist" because I am very dubious about the ability of even the most scrupulously gay-affirmative thinkers to divorce these terms, especially as they relate to the question of ontogeny, from the essentially gay-genocidal nexuses of thought through which they have developed. And beyond that: even where we may think we know the conceptual landscape of their history well enough to do the delicate, always dangerous work of prying them loose from their historical backing to attach to them newly enabling meanings, I fear that the special volatility of postmodern bodily and technological relations may make such an attempt peculiarly liable to tragic misfire. Thus, it would seem to me that gay-affirmative work does well when it aims to minimize its reliance on any particular account of the origin of sexual preference and identity in individuals.

In particular, my fear is that there currently exists no framework in which to ask about the origins or development of individual gay identity that is not already structured by an implicit, trans-individual Western project or fantasy of eradicating that identity. It seems ominously symptomatic that, under the dire homophobic pressures of the last few years, and in the name of Christianity, the subtle constructivist argument that sexual aim is, at least for many people, not a hard-wired biological given but, rather, a social fact deeply embedded in the cultural and linguistic forms of many, many decades is being degraded to the blithe ukase that people are "free at any moment to" (i.e., must immediately) "choose" to adhere to a particular sexual identity (say, at a random hazard, the heterosexual) rather than to its other. (Here we see the disastrously unmarked crossing of phylogenetic with ontogenetic narratives.) To the degree—and it is significantly large—that the gay essentialist/constructivist debate takes its form and premises from, and insistently refers to, a whole history of other nature/nurture or nature/culture debates, it partakes of a tradition of viewing culture as malleable relative to nature: that is, culture, unlike nature, is assumed to be the thing that can be changed; the thing in which "humanity" has, furthermore, a right or even an obligation to intervene. This has certainly been the grounding of, for instance, the feminist formulation of the sex/gender system described above, whose implication is that the more fully gender inequality can be shown to inhere in human culture rather than in biological nature, the more amenable it must be to alteration and reform. I remember the buoyant enthusiasm with which feminist scholars used to greet the finding that one or another brutal form of oppression was not biological but "only" cultural! I have often wondered what the basis was for our optimism about the malleability of culture by any one group or program. At any rate, never so far as I know has there been a sufficiently powerful place from which to argue that such manipulations, however triumphal the ethical imperative behind them, were not a right that belonged to anyone who might have the power to perform them.

The number of persons or institutions by whom the existence of gay people—never mind the existence of *more gay people*—is treated as a precious desideratum, a needed condition of life, is small, even compared to those who may wish for the dignified treatment of any gay people who happen already to exist. Advice on how to make sure your kids turn out gay, not to mention your students, your parishioners, your therapy clients, or your military subordinates, is less ubiquitous than you might think. By contrast, the scope of institutions whose programmatic undertaking is to prevent the development of gay people is unimaginably large. No major institutionalized discourse offers a firm resistance to that undertaking; in the United States, at any rate, most sites of the state, the military, education, law, penal institutions, the church, medicine, mass culture, and the mental health industries enforce it all but unquestioningly, and with little hesitation even at recourse to invasive violence. So for gay and gay-loving people, even though the space of cultural malleability is the only conceivable theatre for our effective politics, every step of this constructivist nature/culture argument holds danger: it is so difficult to intervene in the seemingly natural trajectory that begins by identifying a place of cultural malleability; continues by inventing an ethical or therapeutic mandate for cultural manipulation; and ends in the overarching, hygienic Western fantasy of a world without any more homosexuals in it.

That's one set of dangers, and it is against them, I think, that essentialist understandings of sexual identity accrue a certain gravity. The resistance that seems to be offered by conceptualizing an unalterably *homosexual body*, to the social engineering momentum apparently built into every one of the human sciences of the West, can reassure profoundly. Furthermore, it reaches deeply and, in a sense, protectively into a fraught space of life-or-death struggle that has been more or less abandoned by constructivist gay theory: that is, the experience and identity of gay or proto-gay children. The ability of anyone in the culture to support and honor gay kids may depend on an ability to name them as such, notwithstanding that many gay adults may never have been gay kids and some gay kids may not turn into gay adults. It seems plausible that a lot of the emotional energy behind essentialist historical work has to do not even in the first place with reclaiming the place and eros of Homeric heroes, Renaissance painters, and medieval gay monks, so much as with the far less permissible, vastly more necessary project of recognizing and validating the creativity and heroism of the effeminate boy or tommish girl of the fifties (or sixties or seventies or eighties) whose sense of constituting precisely a *gap* in the discursive fabric of the given has not been done justice, so far, by constructivist work.

At the same time, however, just as it comes to seem questionable to assume that cultural constructs are peculiarly malleable ones, it is also becoming increasingly problematical to assume that grounding an identity in biology or "essential nature" is a stable way of insulating it from societal interference. If anything, the gestalt of assumptions that undergird nature/nurture debates may be in the process of direct reversal. Increasingly it is the conjecture that a particular trait is genetically or biologically based, *not* that it is "only cultural," that seems to trigger an estrus of manipulative fantasy in the technological institutions of the culture. A relative depressiveness about the efficacy of social engineering techniques, a high mania about biological control: the Cartesian bipolar psychosis that always underlay the nature/nurture debates has switched its polar assignments without surrendering a bit of its hold over the collective life. And in this unstable context, the dependence on a specified *homosexual body* to offer resistance to any gay-eradicating momentum is tremblingly vulnerable. AIDS, though it is used to proffer every single day to the news-consuming public the crystallized vision of a world after the homosexual, could never by itself bring about such a world. What whets these fantasies more dangerously, because more blandly, is the presentation, often in ostensibly or authentically gay-affirmative contexts, of biologically based "explanations" for deviant behavior that are absolutely invariably couched in terms of "excess," "deficiency," or "imbalance"— whether in the hormones, in the genetic material, or, as is currently fashionable, in the fetal endocrine environment. If I had ever, in any medium, seen any researcher or popularizer refer even once to any supposed gay-producing circumstance as the *proper* hormone balance, or the *conducive* endocrine environment, for gay generation, I would be less chilled by the breezes of all this technological confidence. As things are, a medicalized dream of the prevention of gay bodies seems to be the less visible, far more respectable underside of the AIDS-fueled public dream of their extirpation. In this unstable balance of assumptions between nature and culture, at any rate, under the overarching, relatively unchallenged aegis of a culture's desire that gay people *not be*, there is no unthreatened, unthreatening conceptual home for a concept of gay origins. We have all the more reason, then, to keep our understanding of gay origin, of gay cultural and material reproduction, plural, multi-capillaried, argus-eyed, respectful, and endlessly cherished.

> *Axiom 5: The historical search for a Great Paradigm Shift may obscure the present conditions of sexual identity.*

Since 1976, when Michel Foucault, in an act of polemical bravado, offered 1870 as the date of birth of modern homosexuality,[40] the most sophisticated historically oriented work in gay studies has been offering ever more precise datings, ever more nuanced narratives of the development of homosexuality "as we know it today."[41] The great value of this scholarly movement has been to subtract from that "as we know it today" the twin positivist assumptions (1) that there must be some *transhistorical* essence of "homosexuality" available to modern knowledge, and (2) that the history of understandings of same-sex relations has been a history of increasingly direct, true knowledge or comprehension of that essence. To the contrary, the recent historicizing work has assumed (1) that the differences between the homosexuality "we know today" and previous arrangements of same-sex relations may be so profound and so integrally rooted in other cultural differences that there may be no continuous, defining essence of "homosexuality" to *be* known; and (2) that modern "sexuality" and hence modern homosexuality are so intimately entangled with the historically distinctive contexts and structures that now count as *knowledge* that such "knowledge" can scarcely be a transparent window onto a separate realm of sexuality but, rather, itself constitutes that sexuality.

These developments have promised to be exciting and productive in the way that the most important work of history or, for that matter, of anthropology may be: in radically defamiliarizing and denaturalizing, not only the past and the distant, but the present. One way, however, in which such an analysis is still incomplete—in which, indeed, it seems

40. Foucault, *History of Sexuality*, p. 43.
41. See, for instance, Alan Bray, *Homosexuality in Renaissance England* (London: Gay Men's Press, 1982); Katz, *Gay/Lesbian Almanac*; Halperin, *One Hundred Years of Homosexuality*; Jeffrey Weeks, *Sex, Politics, and Society: The Regulation of Sexuality since 1800* (London: Longman, 1981); and George Chauncey, Jr., "From Sexual Inversion to Homosexuality: Medicine and the Changing Conceptualization of Female Deviance," *Salmagundi*, no. 58–59 (Fall 1982–Winter 1983): 114–45.

to me that it has tended inadvertently to *re*familiarize, *re*naturalize, damagingly reify an entity that it could be doing much more to subject to analysis—is in counterposing against the alterity of the past a relatively unified homosexuality that "we" *do* "know today." It seems that the topos of "homosexuality as we know it today," or even, to incorporate more fully the antipositivist finding of the Foucauldian shift, "homosexuality as we *conceive of it* today," has provided a rhetorically necessary fulcrum point for the denaturalizing work on the past done by many historians. But an unfortunate side effect of this move has been implicitly to underwrite the notion that "homosexuality as we conceive of it today" itself comprises a coherent definitional field rather than a space of overlapping, contradictory, and conflictual definitional forces. Unfortunately, this presents more than a problem of oversimplification. To the degree that power relations involving modern homo/heterosexual definition have been structured by the very tacitness of the double-binding force fields of conflicting definition—to the degree that, as Chapter 4 puts it more fully, the presumptuous, worldly implication "We Know What That Means" happens to be "the particular lie that animates and perpetuates the mechanism of [modern] homophobic male self-ignorance and violence and manipulability"—to that degree these historical projects, for all their immense care, value, and potential, still risk reinforcing a dangerous consensus of knowingness about the genuinely *un*known, more than vestigially contradictory structurings of contemporary experience.

As an example of this contradiction effect, let me juxtapose two programmatic statements of what seem to be intended as parallel and congruent projects. In the foundational Foucault passage to which I alluded above, the modern category of "homosexuality" that dates from 1870 is said to be

> characterized . . . less by a type of sexual relations than by a certain quality of sexual sensibility, a certain way of inverting the masculine and the feminine in oneself. Homosexuality appeared as one of the forms of sexuality when it was transposed from the practice of sodomy onto a kind of interior androgyny, a hermaphrodism of the soul. The sodomite had been a temporary aberration; the homosexual was now a species.

In Foucault's account, the unidirectional emergence in the late nineteenth century of "the homosexual" as "a species," of homosexuality as a minoritizing identity, is seen as tied to an also unidirectional, and continuing, emergent understanding of homosexuality in terms of gender inversion and gender transitivity. This understanding appears, indeed, according to Foucault, to underlie and constitute the common sense of the homosexuality "we know today." A more recent account by David M. Halperin, on the other hand, explicitly in the spirit and under the influence of Foucault but building, as well, on some intervening research by George Chauncey and others, constructs a rather different narrative—but constructs it, in a sense, *as if it were the same one*:

> Homosexuality and heterosexuality, as we currently understand them, are modern, Western, bourgeois productions. Nothing resembling them can be found in classical antiquity. . . . In London and Paris, in the seventeenth and eighteenth centuries, there appear . . . social gathering-places for persons of the same sex with the same socially deviant attitudes to sex and gender who wish to socialize and to have sex with one another. . . . This phenomenon contributes to the formation of the great nineteenth-century experience of "sexual inversion," or sex-role reversal, in which some forms of sexual deviance are interpreted as, or conflated with, gender deviance. The emergence of homosexuality out of inversion, the formation of a sexual orientation independent of relative degrees of masculinity and femininity, takes place during the latter part of the nineteenth century and comes into its own only in the twentieth. Its highest expression is the "straight-acting and -appearing gay male," a man distinct from other men in absolutely no other respect besides that of his "sexuality."[42]

Halperin offers some discussion of why and how he has been led to differ from Foucault in discussing "inversion" as a stage that in effect preceded "homosexuality." What he does not discuss is that his reading of "homosexuality" as "we currently understand" it—his presumption of the reader's commonsense, present-tense conceptualization of homosexuality, the point from which all the thought experiments of differentiation must proceed—is virtually the opposite of Foucault's. For Halperin, what is presumed to define modern homosexuality "as we understand" it, in the form of the straight-acting and -appearing gay male, is gender intransitivity; for Foucault, it is, in the form of the feminized man or virilized woman, gender transitivity.

What obscures this difference between two historians, I believe, is the underlying structural congruence of the two histories: each is a unidirectional narrative of supersession. Each one makes an overarching point

---

42. Halperin, *One Hundred Years of Homosexuality*, pp. 8–9.

about the complete conceptual alterity of earlier models of same-sex relations. In each history one model of same-sex relations is superseded by another, which may again be superseded by another. In each case the superseded model then drops out of the frame of analysis. For Halperin, the power and interest of a postinversion notion of "sexual orientation independent of relative degrees of masculinity and femininity" seem to indicate that that notion must necessarily be seen as superseding the inversion model; he then seems to assume that any elements of the inversion model still to be found in contemporary understandings of homosexuality may be viewed as mere historical remnants whose process of withering away, however protracted, merits no analytic attention. The end point of Halperin's narrative differs from that of Foucault, but his proceeding does not: just as Halperin, having discovered an important *intervening* model, assumes that it must be a *supervening* one as well, so Foucault had already assumed that the nineteenth-century intervention of a minoritizing discourse of sexual identity in a previously extant, universalizing discourse of "sodomitic" sexual acts must mean, for all intents and purposes, the eclipse of the latter.

This assumption is significant only if—as I will be arguing—the most potent effects of modern homo/heterosexual definition tend to spring precisely from the inexplicitness or denial of the gaps *between* long-coexisting minoritizing and universalizing, or gender-transitive and gender-intransitive, understandings of same-sex relations. If that argument is true, however, then the enactment performed by these historical narratives has some troubling entailments. For someone who lives, for instance, as I do, in a state where certain acts called "sodomy" are criminal regardless of the gender, never mind the homo/heterosexual "identity," of the persons who perform them, the threat of the juxtaposition *on* that prohibition against *acts* of an additional, unrationalized set of sanctions attaching to *identity* can only be exacerbated by the insistence of gay theory that the discourse of acts can represent nothing but an anachronistic vestige. The project of the present book will be to show how issues of modern homo/heterosexual definition are structured, not by the supersession of one model and the consequent withering away of another, but instead by the relations enabled by the unrationalized coexistence of different models during the times they do coexist. This project does not involve the construction of historical narratives alternative to those that have emerged from Foucault and his followers. Rather, it requires a reassignment of attention and emphasis within those valuable narratives—attempting, perhaps, to denarrativize them somewhat by focusing on a performative space of contradiction that they both delineate and, themselves performative, pass over in silence. I have tended, therefore, in these chapters not to stress the alterity of disappeared or now-supposed-alien understandings of same-sex relations but instead to invest attention in those unexpectedly plural, varied, and contradictory historical understandings whose residual—indeed, whose renewed—force seems most palpable today. My first aim is to denaturalize the present, rather than the past—in effect, to render less destructively presumable "homosexuality as we know it today."

Axiom 6: The relation of gay studies to debates on the literary canon is, and had best be, tortuous.

Early on in the work on *Epistemology of the Closet*, in trying to settle on a literary text that would provide a first example for the kind of argument I meant the book to enable, I found myself circling around a text of 1891, a narrative that in spite of its relative brevity has proved a durable and potent centerpiece of gay male intertextuality and indeed has provided a durable and potent physical icon for gay male desire. It tells the story of a young Englishman famous for an extreme beauty of face and figure that seems to betray his aristocratic origin—an origin marked, however, also by mystery and class misalliance. If the gorgeous youth gives his name to the book and stamps his bodily image on it, the narrative is nonetheless more properly the story of a male triangle: a second, older man is tortured by a desire for the youth for which he can find no direct mode of expression, and a third man, emblem of suavity and the world, presides over the dispensation of discursive authority as the beautiful youth murders the tortured lover and is himself, in turn, by the novel's end ritually killed.

But maybe, I thought, one such text would offer an insufficient basis for cultural hypothesis. Might I pick two? It isn't yet commonplace to read *Dorian Gray* and *Billy Budd* by one another's light, but that can only be a testimony to the power of accepted English and American literary canons to insulate and deform the reading of politically important texts. In any gay male canon the two contemporaneous experimental works must be yoked together as overarching gateway texts of our modern period, and the conventionally obvious differences between them of style, literary positioning, national origin, class ethos, structure, and thematics must cease to be taken for granted and must instead become newly salient in the context of their startling erotic congruence. The book of the beautiful male English body foregrounded on an international canvas; the book of its inscription and evocation through a trio of male figures—the lovely boy, the tormented desirer, the deft master of the rules of their discourse; the story in which the lover is murdered by the boy and the boy is himself sacrificed; the deftly magisterial recounting that finally frames, preserves, exploits, and desublimates the male bodily image: *Dorian Gray* and *Billy Budd* are both that book.

The year 1891 is a good moment to which to look for a cross-section of the inaugural discourses of modern homo/heterosexuality—in medicine and psychiatry, in language and law, in the crisis of female status, in the career of imperialism. *Billy Budd* and *Dorian Gray* are among the texts that have set the terms for a modern homosexual identity. And in the Euro-American culture of this past century it has been notable that foundational texts of modern gay culture—*A la recherche du temps perdu* and *Death in Venice*, for instance, along with *Dorian Gray* and *Billy Budd*—have often been the identical texts that mobilized and promulgated the most potent images and categories for (what is now visible as) the canon of homophobic mastery.

Neither *Dorian Gray* nor *Billy Budd* is in the least an obscure text. Both are available in numerous paperback editions, for instance; and, both conveniently short, each differently canonical within a different national narrative, both are taught regularly in academic curricula. As what they are taught, however, and as what canonized, comes so close to disciplining the reading permitted of each that even the contemporaneity of the two texts (*Dorian Gray* was published as a book the year *Billy Budd* was written) may startle. That every major character in the archetypal American "allegory of good and evil" is English; that the archetypal English fin-de-siècle "allegory of art and life" was a sufficiently American event to appear in a Philadelphia publisher's magazine nine months before it became a London book—the canonic regimentation that effaces these international bonds has how much the more scope to efface the intertext and the intersexed. How may the strategy of a new canon operate in this space?

Contemporary discussions of the question of the literary canon tend to be structured either around the possibility of change, of rearrangement and reassignment of texts, within one overarching master-canon of literature—the strategy of adding Mary Shelley to the Norton Anthology—or, more theoretically defensible at the moment, around a vision of an exploding master-canon whose fracture would produce, or at least leave room for, a potentially infinite plurality of mini-canons, each specified as to its thematic or structural or authorial coverage: francophone Canadian or Inuit canons, for instance; clusters of magical realism or national allegory; the blues tradition; working-class narrative; canons of the sublime or the self-reflexive; Afro-Caribbean canons; canons of Anglo-American women's writing.

In fact, though, the most productive canon effects that have been taking place in recent literary studies have occurred, not from within the mechanism either of the master-canon or of a postfractural plurality of canons, but through an interaction between these two models of the canon. In this interaction the new pluralized mini-canons have largely failed to dislodge the master-canon from its empirical centrality in such institutional practices as publishing and teaching, although they have made certain specific works and authors newly available for inclusion in the master-canon. Their more important effect, however, has been to challenge, if not the empirical centrality, then the conceptual anonymity of the master-canon. The most notorious instance of this has occurred with feminist studies in literature, which by on the one hand confronting the master-canon with alternative canons of women's literature, and on the other hand reading rebelliously within the master-canon, has not only somewhat rearranged the table of contents for the master-canon but, more important, given it a title. If it is still in important respects *the* master-canon it nevertheless cannot now escape naming itself with every syllable also *a* particular canon, a canon of mastery, in this case of men's mastery over, and over against, women. Perhaps never again need women—need, one hopes, anybody—feel greeted by the Norton Anthology of mostly white men's Literature with the implied insolent salutation, "I'm nobody. Who are you?"

This is an encouraging story of female canon-formation, working in a sort of pincers movement with a process of feminist canon-*naming*, that has been in various forms a good deal told by now. How much the cheering clarity of this story is indebted, however, to the scarifying coarseness and visibility with which women and men are, in most if not all societies, distinguished publicly and once and for all from one another emerges only when attempts are made to apply the same model to that very differently structured though closely related form of oppression, modern homophobia. It is, as we have seen, only recently—and, I am arguing, only very incompletely and raggedly, although to that extent violently and brutally—that a combination of discursive forces have carved out, for women and for men, a possible though intensively pro-scribed homosexual identity in Euro-American culture. To the extent that such an identity is traceable, there is clearly the possibility, now being realized within literary criticism, for assembling alternative canons of lesbian and gay male writing *as* minority canons, as a literature of oppression and resistance and survival and heroic making. This modern view of lesbians and gay men as a distinctive minority population is of course importantly anachronistic in relation to earlier writing, however; and even in relation to modern writing it seems to falter in important ways in the implicit analysis it offers of the mechanisms of homophobia and of same-sex desire. It is with these complications that the relation between lesbian and gay literature as a minority canon, and the process of making salient the homosocial, homosexual, and homophobic strains and tor-sions in the already existing master-canon, becomes especially revealing.

It's revealing only, however, for those of us for whom relations within and among canons are active relations of thought. From the keepers of a dead canon we hear a rhetorical question—that is to say, a question posed with the arrogant intent of maintaining ignorance. Is there, as Saul Bellow put it, a Tolstoi of the Zulus? Has there been, ask the defenders of a monocultural curriculum, not intending to stay for an answer, has there ever yet been a Socrates of the Orient, an African-American Proust, a female Shakespeare? However assaultive or fatuous, in the context of the current debate the question has not been unproductive. To answer it in good faith has been to broach inquiries across a variety of critical fronts: into the canonical or indeed world-historic texts of non–Euro-American cultures, to begin with, but also into the nonuniversal functions of literacy and the literary, into the contingent and uneven secularization and sacra-lization of an aesthetic realm, into the relations of public to private in the ranking of genres, into the cult of the individual author and the organiza-tion of liberal arts education as an expensive form of masterpiece theatre.

Moreover, the flat insolent question teases by the very difference of its resonance with different projects of inquiry: it stimulates or irritates or reveals differently in the context of oral or written cultures; of the colo-nized or the colonizing, or cultures that have had both experiences; of peoples concentrated or in diaspora; of traditions partially internal or largely external to a dominant culture of the latter twentieth century.

From the point of view of this relatively new and inchoate academic presence, then, the gay studies movement, what distinctive soundings are to be reached by posing the question our way — and staying for an answer? Let's see how it sounds.

Has there ever been a gay Socrates?

Has there ever been a gay Shakespeare?

Has there ever been a gay Proust?

Does the Pope wear a dress? If these questions startle, it is not least as tautologies. A short answer, though a very incomplete one, might be that not only have there been a gay Socrates, Shakespeare, and Proust but that their names are Socrates, Shakespeare, Proust; and, beyond that, legion — dozens or hundreds of the most centrally canonic figures in what the monoculturalists are pleased to consider "our" culture, as indeed, always in different forms and senses, in every other.

What's now in place, in contrast, in most scholarship and most curricula is an even briefer response to questions like these: Don't ask. Or, less laconically: You shouldn't know. The vast preponderance of scholarship and teaching, accordingly, even among liberal academics, does simply neither ask nor know. At the most expansive, there is a series of dismissals of such questions on the grounds that:

1. Passionate language of same-sex attraction was extremely common during whatever period is under discussion — and therefore must have been completely meaningless. Or

2. Same-sex genital relations may have been perfectly common during the period under discussion — but since there was no language about them, *they* must have been completely meaningless. Or

3. Attitudes about homosexuality were intolerant back then, unlike now — so people probably didn't do anything. Or

4. Prohibitions against homosexuality didn't exist back then, unlike now — so if people did anything, it was completely meaningless. Or

5. The word "homosexuality" wasn't coined until 1869 — so everyone before then was heterosexual. (Of course, heterosexuality has always existed.) Or

6. The author under discussion is certified or rumored to have had an attachment to someone of the other sex — so their feelings about people of their own sex must have been completely meaningless. Or (under a perhaps somewhat different rule of admissible evidence)

7. There is no actual proof of homosexuality, such as sperm taken

from the body of another man or a nude photograph with another woman—so the author may be assumed to have been ardently and exclusively heterosexual. Or (as a last resort)

8. The author or the author's important attachments may very well have been homosexual—but it would be provincial to let so insignificant a fact make any difference at all to our understanding of any serious project of life, writing, or thought.

These responses reflect, as we have already seen, some real questions of sexual definition and historicity. But they only reflect them and don't reflect *on* them: the family resemblance among this group of extremely common responses comes from their closeness to the core grammar of *Don't ask; You shouldn't know*. It didn't happen; it doesn't make any difference; it didn't mean anything; it doesn't have interpretive consequences. Stop asking just here; stop asking just now; we know in advance the kind of difference that could be made by the invocation of *this* difference; it makes no difference; it doesn't mean. The most openly repressive projects of censorship, such as William Bennett's literally murderous opposition to serious AIDS education in schools on the grounds that it would communicate a tolerance for the lives of homosexuals, are, through this mobilization of the powerful mechanism of the open secret, made perfectly congruent with the smooth, dismissive knowingness of the urbane and the pseudo-urbane.

And yet the absolute canonical centrality of the list of authors about whom one might think to ask these questions—What was the structure, function, historical surround of same-sex love in and for Homer or Plato or Sappho? What, then, about Euripides or Virgil? If a gay Marlowe, what about Spenser or Milton? Shakespeare? Byron? But what about Shelley? Montaigne, Leopardi...? Leonardo, Michelangelo, but...? Beethoven? Whitman, Thoreau, Dickinson (Dickinson?), Tennyson, Wilde, Woolf, Hopkins, but Brontë? Wittgenstein, but...Nietzsche? Proust, Musil, Kafka, Cather, but...Mann? James, but...Lawrence? Eliot? but...Joyce? The very centrality of this list and its seemingly almost infinite elasticity suggest that no one *can* know *in advance* where the limits of a gay-centered inquiry are to be drawn, or where a gay theorizing of and through even the hegemonic high culture of the Euro-American tradition may need or be able to lead. The emergence, even within the last year or two, of nascent but ambitious programs and courses in gay and lesbian studies, at schools including those of the Ivy League, may now make it possible for the first time to ask these difficult questions from within the very heart of the empowered cultural institutions to which they pertain, as well as from the marginal and endangered institutional positions from which, for so long, the most courageous work in this area has emanated.

Furthermore, as I have been suggesting, the violently contradictory and volatile energies that every morning's newspaper proves to us are circulating even at this moment, in our society, around the issues of homo/heterosexual definition show over and over again how preposterous is anybody's urbane pretense at having a clear, simple story to tell about the outlines and meanings of what and who are homosexual and heterosexual. To be gay, or to be potentially classifiable as gay—that is to say, *to be sexed or gendered*—in this system is to come under the radically overlapping aegises of a universalizing discourse of acts or bonds and at the same time of a minoritizing discourse of kinds of persons. Because of the double binds implicit in the space overlapped by universalizing and minoritizing models, the stakes in matters of definitional control are extremely high.

Obviously, this analysis suggests as one indispensable approach to the traditional Euro-American canon a pedagogy that could treat it neither as something quite exploded nor as something quite stable. A canon seen to be genuinely unified by the maintenance of a particular tension of homo/ heterosexual definition can scarcely be dismantled; but neither can it ever be treated as the repository of reassuring "traditional" truths that could be made matter for any settled consolidation or congratulation. Insofar as the problematics of homo/heterosexual definition, in an intensely homophobic culture, are seen to be precisely internal to the central nexuses of that culture, this canon must always be treated as a loaded one. Considerations of the canon, it becomes clear, while vital in themselves cannot take the place of questions of pedagogic relations within and around the canon. Canonicity itself then seems the necessary wadding of pious obliviousness that allows for the transmission from one generation to another of texts that have the potential to dismantle the impacted foundations upon which a given culture rests.

I anticipate that to an interlocutor like William Bennett such a view would smack of the sinister sublimity peculiar to those of us educated in the dark campus days of the late sixties. I must confess that this demographic specification is exactly true of me. In fact, I can be more precise about where I might have acquired such a view of the high volatility of canonical texts. At the infamous Cornell of the infamous late sixties I was privileged to have teachers who invested in both texts and students their most trenchant passions. Like a lot of intellectually ambitious undergraduates, for instance, I gravitated into the orbit of Allan Bloom; my friends and I imitated, very affectionately and more than superficially, his infusion of every reading project with his own persona and with "p-p-p-passion"—his tattoo on the plosive consonant, part involuntary, part stagecraft, all riveting, dramatizing for us the explosive potential he lent to every interpretive nexus. It was from Bloom, as much as from more explicitly literary and deconstructive theorists or from more leftist ones, that I and some others of that late-sixties generation learned the urgencies and pleasures of reading against the visible grain of any influential text. The so-called conservative practical politics that, even then, so often seemed to make Bloom's vital cross-grained interpretive interventions boil down to a few coarsely ugly stereotypes and prescriptions wasn't quite enough, at least for awhile, to eclipse the lesson that the true sins against the holy ghost would be to read without risking oneself, to write or utter without revealing oneself however esoterically, to interpret without undergoing the perverse danger of setting in motion all the contradictory forces of any only semi-domesticated canonical text.

Now, reading *The Closing of the American Mind*, the splendid pedagogic charms of this great popularizer (i.e., of this great teacher) come flooding back to me. Along with feeling gratitude for his enablement of outrageous but central projects of reading, too, I more specifically recognize in retrospect the actual outlines of what have been for me anti-homophobic canonical reconstructions. For Bloom, that is, as also for a particular gay studies project within the traditional canon, the history of Western thought is importantly constituted and motivated by a priceless history of male-male pedagogic or pederastic relations. In a climactic chapter beguilingly entitled "Our Ignorance," for instance, Bloom encapsulates Western culture as the narrative that goes from the *Phaedrus* to *Death in Venice*. The crisis of Aschenbach's modern culture is seen as the deadeningness of the readings that are performed within its intrinsically explosive canon. As Bloom explains:

> As Aschenbach becomes more and more obsessed by the boy on the beach, quotations from the *Phaedrus* . . . keep coming into his head. . . . The *Phaedrus* was probably one of the things Aschenbach was supposed to have read as a schoolboy while learning Greek. But its content, discourses on the love of a man for a boy, was not supposed to affect him. The dialogue, like so much that was in the German education, was another

scrap of "culture," of historical information, which had not become a part of a vital, coherent whole. This is symptomatic of the deadness of Aschenbach's own cultural activity.[43]

Bloom is frightened by the petrification of these passions within the tradition. The other danger that, in Bloom's view, threatens cultural vitality, however, is not that these desires might be killed but that they might be expressed. For Bloom, and in this I believe he offers an ingenuously faithful and candid representation of Western hegemonic culture, the stimulation and glamorization of the energies of male-male desire (and who could deny that he does an enviable job of glamorizing them?) is an incessant project that must, for the preservation of that self-contradictory tradition, coexist with an equally incessant project of denying, deferring, or silencing their satisfaction. With a mechanistic hydraulicism more reductive than the one he deprecates in Freud, Bloom blames the sexual liberation movements of the sixties—all of them, but of course in this philosophic context the gay movement must take most of the blame—for dissipating the reservoirs of cathectic energy that are supposed to be held, by repression, in an excitable state of readiness to be invested in cultural projects. Instead, as Plato's "diversity of erotic expression" (237) has been frittered away on mere sex, now supposedly licit, "the lion roaring behind the door of the closet" has turned out "to be a little, domesticated cat" (99). In Bloom's sad view, "sexual passion is no longer dangerous in us" (99); "the various liberations wasted that marvelous energy and tension, leaving the students' souls exhausted and flaccid" (50–51).

So Bloom is unapologetically protective of the sanctity of the closet, that curious space that is both internal and marginal to the culture: centrally representative of its motivating passions and contradictions, even while marginalized by its orthodoxies. The modern, normalizing, minoritizing equal-rights movement for people of varying sexual identities is a grave falling-off, in Bloom's view, from the more precarious cultural *privilege* of a past in which "there was a respectable place for marginality, bohemia. But it had to justify its unorthodox practices by its intellectual and artistic achievement" (235). The fragile, precious representational compact by which a small, shadowily identified group both represented

43. Allan Bloom, *The Closing of the American Mind* (New York: Simon & Schuster/ Touchstone, 1988), p. 236. Further citations of this edition will be noted by page numbers in the text.

the hidden, perhaps dangerous truths about a culture to itself, and depended on its exiguous toleration, is by this account exactly like the position of Socrates and, by extension, of the ideal philosopher/teacher—of anyone who uncovers the explosive truths within the body of a culture to a transient young audience whose own hunger for such initiations is likeliest to be, at the very most, nothing more than a phase they are going through. "He is, therefore," Bloom poignantly writes,

> necessarily in the most fundamental tension with everyone except his own kind. He relates to all the others ironically, i.e., with sympathy and playful distance. Changing the character of his relationship to them is impossible because the disproportion between him and them is firmly rooted in nature. Thus, he has no expectation of essential progress. Toleration, not right, is the best he can hope for, and he is kept vigilant by the awareness of the basic fragility of his situation and that of philosophy. (283)

Socrates within the life of the Greeks, like the individual vessel of same-sex desire within the homoerotic tradition of homophobic Western high culture, depends for his survival on the very misrecognitions that his prestige comes from his having the power to demystify. Furthermore, the compact between the philosopher and youth is held together not only by love but by the perhaps necessarily elitist community formed of mutual contempt. He is allowed to despise them for not, he thinks, seeing him for what he is ("Crito, the family man, thinks of Socrates as a good family man. Laches, the soldier, thinks of Socrates as a good soldier" [283]). Meanwhile, they are allowed to condescend to the spectacle of what both are glad to think of as a certain final, irreducible difference from themselves. It's no wonder that such tight knots of desire-laden self-congratulation at one another's expense should be difficult to untie.

What Bloom offers is eloquent as an analysis—if indeed it is meant to be an analysis—of the prestige, magnetism, vulnerability, self-alienation, co-optability, and perhaps ultimately the potential for a certain defiance that inhere in the canonical culture of the closet. However, it is far from being the whole story. One of the things that can be said about the post-Stonewall gay movement, for instance, is that, to the extent that it posited gay women and men as a distinct minority with rights comparable to those of any other minority, it served notice that at least some people were in a position to demand that the representational compact between the closet and the culture be renegotiated or abrogated. Obviously, for many crucial purposes this move has been indispensable. It is heartbreakingly premature for Bloom to worry, at least with regard to homophobic prohibition, that the times are now such that anything goes, that "sexual passion is no longer dangerous in us." Our culture still sees to its being dangerous enough that women and men who find or fear they are homosexual, or are perceived by others to be so, are physically and mentally terrorized through the institutions of law, religion, psychotherapy, mass culture, medicine, the military, commerce and bureaucracy, and brute violence. Political progress on these and similar life-and-death issues has depended precisely on the strength of a minority-model gay activism; it is the normalizing, persuasive analogy between the needs of gay/lesbian students and those of Black or Jewish students, for instance, and the development of the corresponding political techniques that enable progress in such arenas. And *that* side of the needed progress cannot be mobilized from within any closet; it requires very many people's risky and affirming acts of the most explicit self-identification as members of the minority affected.

So, too, at the level of the canon. The invaluable forms of critique and dismantlement within the official tradition, the naming as what it is of a hegemonic, homoerotic/homophobic male canon of cultural mastery and coercive erotic double-binding, can be only part of the strategy of an antihomophobic project. It must work in the kind of pincers movement I have already described with the re-creation of minority gay canons from currently noncanonical material. Most obviously, this would be necessary in order to support lesbian choices, talents, sensibilities, lives, and analyses at the same level of cultural centrality as certain gay male ones: as women of every kind are tangential to the dominant canons of the culture, a fortiori gay women are, and at a terrible price to the culture's vibrance and wealth. Men who write openly as gay men have also often been excluded from the consensus of the traditional canon and may operate more forcefully now within a specifically gay/lesbian canon. Within every other minority canon as well, the work of gay/lesbian inquiry requires to be done. We can't possibly know in advance about the Harlem Renaissance, any more than we can about the New England Renaissance or the English or Italian Renaissance, where the limits of a revelatory inquiry are to be set, once we begin to ask—as it is now beginning to be asked about each of these Renaissances—where and how the power in them of gay desires, people, discourses, prohibitions, and energies were manifest. We know enough already, however, to know with certainty that in each of these Renaissances they were central. (No doubt that's how we will learn to recognize a renaissance when we see one.)

Axiom 7: The paths of allo-identification are likely to be strange and recalcitrant. So are the paths of auto-identification.

In the Introduction to *Between Men* I felt constrained to offer a brief account of how I saw the political/theoretical positioning of "a woman and a feminist writing (in part) about male homosexuality";[44] my account was, essentially, that this was an under-theorized conjunction and it was about time someone put her mind to it. Issues of male homosexuality are, obviously, even more integral to the present volume, and the intervening years have taught me more about how important, not to say mandatory, such an accounting must be — as well as how almost prohibitively difficult. I don't speak here of the question of anyone's "right" to think or write about the subjects on which they feel they have a contribution to make: to the degree that rights can be measured at all, I suppose this one can be measured best by what contribution the work does make, and to whom. Beyond the difficulty of wielding a language of rights, however, I find that abstractive formulations like that phrase in the Introduction to *Between Men* always seem to entail a hidden underpinning of the categorical imperative, one that may dangerously obscure the way political commitments and identifications actually work. Realistically, what brings me to this work can hardly be that I am *a* woman, or *a* feminist, but that I am this particular one. The grounds on which a book like this one might be persuasive or compelling to you, in turn, are unlikely to be its appeal to some *bienpensant*, evenly valenced lambency of your disinterested attention. Realistically, it takes deeply rooted, durable, and often somewhat opaque energies to write a book; it can take them, indeed, to read it. It takes them, as well, to make any political commitment that can be worth anything to anyone.

What, then, would make a good answer to implicit questions about someone's strong group-identification across politically charged boundaries, whether of gender, of class, of race, of sexuality, of nation? It could never be a version of "But everyone *should* be able to make this identifica-

44. *Between Men*, p. 19.

tion." Perhaps everyone should, but everyone does not, and almost no one makes more than a small number of very narrowly channeled ones. (A currently plausible academic ideology, for instance, is that everyone in a position of class privilege *should* group-identify across lines of class; but who hasn't noticed that of the very few U.S. scholars under 50 who have been capable of doing so productively, and over the long haul, most also "happen to have been" red diaper babies?) If the ethical prescription is explanatory at all—and I have doubts about that—it is anything but a full explanation. It often seems to me, to the contrary, that what these implicit questions really ask for is narrative, and of a directly personal sort. When I have experimented with offering such narrative, in relation to this ongoing project, it has been with several aims in mind.[45] I wanted to disarm the categorical imperative that seems to do so much to promote cant and mystification about motives in the world of politically correct academia. I wanted to try opening channels of visibility—toward the speaker, in this case—that might countervail somewhat against the terrible one-directionality of the culture's spectacularizing of gay men, to which it seems almost impossible, in any powerful gay-related project, not also to contribute. I meant, in a sense, to give hostages, though the possible thud of them on the tarmac of some future conflict is not something I can contemplate. I also wanted to offer (though on my own terms) whatever tools I could with which a reader who needed to might begin unknotting certain overdetermined impactions that inevitably structure these arguments. Finally, I have come up with such narrative because I desired and needed to, because its construction has greatly interested me, and what I learned from it has often surprised me.

A note appended to one of these accounts suggested an additional reason: "Part of the motivation behind my work on it," I wrote there, "has been a fantasy that readers or hearers would be variously—in anger, identification, pleasure, envy, 'permission,' exclusion—stimulated to write accounts 'like' this one (whatever that means) of their own, and share those."[46] My impression, indeed, is that some readers of that essay have done so. An implication of that wishful note was that it is not only identifications *across* definitional lines that can evoke or support or even

45. The longest such narrative appears as "A Poem Is Being Written," *Representations*, no. 17 (Winter 1987): 110–43. More fragmentary or oblique ones occur in "Tide and Trust," *Critical Inquiry* 15, no. 4 (Summer 1989): 745–57; in Chapter 4 of the present book; and in "Privilege of Unknowing."
46. "A Poem Is Being Written," p. 137.

require complex and particular narrative explanation; rather, the same is equally true of any person's identification with her or his "own" gender, class, race, sexuality, nation. I think, for instance, of a graduate class I taught a few years ago in gay and lesbian literature. Half the students in the class were men, half women. Throughout the semester all the women, including me, intensely uncomfortable with the dynamics of the class and hyperconscious of the problems of articulating lesbian with gay male perspectives, attributed our discomfort to some obliquity in the class-room relations between ourselves and the men. But by the end of the semester it seemed clear that we were in the grip of some much more intimate dissonance. It seemed that it was among the group of women, all feminists, largely homogeneous in visible respects, that some nerve of individually internal difference had been set painfully, contagiously atremble. Through a process that began, but *only* began, with the percep-tion of some differences among our mostly inexplicit, often somewhat uncrystallized sexual self-definitions, it appeared that each woman in the class possessed (or might, rather, feel we were possessed by) an ability to make one or more of the other women radically and excruciatingly doubt the authority of her own self-definition as a woman; as a feminist; and as the positional subject of a particular sexuality.

I think it probable that most people, especially those involved with any form of politics that touches on issues of identity—race, for instance, as well as sexuality and gender—have observed or been part of many such circuits of intimate denegation, as well as many circuits of its opposite. The political or pedagogical utility or destructiveness of those dissonant dynamics is scarcely a given, though perhaps it must always be aversive to experience them. Such dynamics—the denegating ones along with the consolidating ones—are not epiphenomenal to identity politics, but con-stitute it. After all, to identify *as* must always include multiple processes of identification *with*. It also involves identification *as against*; but even did it not, the relations implicit in *identifying with* are, as psychoanalysis sug-gests, in themselves quite sufficiently fraught with intensities of incor-poration, diminishment, inflation, threat, loss, reparation, and dis-avowal. For a politics like feminism, furthermore, effective moral authority has seemed to depend on its capacity for conscientious and nonperfunctory enfoldment of women alienated from one another in virtually every other relation of life. Given this, there are strong political motives for obscuring any possibility of differentiating between one's identification *as* (a woman) and one's identification *with* (women very differently situated — for bourgeois feminists, this means radically less privileged ones). At least for relatively privileged feminists of my generation, it has been an article of faith, and a deeply educative one, that to conceive of oneself as a woman at all must mean trying to conceive oneself, over and over, as if incarnated in ever more palpably vulnerable situations and embodiments. The costs of this pressure toward mystification — the constant reconflation, as one monolithic act, of *identification with/as* — are, I believe, high for feminism, though its rewards have also been considerable. (Its political efficacy in actually broadening the bases of feminism is still, it seems to me, very much a matter of debate.) *Identification with/as* has a distinctive resonance for women in the oppressively tidy dovetailing between old ideologies of women's traditional "selflessness" and a new one of feminist commitment that seems to begin with a self but is legitimated only by willfully obscuring most of its boundaries.

For better and for worse, mainstream, male-centered gay politics has tended not to be structured as strongly as feminism has by that particular ethical pressure. Yet, as I will be discussing at length in Chapter 3, there is a whole different set of reasons why a problematics of *identification with/ as* seems to be distinctively resonant with issues of male homo/heterosexual definition. *Between Men* tried to demonstrate that modern, homophobic constructions of male heterosexuality have a conceptual dependence on a distinction between men's *identification* (with men) and their *desire* (for women), a distinction whose factitiousness is latent where not patent. The (relatively new) emphasis on the "homo-," on the dimension of sameness, built into modern understandings of relations of sexual desire within a given gender, has had a sustained and active power to expose that factitiousness, to show how close may be the slippage or even the melding between identification and desire. Thus, an entire social region of the vicarious becomes peculiarly charged in association with homo/heterosexual definition. Chapter 3 will argue that processes of homosexual attribution and identification have had a distinctive centrality, in this century, for many stigmatized but extremely potent sets of relations involving projective chains of vicarious investment: sentimentality, kitsch, camp, the knowing, the prurient, the arch, the morbid.

There may, then, be a rich and conflictual salience of the vicarious embedded within gay definition. I don't point that out to offer an excuse for the different, openly vicariating cathexis from outside that motivates this study; it either needs or, perhaps, can have none. But this in turn may suggest some ways in which the particular obliquities of my approach to the subject may bias what I find there. I can say generally that the vicarious investments most visible to me have had to do with my experiences as a woman; as a fat woman; as a nonprocreative adult; as someone who is, under several different discursive regimes, a sexual pervert; and, under some, a Jew. To give an example: I've wondered about my ability to keep generating ideas about "the closet," compared to a relative inability, so far, to have new ideas about the substantive differences made by post-Stonewall imperatives to rupture or vacate that space. (This, obviously, despite every inducement to thought provided by the immeasurable value of "out" liberatory gay politics in the lives around me and my own.) May it not be influenced by the fact that my own relation, as a woman, to gay male discourse and gay men echoes most with the pre-Stonewall gay self-definition of (say) the 1950s? — something, that is, whose names, where they exist at all, are still so exotically coarse and demeaning as to challenge recognition, never mind acknowledgment; leaving, in the stigma-impregnated space of refused recognition, sometimes also a stimulating aether of the unnamed, the lived experiment.

Proust: "The book whose hieroglyphs are not traced by us is the only book that really belongs to us." I feel it about the way the book belongs to me; I hope it about the different way it belongs to some of its readers.

Closet

From the OED:

Closet sb. [a. OF. *closet*, dim. of *clos* :-L. *clausum*]

1.   A room for privacy or retirement; a private room; an inner chamber; formerly often = *bower*; in later use always a small room.

> 1370   A slepe hym toke In hys closet.
>
> 1586   We doe call the most secret place in the house appropriate unto our owne private studies . . . a Closet.
>
> 1611   Let the bridegroome goe forth of his chamber, and the bride out of her closet.
>
> 1750   A sudden intruder into the closet of an author.

b.   *esp.* Such a room as the place of private devotion (with allusion to 1611 version of Matt. vi.6). *arch.*

c.   As the place of private study or secluded speculation; *esp.* in reference to mere theories as opposed to practical measures.

> 1746   The knowledge of the world is only to be acquired in the world, and not in the Closet.

2.   The private apartment of a monarch or potentate.

3. a.   A private repository of valuables or (*esp.* in later use) curiosities; a cabinet. *arch.* or *Obs.*

b.   A small side-room or recess for storing utensils, provisions, etc.; a cupboard.

c.   *Skeleton in the closet* (or *cupboard*): a private or concealed trouble in one's house or circumstances, ever present, and ever liable to come into view.

4.   With special reference to size: Any small room: especially one belonging to or communicating with a larger.

5.   *fig.* The den or lair of a wild beast. *Obs.*

6. a.   *transf.* That which affords retirement like a private chamber, or which encloses like a cabinet; a hidden or secret place, retreat, recess.

> 1450–1530   Went the sonne of god oute of the pryuy closet of the maydens wombe.
>
> 1594   This skinne . . . is also called the little closet of the heart.

7.   Short for 'Closet of ease,' 'water-closet'

> 1662   A Closet of ease.

9.   A sewer. *Sc. Obs.*

[Translating L. *cloaca*: origin doubtful; there is nothing like it in French.]

10.   *attrib.*, as, . . . a place . . . of private study and speculation, as *closet-lucubration, -philosopher, -politician, -speculation, -student, -study,* etc.

> 1649   Reasons, why he should rather pray by the officiating mouth of a Closet-chaplain.
>
> 1649   They knew the King . . . to have suckt from them and their Closetwork all his impotent principles of Tyrannie and Superstition.
>
> 1612–5   There are stage-sins and there are closet-sins.

Epistemology of the Closet

> The lie, the perfect lie, about people we know, about the rela-
> tions we have had with them, about our motive for some action,
> formulated in totally different terms, the lie as to what we are,
> whom we love, what we feel with regard to people who love
> us . . . — that lie is one of the few things in the world that can
> open windows for us on to what is new and unknown, that can
> awaken in us sleeping senses for the contemplation of universes
> that otherwise we should never have known.
>
> Proust, *The Captive*

The epistemology of the closet is not a dated subject or a superseded
regime of knowing. While the events of June, 1969, and later vitally rein-
vigorated many people's sense of the potency, magnetism, and promise of
gay self-disclosure, nevertheless the reign of the telling secret was scarcely
overturned with Stonewall. Quite the opposite, in some ways. To the fine
antennae of public attention the freshness of every drama of (especially
involuntary) gay uncovering seems if anything heightened in surprise and
delectability, rather than staled, by the increasingly intense atmosphere of
public articulations of and about the love that is famous for daring not
speak its name. So resilient and productive a structure of narrative will not
readily surrender its hold on important forms of social meaning. As D. A.
Miller points out in an aegis-creating essay, secrecy can function as

> the subjective practice in which the oppositions of private/public, inside/
> outside, subject/object are established, and the sanctity of their first term
> kept inviolate. And the phenomenon of the "open secret" does not, as one
> might think, bring about the collapse of those binarisms and their ideo-
> logical effects, but rather attests to their fantasmatic recovery.[1]

Even at an individual level, there are remarkably few of even the most
openly gay people who are not deliberately in the closet with someone

---

1. D. A. Miller, "Secret Subjects, Open Secrets," in his *The Novel and the Police*, p. 207.

personally or economically or institutionally important to them. Further-more, the deadly elasticity of heterosexist presumption means that, like Wendy in *Peter Pan*, people find new walls springing up around them even as they drowse: every encounter with a new classful of students, to say nothing of a new boss, social worker, loan officer, landlord, doctor, erects new closets whose fraught and characteristic laws of optics and physics exact from at least gay people new surveys, new calculations, new draughts and requisitions of secrecy or disclosure. Even an out gay person deals daily with interlocutors about whom she doesn't know whether they know or not; it is equally difficult to guess for any given interlocutor whether, if they did know, the knowledge would seem very important. Nor—at the most basic level—is it unaccountable that someone who wanted a job, custody or visiting rights, insurance, protection from violence, from "therapy," from distorting stereotype, from insulting scru-tiny, from simple insult, from forcible interpretation of their bodily product, could deliberately choose to remain in or to reenter the closet in some or all segments of their life. The gay closet is not a feature only of the lives of gay people. But for many gay people it is still the fundamental feature of social life; and there can be few gay people, however courageous and forthright by habit, however fortunate in the support of their immedi-ate communities, in whose lives the closet is not still a shaping presence.

To say, as I will be saying here, that the epistemology of the closet has given an overarching consistency to gay culture and identity throughout this century is not to deny that crucial possibilities around and outside the closet have been subject to most consequential change, for gay people. There are risks in making salient the continuity and centrality of the closet, in a historical narrative that does not have as a fulcrum a saving vision—whether located in past or future—of its apocalyptic rupture. A meditation that lacks that particular utopian organization will risk glam-orizing the closet itself, if only by default; will risk presenting as inevitable or somehow valuable its exactions, its deformations, its disempowerment and sheer pain. If these risks are worth running, it is partly because the nonutopian traditions of gay writing, thought, and culture have remained so inexhaustibly and gorgeously productive for later gay thinkers, in the absence of a rationalizing or often even of a forgiving reading of their politics. The epistemology of the closet has also been, however, on a far vaster scale and with a less honorific inflection, inexhaustibly productive of modern Western culture and history at large. While that may be reason enough for taking it as a subject of interrogation, it should not be reason enough for focusing scrutiny on those who inhabit the closet (however equivocally) to the exclusion of those in the ambient heterosexist culture who enjoin it and whose intimate representational needs it serves in a way less extortionate to themselves.

I scarcely know at this stage a consistent alternative proceeding, however; and it may well be that, for reasons to be discussed, no such consistency is possible. At least to enlarge the circumference of scrutiny and to vary by some new assays of saltation the angle of its address will be among the methodological projects of this discussion.

♦   ♦   ♦

In Montgomery County, Maryland, in 1973, an eighth-grade earth science teacher named Acanfora was transferred to a nonteaching position by the Board of Education when they learned he was gay. When Acanfora spoke to news media, such as "60 Minutes" and the Public Broadcasting System, about his situation, he was refused a new contract entirely. Acanfora sued. The federal district court that first heard his case supported the action and rationale of the Board of Education, holding that Acanfora's recourse to the media had brought undue attention to himself and his sexuality, to a degree that would be deleterious to the educational process. The Fourth Circuit Court of Appeals disagreed. They considered Acanfora's public disclosures to be protected speech under the First Amendment. Although they overruled the lower court's rationale, however, the appellate court affirmed its decision not to allow Acanfora to return to teaching. Indeed, they denied his standing to bring the suit in the first place, on the grounds that he had failed to note on his original employment application that he had been, in college, an officer of a student homophile organization—a notation that would, as school officials admitted in court, have prevented his ever being hired. The rationale for keeping Acanfora out of his classroom was thus no longer that he had disclosed too much about his homosexuality, but quite the opposite, that he had not disclosed enough.[2] The Supreme Court declined to entertain an appeal.

2. On this case see Michael W. La Morte, "Legal Rights and Responsibilities of Homosexuals in Public Education," *Journal of Law and Education* 4, no. 23 (July 1975): 449–67, esp. 450–53; and Jeanne La Borde Scholz, "Comment: Out of the Closet, Out of a Job: Due Process in Teacher Disqualification," *Hastings Law Quarterly* 6 (Winter 1979): 663–717, esp. 682–84.

It is striking that each of the two rulings in *Acanfora* emphasized that the teacher's homosexuality "itself" would not have provided an acceptable ground for denying him employment. Each of the courts relied in its decision on an implicit distinction between the supposedly protected and bracketable fact of Acanfora's homosexuality proper, on the one hand, and on the other hand his highly vulnerable management of information about it. So very vulnerable does this latter exercise prove to be, however, and vulnerable to such a contradictory array of interdictions, that the space for simply existing as a gay person who is a teacher is in fact bayonetted through and through, from both sides, by the vectors of a disclosure at once compulsory and forbidden.

A related incoherence couched in the resonant terms of the distinction of *public* from *private* riddles the contemporary legal space of gay being. When it refused in 1985 to consider an appeal in *Rowland v. Mad River Local School District*, the U.S. Supreme Court let stand the firing of a bisexual guidance counselor for coming out to some of her colleagues; the act of coming out was judged not to be highly protected under the First Amendment because it does not constitute speech on a matter "of public concern." It was, of course, only eighteen months later that the same U.S. Supreme Court ruled, in response to Michael Hardwick's contention that it's nobody's business if he do, that it ain't: if homosexuality is not, however densely adjudicated, to be considered a matter of *public* concern, neither in the Supreme Court's binding opinion does it subsist under the mantle of the *private*.[3]

The most obvious fact about this history of judicial formulations is that it codifies an excruciating system of double binds, systematically oppressing gay people, identities, and acts by undermining through contradictory constraints on discourse the grounds of their very being. That immediately political recognition may be supplemented, however, by a historical hypothesis that goes in the other direction. I want to argue

---

3. Nan Hunter, director of the ACLU's Lesbian and Gay Rights Project, analyzed *Rowland* in "Homophobia and Academic Freedom," a talk at the 1986 Modern Language Association National Convention. There is an interesting analysis of the limitations, for gay-rights purposes, of both the right of privacy and the First Amendment guarantee of free speech, whether considered separately or in tandem, in "Notes: The Constitutional Status of Sexual Orientation: Homosexuality as a Suspect Classification," *Harvard Law Review* 98 (April 1985): 1285–1307, esp. 1288–97. For a discussion of related legal issues that is strikingly apropos of, and useful for, the argument made in *Epistemology of the Closet*, see Janet E. Halley, "The Politics of the Closet: Towards Equal Protection for Gay, Lesbian, and Bisexual Identity," *UCLA Law Review* 36 (1989): 915–76.

that a lot of the energy of attention and demarcation that has swirled around issues of homosexuality since the end of the nineteenth century, in Europe and the United States, has been impelled by the distinctively indicative relation of homosexuality to wider mappings of secrecy and disclosure, and of the private and the public, that were and are critically problematical for the gender, sexual, and economic structures of the heterosexist culture at large, mappings whose enabling but dangerous incoherence has become oppressively, durably condensed in certain figures of homosexuality. "The closet" and "coming out," now verging on all-purpose phrases for the potent crossing and recrossing of almost any politically charged lines of representation, have been the gravest and most magnetic of those figures.

The closet is the defining structure for gay oppression in this century. The legal couching, by civil liberties lawyers, of *Bowers v. Hardwick* as an issue in the first place of a Constitutional right to privacy, and the liberal focus in the aftermath of that decision on the image of the *bedroom invaded by policemen*— "Letting the Cops Back into Michael Hardwick's Bedroom," the *Native* headlined[4]—as though political empowerment were a matter of getting the cops back on the street where they belong and sexuality back into the impermeable space where *it* belongs, are among other things extensions of, and testimony to the power of, the image of the closet. The durability of the image is perpetuated even as its intelligibility is challenged in antihomophobic responses like the following, to *Hardwick*, addressed to gay readers:

> What can you do—alone? The answer is obvious. You're *not* alone, and you can't afford to try to be. That closet door—never very secure as protection—is even more dangerous now. You must come out, for your own sake and for the sake of all of us.[5]

The image of coming out regularly interfaces the image of the closet, and its seemingly unambivalent public siting can be counterposed as a salvational epistemologic certainty against the very equivocal privacy afforded by the closet: "If every gay person came out to his or her family," the same article goes on, "a hundred million Americans could be brought to our side. Employers and straight friends could mean a hundred million more." And yet the Mad River School District's refusal to hear a woman's

---

4. *New York Native*, no. 169 (July 14, 1986): 11.
5. Philip Bockman, "A Fine Day," *New York Native*, no. 175 (August 25, 1986): 13.

coming out as an authentically public speech act is echoed in the frigid response given many acts of coming out: "That's fine, but why did you think I'd want to know about it?"

Gay thinkers of this century have, as we'll see, never been blind to the damaging contradictions of this compromised metaphor of *in* and *out* of the closet of privacy. But its origins in European culture are, as the writings of Foucault have shown, so ramified—and its relation to the "larger," i.e., ostensibly nongay-related, topologies of privacy in the culture is, as the figure of Foucault dramatized, so critical, so enfolding, so representational—that the simple vesting of some alternative metaphor has never, either, been a true possibility.

I recently heard someone on National Public Radio refer to the sixties as the decade when Black people came out of the closet. For that matter, I recently gave an MLA talk purporting to explain how it's possible to come out of the closet as a fat woman. The apparent floating-free from its gay origins of that phrase "coming out of the closet" in recent usage might suggest that the trope of the closet is so close to the heart of some modern preoccupations that it could be, or has been, evacuated of its historical gay specificity. But I hypothesize that exactly the opposite is true. I think that a whole cluster of the most crucial sites for the contestation of meaning in twentieth-century Western culture are consequentially and quite indelibly marked with the historical specificity of homosocial/homosexual definition, notably but not exclusively male, from around the turn of the century.[6] Among those sites are, as I have indicated, the pairings secrecy/disclosure and private/public. Along with and sometimes through these epistemologically charged pairings, condensed in the figures of "the closet" and "coming out," this very specific crisis of definition has then ineffaceably marked other pairings as basic to modern cultural organization as masculine/feminine, majority/minority, innocence/initiation, natural/artificial, new/old, growth/decadence, urbane/provincial, health/illness, same/different, cognition/paranoia, art/kitsch, sincerity/sentimentality, and voluntarity/addiction. So permeative has the

6. A reminder that "the closet" retains (at least the chronic potential of) its gay semantic specification: a media flap in June, 1989, when a Republican National Committee memo calling for House Majority Leader Thomas Foley to "come out of the liberal closet" and comparing his voting record with that of an openly gay Congressman, Barney Frank, was widely perceived (and condemned) as insinuating that Foley himself is gay. The committee's misjudgment about whether it could maintain deniability for the insinuation is an interesting index to how unpredictably full or empty of gay specificity this locution may be perceived to be.

suffusing stain of homo/heterosexual crisis been that to discuss any of these indices in any context, in the absence of an antihomophobic analysis, must perhaps be to perpetuate unknowingly compulsions implicit in each.

For any modern question of sexuality, knowledge/ignorance is more than merely one in a metonymic chain of such binarisms. The process, narrowly bordered at first in European culture but sharply broadened and accelerated after the late eighteenth century, by which "knowledge" and "sex" become conceptually inseparable from one another—so that knowledge means in the first place sexual knowledge; ignorance, sexual ignorance; and epistemological pressure of any sort seems a force increasingly saturated with sexual impulsion—was sketched in Volume I of Foucault's *History of Sexuality*. In a sense, this was a process, protracted almost to retardation, of exfoliating the biblical genesis by which what we now know as sexuality is fruit—apparently the only fruit—to be plucked from the tree of knowledge. Cognition itself, sexuality itself, and transgression itself have always been ready in Western culture to be magnetized into an unyielding though not an unfissured alignment with one another, and the period initiated by Romanticism accomplished this disposition through a remarkably broad confluence of different languages and institutions.

In some texts, such as Diderot's *La Religieuse*, that were influential early in this process, the desire that represents sexuality per se, and hence sexual knowledge and knowledge per se, is a same-sex desire.[7] This possibility, however, was repressed with increasing energy, and hence increasing visibility, as the nineteenth-century culture of the individual proceeded to elaborate a version of knowledge/sexuality increasingly structured by its pointed cognitive *refusal* of sexuality between women, between men. The gradually reifying effect of this refusal[8] meant that by the end of the nineteenth century, when it had become fully current—as obvious to Queen Victoria as to Freud—that knowledge meant sexual knowledge, and secrets sexual secrets, there had in fact developed one particular sexuality that was distinctively constituted *as* secrecy: the perfect object for the by now insatiably exacerbated epistemological/sexual anxiety of the turn-of-the-century subject. Again, it was a long chain of originally scriptural identifications of a sexuality with a particular cog-

7. On this, see my "Privilege of Unknowing."
8. On this, see *Between Men*.

nitive positioning (in this case, St. Paul's routinely reproduced and re-
worked denomination of sodomy as the crime whose name is not to be
uttered, hence whose accessibility to knowledge is uniquely preterited)
that culminated in Lord Alfred Douglas's epochal public utterance, in
1894, "*I am* the Love that dare not speak its name."[9] In such texts as *Billy
Budd* and *Dorian Gray* and through their influence, the subject—the
thematics—of knowledge and ignorance themselves, of innocence and
initiation, of secrecy and disclosure, became not contingently but integrally infused with one particular object of cognition: no longer sexuality
as a whole but even more specifically, now, the homosexual topic. And the
condensation of the world of possibilities surrounding same-sex sexuality—including, shall we say, both gay desires and the most rabid pho-
bias against them—the condensation of this plurality to *the homosexual
topic* that now formed the accusative case of modern processes of personal knowing, was not the least infliction of the turn-of-the-century crisis
of sexual definition.

To explore the differences it makes when secrecy itself becomes manifest as *this* secret, let me begin by twining together in a short anachronistic braid a variety of exemplary narratives—literary, biographical,
imaginary—that begin with the moment on July 1, 1986, when the
decision in *Bowers v. Hardwick* was announced, a moment which, sand-
wiched between a weekend of Gay Pride parades nationwide, the announcement of a vengeful new AIDS policy by the Justice Department,
and an upcoming media-riveting long weekend of hilarity or hysteria
focused on the national fetishization in a huge hollow blind spike-headed
female body of the abstraction Liberty, and occurring in an ambient
medium for gay men and their families and friends of wave on wave of
renewed loss, mourning, and refreshed personal fear, left many people
feeling as if at any rate one's own particular car had finally let go forever of
the tracks of the roller coaster.

In many discussions I heard or participated in immediately after the
Supreme Court ruling in *Bowers v. Hardwick*, antihomophobic or gay
women and men speculated—more or less empathetically or ven-
omously—about the sexuality of the people most involved with the decision. The question kept coming up, in different tones, of what it could
have felt like to be a closeted gay court assistant, or clerk, or justice, who

---

9. Lord Alfred Douglas, "Two Loves," *The Chameleon* 1 (1894): 28 (emphasis
added).

might have had some degree, even a very high one, of instrumentality in conceiving or formulating or "refining" or logistically facilitating this ruling, these ignominious majority opinions, the assaultive sentences in which they were framed.

That train of painful imaginings was fraught with the epistemological distinctiveness of gay identity and gay situation in our culture. Vibrantly resonant as the image of the closet is for many modern oppressions, it is indicative for homophobia in a way it cannot be for other oppressions. Racism, for instance, is based on a stigma that is visible in all but exceptional cases (cases that are neither rare nor irrelevant, but that de-lineate the outlines rather than coloring the center of racial experience); so are the oppressions based on gender, age, size, physical handicap. Eth-nic/cultural/religious oppressions such as anti-Semitism are more analo-gous in that the stigmatized individual has at least notionally some discretion—although, importantly, it is never to be taken for granted how much—over other people's knowledge of her or his membership in the group: one could "come out as" a Jew or Gypsy, in a heterogeneous urbanized society, much more intelligibly than one could typically "come out as," say, female, Black, old, a wheelchair user, or fat. A (for instance) Jewish or Gypsy identity, and hence a Jewish or Gypsy secrecy or closet, would nonetheless differ again from the distinctive gay versions of these things in its clear ancestral linearity and answerability, in the roots (how-ever tortuous and ambivalent) of cultural identification through each individual's originary culture of (at a minimum) the family.

Proust, in fact, insistently suggests as a sort of limit-case of one kind of coming out precisely the drama of Jewish self-identification, embodied in the Book of Esther and in Racine's recasting of it that is quoted throughout the "Sodom and Gomorrah" books of *A la recherche*. The story of Esther seems a model for a certain simplified but highly potent imagining of coming out and its transformative potential. In concealing her Judaism from her husband, King Assuérus (Ahasuerus), Esther the Queen feels she is concealing, simply, her identity: "The King is to this day unaware who I am."[10] Esther's deception is made necessary by the powerful ideology that makes Assuérus categorize her people as unclean ("cette source impure" [1039]) and an abomination against nature ("Il nous croit en horreur à toute la nature" [174]). The sincere, relatively abstract Jew-hatred of this

---

10. Jean Racine, *Esther*, ed. H. R. Roach (London: George G. Harrap, 1949), line 89; my translation. Further citations of this play will be noted by line number in the text.

fuddled but omnipotent king undergoes constant stimulation from the grandiose cynicism of his advisor Aman (Haman), who dreams of an entire planet exemplarily cleansed of the perverse element.

> I want it said one day in awestruck centuries:
> "There once used to be Jews, there was an insolent race;
> widespread, they used to cover the whole face of the earth;
> a single one dared draw on himself the wrath of Aman,
> at once they disappeared, every one, from the earth."
> (476–80)

The king acquiesces in Aman's genocidal plot, and Esther is told by her cousin, guardian, and Jewish conscience Mardochée (Mordecai) that the time for her revelation has come; at this moment the particular operation of suspense around her would be recognizable to any gay person who has inched toward coming out to homophobic parents. "And if I perish, I perish," she says in the Bible (Esther 4:16). That the avowal of her secret identity will have an immense potency is clear, is the premise of the story. All that remains to be seen is whether under its explosive pressure the king's "political" animus against her kind will demolish his "personal" love for her, or vice versa: will he declare her as good as, or better, dead? Or will he soon be found at a neighborhood bookstore, hoping not to be recognized by the salesperson who is ringing up his copy of *Loving Someone Jewish*?

The biblical story and Racinian play, bearable to read in their balance of the holocaustal with the intimate only because one knows how the story will end,[11] are enactments of a particular dream or fantasy of coming out. Esther's eloquence, in the event, is resisted by only five lines of her husband's demurral or shock: essentially at the instant she names herself, both her ruler and Aman see that the anti-Semites are lost ("*AMAN, tout bas*: Je tremble" [1033]). Revelation of identity in the space of intimate love effortlessly overturns an entire public systematics of the natural and the unnatural, the pure and the impure. The peculiar strike that the story makes to the heart is that Esther's small, individual ability to risk losing the love and countenance of her master has the power to save not only her own space in life but her people.

It would not be hard to imagine a version of *Esther* set in the Supreme

---

11. It is worth remembering, of course, that the biblical story still ends with mass slaughter: while Racine's king *revokes* his orders (1197), the biblical king *reverses* his (Esther 8:5), licensing the Jews' killing of "seventy and five thousand" (9:16) of their enemies, including children and women (8:11).

Court in the days immediately before the decision in *Bowers v. Hardwick*. Cast as the ingenue in the title role a hypothetical closeted gay clerk, as Assuérus a hypothetical Justice of the same gender who is about to make a majority of five in support of the Georgia law. The Justice has grown fond of the clerk, oddly fonder than s/he is used to being of clerks, and . . . In our compulsive recursions to the question of the sexualities of court personnel, such a scenario was close to the minds of my friends and me in many forms. In the passionate dissenting opinions, were there not the traces of others' comings-out already performed; could even the dissents themselves represent such performances, Justice coming out to Justice? With the blood-let tatters of what risky comings-out achieved and then overridden — friends', clerks', employees', children's — was the imperious prose of the majority opinions lined? More painful and frequent were thoughts of all the coming out that had not happened, of the women and men who had not in some more modern idiom said, with Esther,

> I dare to beg you, both for my own life
> and the sad days of an ill-fated people
> that you have condemned to perish with me.
> (1029–31)

What was lost in the absence of such scenes was not, either, the opportunity to evoke with eloquence a perhaps demeaning pathos like Esther's. It was something much more precious: evocation, articulation, of the dumb Assuérus in all his imperial ineloquent bathos of unknowing: "A périr? Vous? Quel peuple?" ("To perish? You? What people?" [1032]). "What people?" indeed — why, as it oddly happens, the very people whose eradication he personally is just on the point of effecting. But only with the utterance of these blank syllables, making the weight of Assuérus's power-ful ignorance suddenly audible — not least to him — in the same register as the weight of Esther's and Mardochée's private knowledge, can any open flow of power become possible. It is here that Aman begins to tremble.

Just so with coming out: it can bring about the revelation of a powerful unknowing *as* unknowing, not as a vacuum or as the blank it can pretend to be but as a weighty and occupied and consequential epistemological space. Esther's avowal allows Assuérus to make visible two such spaces at once: "You?" "What people?" He has been blindly presuming about herself,[12] and simply blind to the race to whose extinction he has pledged

---

12. In Voltaire's words, "un roi insensé qui a passé six mois avec sa femme sans savoir, sans s'informer même qui elle est" (in Racine, *Esther*, pp. 83–84).

himself. What? *you're* one of *those?* Huh? *you're* a *what?* This frightening thunder can also, however, be the sound of manna falling.

◆   ◆   ◆

There is no question that to fixate, as I have done, on the scenario sketched here more than flirts with sentimentality. This is true for quite explicable reasons. First, we have too much cause to know how limited a leverage any individual revelation can exercise over collectively scaled and institutionally embodied oppressions. Acknowledgment of this disproportion does not mean that the consequences of such acts as coming out can be circumscribed within *predetermined* boundaries, as if between "personal" and "political" realms, nor does it require us to deny how disproportionately powerful and disruptive such acts can be. But the brute incommensurability has nonetheless to be acknowledged. In the theatrical display of an *already institutionalized* ignorance no transformative potential is to be looked for.

There is another whole family of reasons why too long a lingering on moments of *Esther*-style avowal must misrepresent the truths of homophobic oppression; these go back to the important differences between Jewish (here I mean Racinian-Jewish) and gay identity and oppression. Even in the "Sodom and Gomorrah" books of Proust, after all, and especially in *La Prisonnière*, where *Esther* is so insistently invoked, the play does not offer an efficacious model of transformative revelation. To the contrary: *La Prisonnière* is, notably, the book whose Racine-quoting hero has the most disastrous incapacity either to come out or *to be come out to*.

The suggested closeted Supreme Court clerk who struggled with the possibility of a self-revelation that *might* perceptibly strengthen gay sisters and brothers, but *would* radically endanger at least the foreseen course of her or his own life, would have an imagination filled with possibilities beyond those foreseen by Esther in her moment of risk. It is these possibilities that mark the distinctive structures of the epistemology of the closet. The clerk's authority to describe her or his own sexuality might well be impeached; the avowal might well only further perturb an already stirred-up current of the open secret; the avowal might well represent an aggression against someone with whom the clerk felt, after all, a real bond; the nongay-identified Justice might well feel too shaken in her or his own self-perception, or in the perception of the bond with the clerk, to respond with anything but an increased rigor; the clerk might well, through the avowal, be getting dangerously into the vicinity of the explosive-mined closet of a covertly gay Justice; the clerk might well fear being too isolated or self-doubting to be able to sustain the consequences of the avowal; the intersection of gay revelation with underlying gender expectations might well be too confusing or disorienting, for one or the other, to provide an intelligible basis for change.

To spell these risks and circumscriptions out more fully in the comparison with *Esther*:

1. Although neither the Bible nor Racine indicates in what, if any, religious behaviors or beliefs Esther's Jewish identity may be manifested, *there is no suggestion that that identity might be a debatable, a porous, a mutable fact about her.* "Esther, my lord, had a Jew for her father" (1033) — ergo, Esther is a Jew. Taken aback though he is by this announcement, Assuérus does not suggest that Esther is going through a phase, or is just angry at Gentiles, or could change if she only loved him enough to get counseling. Nor do such undermining possibilities occur to Esther. The Jewish identity in this play — whatever it may consist of in real life in a given historical context — has a solidity whose very unequivocalness grounds the story of Esther's equivocation and her subsequent self-disclosure. In the processes of gay self-disclosure, by contrast, in a twentieth-century context, questions of authority and evidence can be the first to arise. "How do you know you're really gay? Why be in such a hurry to jump to conclusions? After all, what you're saying is only based on a few feelings, not real actions [*or alternatively*: on a few actions, not necessarily your real feelings]; hadn't you better talk to a therapist and find out?" Such responses — and their occurrence in the people come out to can seem a belated echo of their occurrence in the person coming out — reveal how problematical at present is the very concept of gay identity, as well as how intensely it is resisted and how far authority over its definition has been distanced from the gay subject her- or himself.

2. *Esther expects Assuérus to be altogether surprised by her self-disclosure; and he is.* Her confident sense of control over other people's knowledge about her is in contrast to the radical uncertainty closeted gay people are likely to feel about who is in control of information about their sexual identity. This has something to do with a realism about secrets that is greater in most people's lives than it is in Bible stories; but it has much more to do with complications in the notion of gay identity, so that no one person can take control over all the multiple, often contradictory codes by which information about sexual identity and activity can seem to be conveyed. In many, if not most, relationships, coming out is a matter of

crystallizing intuitions or convictions that had been in the air for a while already and had already established their own power-circuits of silent contempt, silent blackmail, silent glamorization, silent complicity. After all, the position of those who think they *know something about one that one may not know oneself* is an excited and empowered one—whether what they think one doesn't know is that one somehow *is* homosexual, or merely that one's supposed secret is known to them. The glass closet can license insult ("I'd never have said those things if I'd *known* you were gay!"—yeah, sure); it can also license far warmer relations, but (and) relations whose potential for exploitiveness is built into the optics of the asymmetrical, the specularized, and the inexplicit.[13] There are sunny and apparently simplifying versions of coming out under these circumstances: a woman painfully decides to tell her mother that she's a lesbian, and her mother responds, "Yeah, I sort of thought you might be when you and Joan started sleeping together ten years ago." More often this fact makes the closet and its exits not more but less straightforward, however; not, often, more equable, but more volatile or even violent. Living in and hence coming out of the closet are never matters of the purely hermetic; the personal and political geographies to be surveyed here are instead the more imponderable and convulsive ones of the open secret.

3. *Esther worries that her revelation might destroy her or fail to help her people, but it does not seem to her likely to damage Assuérus, and it does not indeed damage him.* When gay people in a homophobic society come out, on the other hand, perhaps especially to parents or spouses, it is with the consciousness of a potential for serious injury that is likely to go in both directions. The pathogenic secret itself, even, can circulate contagiously *as* a secret: a mother says that her adult child's coming out of the closet with her has plunged her, in turn, into the closet in her conservative community. In fantasy, though not in fantasy only, against the fear of being killed or wished dead by (say) one's parents in such a revelation there is apt to recoil the often more intensely imagined possibility of its killing *them*. There is no guarantee that being under threat from a double-edged weapon is a more powerful position than getting the ordinary axe, but it is certain to be more destabilizing.

4. The inert substance of *Assuérus seems to have no definitional in-volvement with the religious/ethnic identity of Esther.* He sees neither himself nor their relationship differently when he sees that she is different

---

13. On this, see "Privilege of Unknowing," esp. p. 120.

from what he had thought her. The double-edged potential for injury in
the scene of gay coming out, by contrast, results partly from the fact that
the erotic identity of the person who receives the disclosure is apt also to
be implicated in, hence perturbed by it. This is true first and generally
because erotic identity, of all things, is never to be circumscribed simply as
itself, can never not be relational, is never to be perceived or known by
anyone outside of a structure of transference and countertransference.
Second and specifically it is true because the incoherences and contradictions of homosexual identity in twentieth-century culture are responsive
to and hence evocative of the incoherences and contradictions of compulsory heterosexuality.

5. *There is no suggestion that Assuérus might himself be a Jew in
disguise.* But it is entirely within the experience of gay people to find that a
homophobic figure in power has, if anything, a disproportionate likelihood of being gay and closeted. Some examples and implications of this
are discussed toward the end of Chapter 5; there is more to this story. Let it
stand here merely to demonstrate again that gay identity is a convoluted
and off-centering possession if it is a possession at all; even to come out
does not end anyone's relation to the closet, including turbulently the
closet of the other.

6. *Esther knows who her people are and has an immediate answerability
to them.* Unlike gay people, who seldom grow up in gay families; who are
exposed to their culture's, if not their parents', high ambient homophobia
long before either they or those who care for them know that they are
among those who most urgently need to define themselves against it; who
have with difficulty and always belatedly to patch together from fragments a community, a usable heritage, a politics of survival or resistance;
unlike these, Esther has intact and to hand the identity and history and
commitments she was brought up in, personified and legitimated in a
visible figure of authority, her guardian Mardochée.

7. Correspondingly, *Esther's avowal occurs within and perpetuates a
coherent system of gender subordination.* Nothing is more explicit, in the
Bible, about Esther's marriage than its origin in a crisis of patriarchy and
its value as a preservative of female discipline. When the Gentile Vashti,
her predecessor as Ahasuerus's queen, had refused to be put on exhibition
to his drunk men friends, "the wise men, which knew the times," saw that

> Vashti the queen hath not done wrong to the king only, but also to all the
> princes, and to all the people that are in all the provinces of the king

Ahasuerus. For this deed of the queen shall come abroad unto all women, so that they shall despise their husbands in their eyes, when it shall be reported.

(Esther 1:13–17)

Esther the Jew is introduced onto this scene as a salvific ideal of female submissiveness, her single moment of risk with the king given point by her customary pliancy. (Even today, Jewish little girls are educated in gender roles—fondness for being looked at, fearlessness in defense of "their people," nonsolidarity with their sex—through masquerading as Queen Esther at Purim; I have a snapshot of myself at about five, barefoot in the pretty "Queen Esther" dress my grandmother made [white satin, gold spangles], making a careful eyes-down toe-pointed curtsey at [presumably] my father, who is manifest in the picture only as the flashgun that hurls my shadow, pillaring up tall and black, over the dwarfed sofa onto the wall behind me.) Moreover, the literal patriarchism that makes coming out to *parents* the best emotional analogy to Esther's self-disclosure to her *husband* is shown with unusual clarity to function through the male traffic in women: Esther's real mission, as a wife, is to get her guardian Mardochée installed in place of Aman as the king's favorite and advisor. And the instability and danger that by contrast lurk in the Gentile Aman's relation to the king seem, Iago-like, to attach to the inadequate heterosexual buffering of the inexplicit intensities between them. If the story of Esther reflects a firm Jewish choice of a minority politics based on a conservative reinscription of gender roles, however, such a choice has never been able to be made intelligibly by gay people in a modern culture (although there have been repeated attempts at making it, especially by men). Instead, both within and outside of homosexual-rights movements, the contradictory understandings of same-sex bonding and desire and of male and female gay identity have crossed and recrossed the definitional lines of gender identity with such disruptive frequency that the concepts "minority" and "gender" themselves have lost a good deal of their categorizing (though certainly not of their performative) force.

Each of these complicating possibilities stems at least partly from the plurality and the cumulative incoherence of modern ways of conceptualizing same-sex desire and, hence, gay identity; an incoherence that answers, too, to the incoherence with which *hetero*sexual desire and identity are conceptualized. A long, populous theoretical project of interrogating and historicizing the self-evidence of the pseudo-symmetrical opposition homosexual/heterosexual (or gay/straight) as categories of persons will be assumed rather than summarized here. Foucault among other historians locates in about the nineteenth century a shift in European thought from viewing same-sex sexuality as a matter of prohibited and isolated genital *acts* (acts to which, in that view, anyone might be liable who did not have their appetites in general under close control) to viewing it as a function of stable definitions of *identity* (so that one's personality structure might mark one as *a homosexual*, even, perhaps, in the absence of any genital activity at all). Thus, according to Alan Bray, "To talk of an individual [in the Renaissance] as being or not being 'a homosexual' is an anachronism and ruinously misleading,"[14] whereas the period stretching roughly between Wilde and Proust was prodigally productive of attempts to name, explain, and define this new kind of creature, the homosexual person — a project so urgent that it spawned in its rage of distinction an even newer category, that of the heterosexual person.[15]

To question the natural self-evidence of this opposition between gay and straight as distinct kinds of persons is not, however, as we saw in the Introduction, to dismantle it. Perhaps no one should wish it to do so; substantial groups of women and men under this representational regime have found that the nominative category "homosexual," or its more recent near-synonyms, does have a real power to organize and describe their experience of their own sexuality and identity, enough at any rate to make their self-application of it (even when only tacit) worth the enormous accompanying costs. If only for this reason, the categorization commands respect. And even more at the level of groups than of individuals, the durability of any politics or ideology that would be so much as *permissive* of same-sex sexuality has seemed, in this century, to depend on a definition of homosexual persons as a distinct, minority population, however produced or labeled.[16] Far beyond any cognitively or politically enabling effects on the people whom it claims to describe, moreover, the nominative category of "the homosexual" has robustly failed to disintegrate under the pressure of decade after decade, battery after battery of deconstructive exposure — evidently not in the first place because of its meaningfulness to those whom it defines but because of its indispensableness to those who define themselves as against it.

For surely, if paradoxically, it is the paranoid insistence with which the

14. Bray, *Homosexuality*, p. 16.
15. On this, see Katz, *Gay/Lesbian Almanac*, pp. 147–50, and the other works cited in note 1 to the Introduction.
16. Conceivably, contemporary liberal/radical feminism, on the spectrum stretching from NOW to something short of radical separatism, could prove to be something of an exception to this rule — though, of course, already a much compromised one.

definitional barriers between "the homosexual" (minority) and "the heterosexual" (majority) are fortified, in this century, by nonhomosexuals,
and especially by men against men, that most saps one's ability to believe
in "the homosexual" as an unproblematically discrete category of persons. Even the homophobic fifties folk wisdom of *Tea and Sympathy*
detects that the man who most electrifies those barriers is the one whose
own current is at most intermittently direct. It was in the period of the so-
called "invention of the 'homosexual'" that Freud gave psychological
texture and credibility to a countervalent, universalizing mapping of this
territory, based on the supposed protean mobility of sexual desire and on
the potential bisexuality of every human creature; a mapping that implies
no presumption that one's sexual penchant will always incline toward
persons of a single gender, and that offers, additionally, a richly denaturalizing description of the psychological motives and mechanisms
of male paranoid, projective homophobic definition and enforcement.
Freud's antiminoritizing account only gained, moreover, in influence by
being articulated through a developmental narrative in which heterosexist
and masculinist ethical sanctions found ready camouflage. If the new
common wisdom that hotly overt homophobes are men who are "insecure
about their masculinity" supplements the implausible, necessary illusion
that there could be a *secure* version of masculinity (known, presumably, by
the coolness of its homophobic enforcement) and a stable, intelligible way
for men to feel about other men in modern heterosexual capitalist patriarchy, what tighter turn could there be to the screw of an already off-
center, always at fault, endlessly blackmailable male identity ready to be
manipulated into any labor of channeled violence?[17]

It remained for work emerging from the later feminist and gay movements to begin to clarify why the male paranoid project had become so
urgent in the maintenance of gender subordination; and it remained for a
stunningly efficacious coup of feminist redefinition to transform lesbianism, in a predominant view, from a matter of female virilization to one of
woman-identification.[18] Although the post-Stonewall, predominantly
male gay liberation movement has had a more distinct political presence
than radical lesbianism and has presented potent new images of gay
people and gay communities, along with a stirring new family of narrative

17. For a fuller discussion of this, see Chapter 4.
18. See, for example, Radicalesbians, "The Woman Identified Woman," reprinted in
Anne Koedt, Ellen Levine, and Anita Rapone, eds., *Radical Feminism* (New York:
Quadrangle, 1973), pp. 240–45; and Rich, "Compulsory Heterosexuality."

structures attached to coming out, it has offered few new analytic facilities for the question of homo/heterosexual definition prior to the moment of individual coming out. That has not, indeed, been its project. In fact, except for a newly productive interest in historicizing gay definition itself, the array of analytic tools available today to anyone thinking about issues of homo/heterosexual definition is remarkably little enriched from that available to, say, Proust. Of the strange plethora of "explanatory" schemas newly available to Proust and his contemporaries, especially in support of minoritizing views, some have been superseded, forgotten, or rendered by history too unpalatable to be appealed to explicitly. (Many of the supposedly lost ones do survive, if not in sexological terminology, then in folk wisdom and "commonsense." One is never surprised, either, when they reemerge under new names on the Science page of the *Times*; the menwomen of Sodom matriculate as the "sissy boys" of Yale University Press.)[19] But there are few new entries. Most moderately to well-educated Western people in this century seem to share a similar understanding of homosexual definition, independent of whether they themselves are gay or straight, homophobic or antihomophobic. That understanding is close to what Proust's probably was, what for that matter mine is and probably yours. That is to say, it is organized around a radical and irreducible incoherence. It holds the minoritizing view that there is a distinct population of persons who "really are" gay; at the same time, it holds the universalizing views that sexual desire is an unpredictably powerful solvent of stable identities; that apparently heterosexual persons and object choices are strongly marked by same-sex influences and desires, and vice versa for apparently homosexual ones; and that at least male heterosexual identity and modern masculinist culture may require for their maintenance the scapegoating crystallization of a same-sex male desire that is widespread and in the first place internal.[20]

19. I'm referring here to the publicity given to Richard Green's *The "Sissy Boy Syndrome" and the Development of Homosexuality* on its 1987 publication. The intensely stereotypical, homophobic journalism that appeared on the occasion seemed to be legitimated by the book itself, which seemed, in turn, to be legitimated by the status of Yale University Press *itself*.

20. Anyone who imagines that this perception is confined to antihomophobes should listen, for instance, to the college football coach's ritualistic scapegoating and abjection of his team's "sissy" (or worse) personality traits. D. A. Miller's "*Cage aux folles*: Sensation and Gender in Wilkie Collins's *The Woman in White*" (in his *The Novel and the Police*, pp. 146–91, esp. pp. 186–90) makes especially forcefully the point (oughtn't it always to have been obvious?) that this whole family of perceptions is if anything less distinctively the property of cultural criticism than of cultural enforcement.

It has been the project of many, many writers and thinkers of many different kinds to adjudicate between the minoritizing and universalizing views of sexual definition and to resolve this conceptual incoherence. With whatever success, on their own terms, they have accomplished the project, none of them has budged in one direction or other the absolute hold of this yoking of contradictory views on modern discourse. A higher *valuation* on the transformative and labile play of desire, a higher *valuation* on gay identity and gay community: neither of these, nor their opposite, often far more potent depreciations, seems to get any purchase on the stranglehold of the available and ruling paradigm-clash. And this incoherence has prevailed for at least three-quarters of a century. Sometimes, but not always, it has taken the form of a confrontation or nonconfrontation between politics and theory. A perfect example of this potent incoherence was the anomalous legal situation of gay people and acts in this country after one recent legal ruling. The Supreme Court in *Bowers v. Hardwick* notoriously left the individual states free to prohibit any *acts* they wish to define as "sodomy," by whomsoever performed, with no fear at all of impinging on any rights, and particularly privacy rights, safeguarded by the Constitution; yet only shortly thereafter a panel of the Ninth Circuit Court of Appeals ruled (in *Sergeant Perry J. Watkins v. United States Army*) that homosexual *persons*, as a particular kind of person, *are* entitled to Constitutional protections under the Equal Protection clause.[21] To be gay in this system is to come under the radically overlapping aegises of a universalizing discourse of acts and a minoritizing discourse of persons. Just at the moment, at least within the discourse of law, the former of these prohibits what the latter of them protects; but in the concurrent public-health constructions related to AIDS, for instance, it is far from clear that a minoritizing discourse of persons ("risk groups") is not even more oppressive than the competing, universalizing discourse of acts ("safer sex"). In the double binds implicit in the space overlapped by the two, at any rate, every matter of definitional control is fraught with consequence.

The energy-expensive but apparently static clinch between minoritizing and universalizing views of *homo/heterosexual definition* is not, either, the only major conceptual siege under which modern homosexual and heterosexist fates are enacted. The second one, as important as the first

21. When Watkins's reinstatement in the army was supported by the full Ninth Circuit Court of Appeals in a 1989 ruling, however, it was on narrower grounds.

and intimately entangled with it, has to do with defining the relation to gender of homosexual persons and same-sex desires. (It was in this conceptual register that the radical-feminist reframing of lesbianism as woman-identification was such a powerful move.) Enduringly since at least the turn of the century, there have presided two contradictory *tropes of gender* through which same-sex desire could be understood. On the one hand there was, and there persists, differently coded (in the homophobic folklore and science surrounding those "sissy boys" and their mannish sisters, but also in the heart and guts of much living gay and lesbian culture), the trope of inversion, *anima muliebris in corpore virili inclusa* — "a woman's soul trapped in a man's body" — and vice versa. As such writers as Christopher Craft have made clear, one vital impulse of this trope is the preservation of an essential *heterosexuality* within desire itself, through a particular reading of the homosexuality of persons: desire, in this view, by definition subsists in the current that runs between one male self and one female self, in whatever sex of bodies these selves may be manifested.[22] Proust was not the first to demonstrate — nor, for that matter, was the Shakespeare of the comedies — that while these attributions of "true" "inner" heterogender may be made to stick, in a haphazard way, so long as dyads of people are all that are in question, the broadening of view to include any larger circuit of desire must necessarily reduce the inversion or liminality trope to a choreography of breathless farce. Not a jot the less for that has the trope of inversion remained a fixture of modern discourse of same-sex desire; indeed, under the banners of androgyny or, more graphically, "genderfuck," the dizzying instability of this model has itself become a token of value.

Charged as it may be with value, the persistence of the inversion trope has been yoked, however, to that of its contradictory counterpart, the trope of gender separatism. Under this latter view, far from its being of the essence of desire to cross boundaries of gender, it is instead the most natural thing in the world that people of the same gender, people grouped together under the single most determinative diacritical mark of social organization, people whose economic, institutional, emotional, physical needs and knowledges may have so much in common, should bond together also on the axis of sexual desire. As the substitution of the phrase "woman-identified woman" for "lesbian" suggests, as indeed does the

---

22. Christopher Craft, "'Kiss Me with Those Red Lips': Gender and Inversion in Bram Stoker's *Dracula*," *Representations*, no. 8 (Fall 1984): 107–34, esp. 114.

	Separatist:	Integrative:
Homo/hetero *sexual* definition:	*Minoritizing*, e.g., gay identity, "essentialist," third-sex models, civil rights models	*Universalizing*, e.g., bisexual potential, "social constructionist," "sodomy" models, "lesbian continuum"
Gender definition:	*Gender separatist*, e.g., homosocial continuum, lesbian separatist, manhood-initiation models	*Inversion/liminality/ transitivity*, e.g., cross-sex, androgyny, gay/lesbian solidarity models

Figure 2.   Models of Gay/Straight Definition
in Terms of Overlapping Sexuality and Gender

concept of the continuum of male or female homosocial desire, this trope tends to reassimilate to one another identification and desire, where inversion models, by contrast, depend on their distinctness. Gender-separatist models would thus place the woman-loving woman and the man-loving man each at the "natural" defining center of their own gender, again in contrast to inversion models that locate gay people — whether biologically or culturally — at the threshold between genders (see Figure 2).

The immanence of each of these models throughout the history of modern gay definition is clear from the early split in the German homosexual rights movement between Magnus Hirschfeld, founder (in 1897) of the Scientific-Humanitarian Committee, a believer in the "third sex" who posited, in Don Mager's paraphrase, "an exact equation . . . between cross-gender behaviors and homosexual desire"; and Benedict Friedländer, co-founder (in 1902) of the Community of the Special, who concluded to the contrary "that homosexuality was the highest, most perfect evolutionary stage of gender differentiation."[23] As James Steakley explains, "the true *typus inversus*," according to this latter argument, "as distinct from the effeminate homosexual, was seen as the founder of

23. Don Mager, "Gay Theories of Gender Role Deviance," *SubStance* 46 (1985): 32–48; quoted from 35–36. His sources here are John Lauritsen and David Thorstad, *The Early Homosexual Rights Movement* (New York: Times Change Press, 1974), and James D. Steakley, *The Homosexual Emancipation Movement in Germany* (New York: Arno Press, 1975).

patriarchal society and ranked above the heterosexual in terms of his capacity for leadership and heroism."[24]

Like the dynamic impasse between minoritizing and universalizing views of homosexual definition, that between transitive and separatist tropes of homosexual gender has its own complicated history, an especially crucial one for any understanding of modern gender asymmetry, oppression, and resistance. One thing that does emerge with clarity from this complex and contradictory map of sexual and gender definition is that the possible grounds to be found there for alliance and cross-identification among various groups will also be plural. To take the issue of gender definition alone: under a gender-separatist topos, lesbians have looked for identifications and alliances among women in general, including straight women (as in Adrienne Rich's "lesbian continuum" model); and gay men, as in Friedländer's model — or more recent "male liberation" models — of masculinity, might look for them among men in general, including straight men. "The erotic and social presumption of women is our enemy," Friedländer wrote in his "Seven Theses on Homosexuality" (1908).[25] Under a topos of gender inversion or liminality, in contrast, gay men have looked to identify with straight women (on the grounds that they are also "feminine" or also desire men), or with lesbians (on the grounds that they occupy a similarly liminal position); while lesbians have analogously looked to identify with gay men or, though this latter identification has not been strong since second-wave feminism, with straight men. (Of course, the political outcomes of all these trajectories of potential identification have been radically, often violently, shaped by differential historical forces, notably homophobia and sexism.) Note, however, that this schematization over "the issue of gender definition alone" also does impinge on the issue of homo/heterosexual definition, as well, and in an unexpectedly chiasmic way. Gender-*separatist* models like Rich's or Friedländer's seem to tend toward *universalizing* understandings of homo/heterosexual potential. To the degree that gender-*integrative* inversion or liminality models, such as Hirschfeld's "third-sex" model, suggest an alliance or identity between lesbians and gay men, on the other hand, they tend toward gay-*separatist*, minoritizing models of specifically gay identity and politics. Steakley makes a useful series of comparisons between Hirschfeld's Scientific-Humanitarian Committee and Friedländer's Com-

24. Steakley, *The Homosexual Emancipation Movement in Germany*, p. 54.
25. Steakley, *The Homosexual Emancipation Movement in Germany*, p. 68.

munity of the Special: "Within the homosexual emancipation movement there was a deep factionalization between the Committee and the Community. . . . [T]he Committee was an organization of men and women, whereas the Community was exclusively male. . . . The Committee called homosexuals a third sex in an effort to win the basic rights accorded the other two; the Community scorned this as a beggarly plea for mercy and touted the notion of supervirile bisexuality."[26] These crossings are quite contingent, however; Freud's universalizing understanding of sexual definition seems to go with an integrative, inversion model of gender definition, for instance. And, more broadly, the routes to be taken across this misleadingly symmetrical map are fractured in a particular historical situation by the profound asymmetries of gender oppression and heterosexist oppression.

Like the effect of the minoritizing/universalizing impasse, in short, that of the impasse of gender definition must be seen first of all in the creation of a field of intractable, highly structured discursive incoherence at a crucial node of social organization, in this case the node at which *any* gender is discriminated. I have no optimism at all about the availability of a standpoint of thought from which either question could be intelligibly, never mind efficaciously, adjudicated, given that the same yoking of contradictions has presided over all the thought on the subject, and all its violent and pregnant modern history, that has gone to form our own thought. Instead, the more promising project would seem to be a study of the incoherent dispensation itself, the indisseverable girdle of incongruities under whose discomfiting span, for most of a century, have unfolded both the most generative and the most murderous plots of our culture.

26. Steakley, *The Homosexual Emancipation Movement in Germany*, pp. 60–61.

2

Some Binarisms (I)
Billy Budd: *After the Homosexual*

I would like this chapter and the next one to accomplish three main tasks. First, they aim, between them, to provide a set of terms and associations to introduce each of the binarisms around which other issues in the book, in the century, are organized. Second, they will offer something in the way of a reading of each of two texts—an essentially continuous reading of *Billy Budd* in this chapter, and in the next, a Nietzsche-inflected and thematically oriented set of readings of and around *Dorian Gray*. Finally, the chapters mean to give something of a texture, albeit a necessarily anachronizing one, to a particular historical moment, culminating in 1891, a moment from the very midst of the process from which a modern homosexual identity and a modern problematic of sexual orientation could be said to date.

In the last chapter I suggested that the current impasse within gay theory between "constructivist" and "essentialist" understandings of homosexuality is the most recent link in a more enduring chain of conceptual impasses, a deadlock between what I have been calling more generally *universalizing* and *minoritizing* accounts of the relation of homosexual desires or persons to the wider field of all desires or persons. I argued, too, that not the correctness or prevalence of one or the other side of this enduring deadlock but, rather, the persistence of the deadlock itself has been the single most powerful feature of the important twentieth-century understandings of sexuality whether hetero or homo, and a determining feature too of all the social relations routed, in this sexualized century, through understandings of sexuality. This deadlock has by now been too deeply constitutive of our very resources for asking questions about sexuality for us to have any realistic hope of adjudicating it in the future. What we can do is to understand better the structuring, the mechanisms, and the immense consequences of the incoherent dispensation under which we now live.

camping vping
thru opera version!

This argument, as I explained in the Introduction, is a deconstructive one, in a fairly specific sense. Accordingly, my discussion of each of these structuring binarisms as it functions within a specific cultural text will follow a process cognate to the one described there. It will move through a deconstructive description of the instability of the binarism itself, usually couched as the simultaneous interiority and exteriority of a marginalized to a normative term, toward an examination of the resulting definitional incoherence: its functional potential and realization, its power effects, the affordances for its mobilization within a particular discursive context, and finally the distinctive entanglement with it of the newly crucial issues of homo/heterosexual definition.

The crisis of sexual definition whose terms, both minoritizing and universalizing, were crystallizing so rapidly by 1891 provides the structure of *Billy Budd*. There is *a homosexual* in this text—a homosexual person, presented as different in his essential nature from the normal men around him. That person is John Claggart. At the same time, *every* impulse of *every* person in this book that could at all be called desire could be called homosexual desire, being directed by men exclusively toward men. The intimate strangleholds of interrepresentation between that exemplar of a new species, the homosexual man, and his thereby radically reorganized surround of male erotic relations seem to make it irresistible to bring to *Billy Budd* all *our* intimate, paralyzing questions about the essential truths of "homosexuality." (When Benjamin Britten and E. M. Forster agreed to collaborate on an opera, for instance, the epiphany of doing *Billy Budd* came to each of them independently; and of course the book has made a centerpiece for gay, gay-affirmative, or gay-related readings of American culture, and for readings by gay critics.)[1] But while that readerly demand can forge a magnetic relation to the book, the relation is bound to be structured—not at all to say dissipated—by the fact that *Billy Budd* is already organized around the same, potentially paralytic demand for essence. The more apertive questions to bring to it might then be different ones: for instance, how the definitional stranglehold works, and for whom; where the points of volatility or leverage in it might be, and, again, for whom.

---

1. Examples: F. O. Matthiessen, *American Renaissance: Art and Expression in the Age of Emerson and Whitman* (London: Oxford University Press, 1941), pp. 500–514; Robert K. Martin, *Hero, Captain, and Stranger: Male Friendship, Social Critique, and Literary Form in the Sea Novels of Herman Melville* (Chapel Hill: University of North Carolina Press, 1986), pp. 107–24; Joseph Allen Boone, *Tradition Counter Tradition: Love and the Form of Fiction* (Chicago: University of Chicago Press, 1987), pp. 259–66.

If *Billy Budd* won't tell us whether it is of the essence of male homosexual desire to wash across whole cultures or to constitute a distinct minority of individuals, neither will it answer the crucial question of a potentially utopian politics that, again, it all but forces us to ask. Is men's desire for other men the great preservative of the masculinist hierarchies of Western culture, or is it among the most potent of the threats against them? *Billy Budd* seems to pose the question frontally. The male body lovely to male eyes: is this figure "the fighting peacemaker"[2] precious to a ship's captain, the "cynosure" [1359] of male loves whose magnetism for his fellows ("they took to him like hornets to treacle" [1356]) can turn the forecastle that had been a "rat-pit of quarrels" (1356) into "the happy family" (1357) of commercial or warlike solidarity? Or to the contrary, does his focusing of male same-sex desire render him the exact, catalytic image of revolution — of that threat or promise of armed insurrection that, an early draft says, embodies "a crisis for Christendom not exceeded . . . by any other recorded era" (1476*n*.1405.31), and under the urgency of whose incessant evocation the narrative proceeds?[3] *Billy Budd* is unequivocal about the hierarchy-respecting inclinations of its hero. But these notwithstanding, it remains for the very last moments of the novella to show whether his ultimate effect on the personnel of the man-o'-war *Bellipotent* will be to trigger violent revolt or, in the actual denouement that is reclaimed from mutiny by a seeming hair's breadth, to reconsolidate the more inescapably the hierarchies of discipline and national defense.

If, again, as we will be suggesting, the expressive constraints on mutiny make it analogous to the excess of male-male desire, its "final suppression" nonetheless is also said to depend upon an arbitrary surplus of male

2. Herman Melville, *Pierre; Israel Potter; The Piazza Tales; The Confidence-Man; Uncollected Prose; Billy Budd* (New York: Library of America, 1984), p. 1357. Further citations from *Billy Budd* will be given by page number in the text.

3. Note that I am *not* here distinguishing the peaceable trader *Rights of Man* from the man-o'-war *Bellipotent*. The merchant marine and the military navy are two distinct faces of the same national polity; Billy Budd is desired by each community, and for approximately the same potentials in him. The hierarchies of the *Rights of Man*, and its forms of enforcement, are vastly less exacerbated than those of the *Bellipotent*, but both are hierarchical, and the symbiosis between the two systems makes any attempt to disjoin them symbolically a difficult one.

It may be worth adding that if, as this chapter will argue, the last third of *Billy Budd* is a symptomatic Western fantasy about a life *after the homosexual*, the *Rights of Man* parts correspondingly represent the fantasy of life *before the homosexual* — before, that is, the specification of a distinct homosexual identity. To the extent that it is a fantasy of *before*, it is also already structured, therefore, by a full and self-contradictory notion of *the homosexual*.

attachment, "the unswerving loyalty of the marine corps and a voluntary resumption of loyalty among influential sections of the crews" (1364). The relation of the health of the male-male disciplinary system when it is "healthy" to its insubordinate virulence when it is "diseased" is oddly insusceptible of explanation. "To some extent the Nore Mutiny may be regarded as analogous to the distempering irruption of contagious fever in a frame constitutionally sound, and which anon throws it off" (1365). But there's a lot of that going around: a few pages later, "Discontent foreran the Two Mutinies, and more or less it lurkingly survived them. Hence it was not unreasonable to apprehend some return of trouble sporadic or general" (1368). The only barely not aleatory closeness of shave by which, at the end of *Billy Budd*, the command of the *Bellipotent* averts mutiny should warn us again: this is a dangerous book to come to with questions about the *essential nature* of men's desire for men. A book about the placement and re-placement of the barest of thresholds, it continues to mobilize desires that could go either way. A better way of asking the question might then be, What are the operations necessary to deploy male-male desire as the glue rather than as the solvent of a hierarchical male disciplinary order?

But first, we need to reconstruct how we have gone about recognizing the homosexual in the text.

Knowledge/Ignorance; Natural/Unnatural

In the famous passages of *Billy Budd* in which the narrator claims to try to illuminate for the reader's putatively "normal nature" (1382) the peculiarly difficult riddle of "the hidden nature of the master-at-arms" Claggart (riddle on which after all, the narrator says, "the point of the present story turn[s]" [1384]), the answer to the riddle seems to involve not the substitution of semantically more satisfying alternatives to the epithet "hidden" but merely a series of intensifications of it. Sentence after sentence is produced in which, as Barbara Johnson points out in her elegant essay "Melville's Fist," "what we learn about the master-at-arms is that we cannot learn anything":[4] the adjectives applied to him in chapter 11 include "mysterious," "exceptional," "peculiar," "exceptional" again, "obscure," "phenomenal," "notable," "phenomenal" again, "exceptional" again, "secretive." "Dark sayings are these, some will say" (1384). In-

---

4. Barbara Johnson, "Melville's Fist: The Execution of *Billy Budd*," *Studies in Romanticism* 18 (Winter 1979): 567–99; quoted from p. 582.

deed. These representationally vacant, epistemologically arousing place-markers take what semantic coloration they have from a parallel and equally abstract chain of damning ethical designations—"the direct reverse of a saint," "depravity," "depravity," "depravity," "wantonness of atrocity," "the mania of an evil nature"—and from the adduced proximity, in a perhaps discarded draft of the next chapter, of three specific, diagnostic professions, law, medicine, and religion, each however said to be reduced to "perplexing strife" by "the phenomenon" that can by now be referred to only, but perhaps satisfactorily, as "it" (1475*n*.1384.3).[5] And, oh by the way, "it" has something to do with—"it" is prone, in the double shape of envy (antipathy, desire) to being fermented by—the welkin eyes, dyed cheeks, supple joints, and dancing yellow curls (1385) of a lad like Billy Budd.

Even the language by which Claggart's nameless peculiarity is specified as part of his ontological essence is more equivocal than readers are accustomed to note. The narrator labels this human specimen with a definition attributed to Plato: "Natural depravity: a depravity according to nature" (1383). The narrative does not pause to remark, however, that the platonic "definition" is worse than tautological, suggesting as it does two diametrically opposite meanings. "A depravity according to nature," like "natural depravity," might denote something that is depraved when measured against the external standard of nature—that is, something whose depravity is unnatural. Either of the same two phrases might also denote, however, something whose proper nature it is to be depraved—that is, something whose depravity is natural.[6] So all the definition accomplishes here is to carry the damning ethical sanctions already accumulated into a new semantic field, that of nature and the *contra naturam*—a field already entangled for centuries with proto-forms of the struggles around homosexual definition.[7]

5. "Pride," indeed, "envy," and "despair," nouns that could be substantive, are finally produced as if in explanation—but produced also as if synonymous with one another, and as part of a stylized biblical/Miltonic scenario ("serpent," "elemental evil") that barely if at all fails to resubmerge their psychological specificity in the vacant, bipolar ethical categories of the preceding two chapters. To the degree that the three nouns mean each other, they mean nothing but the category "evil"—a category whose constituents then remain to be specified.

6. The Library of America editors note, "Hayford and Sealts identify [the translation from which Melville quotes] as the Bohn edition of Plato's works . . . , in which 'the list of definitions' is included and 'Natural Depravity' is defined as 'a badness by nature, and a sinning in that, which is according to nature.'" In short, the same contradiction made only more explicit.

7. See, for instance, John Boswell, *Christianity, Social Tolerance, and Homosexuality:*

What *was*—Melville asks it—the matter with the master-at-arms? If there is a full answer to this question at all then there are two full answers. Briefly these would be, first, that Claggart is depraved because he is, in his desires, a pervert, of a sort that by 1891 had names in several taxonomic systems although scarcely yet, in English, the name "homosexual"; or, second, that Claggart is depraved not because of the male-directed nature of his desire, here seen as natural or innocuous, but, rather, because he feels toward his own desires only terror and loathing (call this "phobia"). The relation between these possible two answers—that Claggart is depraved because homosexual, or alternatively depraved because homophobic—is of course an odd problem. Suffice it here to say that either could qualify him for, and certainly neither would disqualify him from, a designation like "homosexual."

Arguably, however, there can be no full or substantive answer at all to the question; even as it invokes the (stymied) expertise of certain taxonomic professions, the narrative has nonetheless gone to considerable lengths to invite the purgative reading that "Melville's Fist" exemplarily performs, the reading in which Claggart represents a pure *epistemological essence*, a form and a theory of knowing untinctured by the actual stuff that he either knows or comprises. Claggart, in this reading, "is thus a personification of ambiguity and ambivalence, of the distance between signifier and signified, of the separation between being and doing. . . . He is properly an ironic reader, who, assuming the sign to be arbitrary and unmotivated, reverses the value signs of appearances."[8]

That Claggart displays, as indeed he does prominently, the allegorical label of a certain pure epistemological extremity is not, however, enough to drive doctor, lawyer, clergyman, once summoned, from their place of consultation at the door of the text. Rather, doesn't it associate the abstractive epistemological pressure Claggart embodies *with* the diagnostic specifications—diagnostic and therefore demeaning—of these institutions of expertise?[9] The rhetorical impaction here between a thematically evacuated abstraction of knowledge and a theoretically jejune

---

Gay People in Western Europe from the Beginning of the Christian Era to the Fourteenth Century (Chicago: University of Chicago Press, 1980), pp. 303–32.

8. Johnson, "Melville's Fist," p. 573.

9. In, however, a metonymy none the less durable for its apparent contingency; none the less efficient for the logical contradiction between diagnosis on the one hand and, on the other, the epistemological imperative to uncouple from one another "being and doing."

empiricism of taxonomy effects, I believe, finally a crossing whereby the (structurally generalized) vessels of "knowledge itself" do come to take their shape from the (thematically specified) thing known, or person knowing. The shape taken — the form of knowledge that represents at the same time "knowledge itself" and a diagnosable pathology of cognition, or the cognition of a diagnosable pathology — must, in accordance with the double presentation of Claggart's particular depravity, be described by some such condensation as "homosexual-homophobic knowing." In a more succinct formulation, paranoia.

Urbane/Provincial; Innocence/Initiation; Man/Boy

I have described this crossing of epistemology with thematics as a "rhetorical impaction." The adjective is appropriate because such a crossing can be effected only through a distinctive *reader*-relation imposed by text and narrator. The inexplicit compact by which novel-readers voluntarily plunge into worlds that strip them, however temporarily, of the painfully acquired cognitive maps of their ordinary lives (awfulness of going to a party without knowing anyone) on condition of an invisibility that promises cognitive exemption and eventual privilege, creates, especially at the beginning of books, a space of high anxiety and dependence. In this space a reader's identification with modes of categorization ascribed to her by a narrator may be almost vindictively eager. Any appeal, for instance, to or beyond "knowledge of the world" depends for its enormous novelistic force on the anxious surplus of this early overidentification with the novel's organizing eye. "Worldly" or "urbane" is par excellence one of those categories that, appearing to be a flatly descriptive attribution attached to one person, actually describes or creates a chain of perceptual angles: it is the cognitive privilege of the person described over a separate, perceived world that is actually attested, and by a speaker who through that attestation lays claim in turn to an even more inclusive angle of cognitive distancing and privilege over both the "urbane" character and the "world." The position of a reader in this chain of privilege is fraught with promise and vulnerability. The ostentatious presumption by the narrator that a reader is similarly entitled — rather than, what in truth she necessarily is, disoriented — sets up relations of flattery, threat, and complicity between reader and narrator that may in turn restructure the perception of the conformation originally associated with the "worldly."

Any reassurance for the reader must come through her cultivated and ungrounded precocity at wielding, through and perhaps beyond the terms of the book, not merely the *material of worldliness* but, with it, the *relations of worldliness*, the sense of differentials or thresholds whose manipulation constitutes a "true" knowledge of the world. Thus, for instance, at the beginning of *The Bostonians* the Southerner Basil Ransom, introduced as "provincial,"[10] is shown to be most "'Boeotian,'" not by his failure to pigeonhole the woman-centered Boston spinster Olive Chancellor, but by his unshared satisfaction in what are described to us as the crude tools — the category "morbid" — he has for doing so (11). She has much better tools for classifying him, but is in turn the more deeply discredited by her provinciality in wielding so judgmentally the very term "provincial" (31). James himself, meanwhile, who is after all the one responsible for casting the erotic drama in the framework of "provinciality" from his choice of title onward, unlike Olive succeeds for a long time in protecting himself from the contagion of wielding that attribution — by so exacerbating and so promising to soothe in the reader the anxiety of the reader's own positioning in this projectile drama.

Like *The Bostonians* but by a more definitive, less contingent path, *Billy Budd* enforces, through the reader's drama of disorientation and tentative empowerment, an equation between cognitive mastery of the world in general and mastery of the terms of homoerotic desire in particular.

> But for the adequate comprehending of Claggart by a normal nature these hints are insufficient. To pass from a normal nature to him one must cross "the deadly space between." And this is best done by indirection.
>
> Long ago an honest scholar, my senior, said to me in reference to one who like himself is now no more, a man so unimpeachably respectable that against him nothing was ever openly said though among the few something was whispered, "Yes, X— is a nut not to be cracked by the tap of a lady's fan. You are aware that I am the adherent of no organized religion, much less of any philosophy built into a system. Well, for all that, I think that to try and get into X—, enter his labyrinth and get out again, without a clue derived from some source other than what is known as 'knowledge of the world' — that were hardly possible, at least for me."
>
> . . . At the time, my inexperience was such that I did not quite see the drift of all this. It may be that I see it now. (1382)

Where the reader is in all this is no simple matter: where, after all, can the reader wish to be? The terrorism wielded by the narrator's mystifications

---

10. Henry James, *The Bostonians* (Harmondsworth, Middlesex: Penguin, 1966), p. 6. Further citations from *The Bostonians* will be given by page numbers in the text.

makes the role of "normal" incomprehension at once compulsory and contemptible. The close frame of a male-homosocial pedagogy within which alone the question of X—— can be more than whispered (though still not so much as asked), but "*against*" which the question of X—— must be all the more sharply distinguished, is specified as a bygone possibility at the same time as it is teasingly proffered by the narrator to the reader. Knowledge of X——, in an image whose ghastliness is scarcely mitigated by its disguise as commonplace, is presented as a testicular violence against him, while to fail to crack his nut is oneself to be feminized and accessorized. The worst news, however, is that knowledge of X—— and "'knowledge of the world'" turn out to be not only not enough, but more dangerous than no knowledge at all: to know X—— is not, after all, to deliver the single *coup* of the nutcracker but, rather, with a violence suddenly made vulnerability "to get into X——, enter his labyrinth"—requiring the emergency rescue of some yet more ineffable form of cognition to prevent the direst reversal of the violent power relations of knowledge.

The reader, thus, is invented as a subject in relation to the "world" of the novel by an act of interpellation that is efficacious to the degree that it is contradictory, appealing to the reader on the basis of an assumed sharing of cognitive authority whose ground is hollowed out in the very act of the appeal. The reader is both threatened with and incited to violence at the same time as knowledge. This is also the rhetorical structure of a pivotal moment of the plot of *Billy Budd*. The sudden blow by which Billy murders Claggart in their confrontation under the eye of Vere is preceded by two interpellatory imperatives addressed by Vere to Billy. The first of these instructs Billy, "'Speak, man!... Speak! defend yourself!'" The second of them, brought home to Billy's body by Vere's simultaneous physical touch, is "'There is no hurry, my boy. Take your time, take your time'" (1404). It is possible that Billy could have succeeded in making himself intelligible as either "man" or "boy." But the instruction to him to defer as a boy, simply juxtaposed on the instruction to expedite as a man, "touching Billy's heart to the quick" also ignites it to violence: "The next instant, quick as the flame from a discharged cannon at night, his right arm shot out, and Claggart dropped to the deck." It is, of course, at this moment of Claggart's murder that Billy has been propelled once and for all across the initiatory threshold and into the toils of Claggart's phobic desire. The death of the text's homosexual marks, for reasons we must discuss later, not a terminus but an initiation for the text, as well, into the narrative circulation of male desire.

In *Billy Budd*'s threatening staging, then, *knowledge of the world*, which is linked to the ability to recognize same-sex desire, while compulsory for inhabitants and readers of the world, is also a form of vulnerability as much as it is of mastery. Some further, higher, differently structured way of knowing is required of the person who would wish for whatever reason to "enter [Claggart's] labyrinth *and get out again*." We have already suggested, in a formulation that will require more discussion, that the form of knowledge circulated around and by Claggart ought to be called paranoia. If that is true, then what form of knowledge can in this world be distinguished from paranoia, and how?

Cognition/Paranoia; Secrecy/Disclosure

If it is justifiable to suggest that the form of knowledge — one marked by his own wracking juncture of same-sex desire with homophobia — by which Claggart is typically known to others is the same as that by which he himself knows others, that records the identifying interspecularity and fatal *symmetry* of paranoid knowledge. To know and to be known become the same process. "An uncommon prudence is habitual with the subtler depravity, for it has everything to hide. And in case of an injury but suspected, its secretiveness voluntarily cuts it off from enlightenment or disillusion; and, not unreluctantly, action is taken upon surmise as upon certainty" (1387). The doubling of protective with projective aptitudes is recorded in the very title of the master-at-arms's job, which

> may to landsmen seem somewhat equivocal. Originally, doubtless, that petty officer's function was the instruction of the men in the use of arms. . . . But very long ago . . . that function ceased; the master-at-arms of a great warship becoming a sort of chief of police charged among other matters with the duty of preserving order on the populous lower gun decks. (1372)

The projective mutual accusation of two mirror-image men, drawn together in a bond that renders desire indistinguishable from predation, is the typifying gesture of paranoid knowledge. "It takes one to know one" is its epistemological principle, for it is able, in Melville's phrase, to form no conception of an unreciprocated emotion (1387). And its disciplinary processes are all tuned to the note of police entrapment. The politics of

the agent provocateur makes the conditions of Claggart's life and consciousness; as we shall see, if there is a knowledge that "transcends"
paranoia, it will also be reflected, in *Billy Budd*, in a politics that claims
both to utilize and to "place" the paralytic mirror-violence of entrapment
that Claggart embodies.

Both the efficacy of policing-by-entrapment and the vulnerability of
this policial technique to extreme reversals depend on the structuring of
the policed desire, within a particular culture and moment, as an open
secret. The particular form of the open secret on the *Bellipotent* is the
potential among its men for mutiny. Not an alternative to the plot of male-
male desire and prohibition in *Billy Budd*, the mutiny plot is the form it
takes at the (inseparable) level of the collective. The early evocations of
mutiny in the novella suggest that the difficulty of learning about it is like
the difficulty of learning about such scandalous secrets as proscribed
sexuality. Both are euphemized as "aught amiss." As with that other
"'deadly space between'" (1382), the terms in which mutiny can be
described must be confined to references that evoke recognizant knowledge in those who already possess it without igniting it in those who may
not:

> Such an episode in the Island's grand naval story her naval historians
> naturally abridge, one of them (William James) candidly acknowledging
> that fain would he pass it over did not "impartiality forbid fastidiousness."
> And yet his mention is less a narration than a reference, having to do
> hardly at all with details. Nor are these readily to be found in the
> libraries. . . . Such events cannot be ignored, but there is a considerate
> way of historically treating them. If a well-constituted individual refrains
> from blazoning aught amiss or calamitous in his family, a nation in the
> like circumstances may without reproach be equally discreet. (1364)

Or, again,

> If possible, not to let the men so much as surmise that their officers
> anticipate aught amiss from them is the tacit rule in a military ship. And
> the more that some sort of trouble should really be apprehended, the more
> do the officers keep that apprehension to themselves. (1421)

Specifically, in Captain Vere's exposition and orders around the disciplining of Billy Budd, "the word *mutiny* was not named" (1420).

The potential for mutiny in the British navy fed, of course, on the
involuntarity of the servitude of many of the men aboard; and the question of impressment, which is to say of the entire circumstances by which

these men come to be under the authority they are under, represents the open secret writ—in, for that matter, the only handwriting that can ever express the open secret—large. A "notorious" matter about which there was "little or no secret," nevertheless "such sanctioned irregularities, which for obvious reasons the government would hardly think to parade . . . consequently . . . have all but dropped into oblivion"; "it would not perhaps be easy at the present day directly to prove or disprove the allegation" (1374). "The fact that nobody could substantiate this report was, of course, nothing against its secret currency" (1373). There is no right way of treating such information, and every way of treating it becomes charged with potent excess meanings. Claggart refers to it periphrastically as the fact that certain men "had entered His Majesty's service under another form than enlistment"—

> At this point Captain Vere with some impatience interrupted him: "Be direct, man; say *impressed men.*"
> Claggart made a gesture of subservience.

But immediately afterwards, on Claggart's concluding, with the pre-scribed directness,

> "God forbid, your honor, that the *Indomitable's* should be the experi-ence of the—"
> "Never mind that!" here peremptorily broke in the superior, his face altering with anger. . . . Under the circumstances he was indignant at the purposed allusion. When the commissioned officers themselves were on all occasions very heedful how they referred to the recent events in the fleet, for a petty officer unnecessarily to allude to them in the presence of his captain, this struck him as a most immodest presumption. Besides, to his quick sense of self-respect it even looked under the circumstances something like an attempt to alarm him. (1398–99)

With the characteristic symmetry of the paranoid, open-secret struc-ture, too, the moral stain associated with the navy's recruiting method adheres to its objects at least as damagingly as to its agents. "The promiscuous lame ducks of morality," "drafts culled direct from the jails," "any questionable fellow at large" (1374) (under the eye of paranoia the only man more "questionable" than the one in prison is the one out of it)—these descriptions mark what is morally presumed of any man who has come into any relation at all to the entrapping contagions of His Majesty's discipline. The phrases just quoted are not, indeed, though they might be, from a context descriptive of the most powerless of the impressed men, but from one of the passages devoted to explicating the master-at-arms; thus they especially foreground the symmetrical undecidability of Claggart's own position between being stigmatized agent and stigmatized object of military compulsion. Naturally, the resources of the master-at-arms for understanding the men over whom he is to exercise discipline replicate so faithfully the disciplinary imperative itself that they can convey to him nothing but mirrorings of the panic of his own position. The very accuracy with which he understands his position makes him fatally credulous of any suggested threat to discipline or to himself: "The master-at-arms never suspected the veracity of these [false] reports . . . for he well knew how secretly unpopular may become a master-at-arms, at least a master-at-arms of those days, zealous in his function" (1386).

The attempted entrapment of Billy by the after-guardsman (one of the "implicit tools" [1386] of the master-at-arms) only accentuates the mirroring structure of this form of enforcement, as well as the ineradicable double entendre in this book between the mutiny question and the homosexuality question. The place of his temptation is too dark to enable Billy to see the features of the agent provocateur; had he done so, he might have been startled by the parodic resemblance of "that equivocal young person" (1395) to his welkin-eyed self: by "his round freckled face and glassy eyes of pale blue, veiled with lashes all but white . . . a genial fellow enough to look at, and something of a rattlebrain, to all appearance. Rather chubby too for a sailor" (1391). This nautical tempter, having failed to put on Billy's Nautilus body at the same time as his coloring and vapidity, attempts (whether out of envy or sheer "precocity of crookedness" [1395]) to entrap Billy by his own pseudo self-disclosure into joining a group of supposed confreres: "'You were impressed, weren't you? Well, so was I'; and he paused, as to mark the effect. . . . 'We are not the only impressed ones, Billy. There's a gang of us'" (1389). The further indignity of a display of coins ("see, they are yours, Billy, if you'll only—" [1389]) prompts Billy to put an end to the "abrupt proposition" in classically phobic style ("in his disgustful recoil from an overture which though he but ill comprehended he instinctively knew must involve evil of some sort" [1390]), mobilizing his poor resources of ignorance, rudimentary taxonomy, and physical violence: "D-d-damme, I don't know what you are d-driving at, or what you mean, but you had better g-g-go where you belong! . . . If you d-don't start, I'll t-t-toss you back over the r-rail!"

A more ingenuous and less paranoid personality structure than Billy's, we are repeatedly informed, it would be impossible to imagine. Who could be more immune to paranoid contagion than a person with no cognition at all? Yet even the determined resistance posed by Billy's stupidity can be made, under the right pressure of events, to answer actively as a mirror to the exactions of paranoid desire. In Robert K. Martin's acute summary of the murder itself, for instance,

> Claggart's desire for Billy is not only a desire to hurt Billy, but also a desire to *provoke* Billy, so that *he* (Claggart) can be raped by Billy. His false accusation achieves this purpose by finally provoking Billy to raise his arm. . . . When Billy strikes Claggart, he in some way fulfills Claggart's desire: Claggart dies instantly, at last possessed by that which he has sought to possess.[11]

Discipline/Terrorism

It is easy to forget, however, that the pressure under which Billy and Claggart are finally, in the scene of Claggart's murder, faced off as if symmetrically against one another is not simply the pressure of Claggart's position and desire. Rather, it is the pressure of *Vere's mobilization of Claggart's position and desire*. I mean to argue that the force and direction of paranoid knowing — of, in the past century, the homophobic/homosexual momentum around men's desire for men — are manipulable, though not reliably so, by certain apparently nonparanoid processes of reframing and redefinition affecting the binarisms we are discussing, and exemplified by Captain Vere.

One useful distinction to adduce, though as an opposition it will prove no more absolute than those others we already have in play, could be between two structures of enforcement. From the inefficient, paranoiacally organized structure we have already discussed, symmetrical and "one-on-one," based on entrapment and the agent provocateur, *Billy Budd* suggests that it may be possible to differentiate another: the more efficient because spectacular one of exemplary violence, the male body elevated for display. "War looks but to the frontage, the appearance. And the Mutiny Act, War's child, takes after the father" (1416), Vere reflects, railroading Billy's death sentence through his drumhead court. The bodies of executed men already preside over the prehistory of the book, where discipline after the Great Mutiny is shown to have been "confirmed

---

11. Martin, *Hero, Captain, and Stranger*, p. 112.

only when its ringleaders were hung for an admonitory spectacle to the anchored fleet" (1477n.1405.31). The sacrificial body of Lord Nelson, both in life and in death, has itself been an admonitory spectacle of great magnetism. "Unnecessary" and "foolhardy," Nelson's "ornate publication of his person in battle" (1366) represents, as conspicuous consumption, a form of discipline-through-embodiment that is explicitly distinguished from the terroristic:

> danger was apprehended from the temper of the men; and it was thought that an officer like Nelson was the one, not indeed to terrorize the crew into base subjection, but to win them, by force of his mere presence and heroic personality, back to an allegiance if not as enthusiastic as his own yet as true. (1368)

At Trafalgar, "under the presentiment of the most magnificent of all victories to be crowned by his own glorious death, a sort of priestly motive led him to dress his person in the jewelled vouchers of his own shining deeds" — a coup de theatre that lends his very name, for a posthumous eternity of sailors, the arousing and marshaling effect of "a trumpet to the blood" (1367).

And of course, at a more routine level but scarcely less grievous, there is the galvanizing

> impression made upon [Billy] by the first formal gangway-punishment he had ever witnessed. . . . When Billy saw the culprit's naked back under the scourge, gridironed with red welts and worse, when he marked the dire expression on the liberated man's face as with his woolen shift flung over him by the executioner he rushed forward from the spot to bury himself in the crowd, Billy was horrified. He resolved that never through remissness would he make himself liable to such a visitation or do or omit aught that might merit even verbal reproof. (1376–77)

Among the three endings of *Billy Budd*, the central one traces the ultimate "publication" of his own person, once hanged by the neck until dead, for precisely this exemplary purpose, multiplying through the organ of "an authorized weekly publication" (1432) — as indeed the novella itself does whenever it is reprinted and read — the highly performative, not to say wishful news, "'The criminal paid the penalty of his crime. The promptitude of the punishment has proved salutary. Nothing amiss is now apprehended'" (1433).

The association of Captain Vere with on the one hand the cognitive category of discipline, and on the other the physical image of the single human body elevated from the common horizon of view, is stamped by the story even on his firmamental nickname, "Starry Vere." This comes, we are told, from lines in "Upon Appleton House,"

> This 'tis to have been from the first
> In a domestic heaven nursed,
> Under the discipline severe
> Of Fairfax and the starry Vere.
>   (1370)

Again, the inflexibility of Vere's converse is attributed by the narrator to a constitutional "directness, sometimes far-reaching like that of a migratory fowl that in its flight never heeds when it crosses a frontier" (1372). Vere's discipline is thus associated with physical elevation in two ways. First, his preferred form of discipline depends, as we have seen, on positioning some male body not his own in a sacrificial "bad eminence" of punitive visibility, an eminence that (in his intention) forms the organizing summit of what thereby becomes a triangle or pyramid of male relations, a "wedged mass of upturned faces" (1427), the men at whom the spectacle is aimed being braced by their shared witness of it into a supposedly stabilized clutch of subordination. In another version of Vere's disciplinary triangle, however, his own seeing eye, not the looked-upon body of some other man who has been made an example of, makes the apex of the disciplinary figure.

The defining example of this latter tableau is the way Vere chooses to handle Claggart's insinuations to him about Billy Budd: he cannot rest until the stage is set on which he may stand "prepared to scrutinize the mutually confronting visages" (1403) of the two men who are or are soon to be locked in a mutually fatal knot of paranoid symmetry. The geometric symmetry of their confrontation seems to be essential to Vere's achieving the elevated distance to which he aspires. At the same time, it is Vere's desire to adjudicate from such a disciplinary distance, one defined by its very difference from the mutual confrontation of symmetrical visages, that completes the mutuality and entirely *creates* the fatality of the paranoid knot of Claggart and Billy Budd.[12] At the crudest level, had Vere been content either to hear the two men's depositions separately or to

---

12. And even after Claggart's death, Vere's fine sense of space persists in keeping the two men confronted: his drumhead court takes place in a room flanked by two "compartments," in one of which Claggart's body lies, "opposite that where the foretopman remained immured" (1406).

grant them an official hearing—to confront each with his own visage, or each with the collective visage of a court-martial, rather than each with the other's visage under Vere's "impartial" eye—then neither of the men would have been murdered.

Vere's discipline both requires and enforces the paranoid symmetry against which it is defined, then, just as it will not dispense with the system of police entrapment whose squalid techniques provide at once foil and fodder for the celestial justice-machine.[13] It is Vere's "judicious" justice that solders Billy into the vis-à-vis from which—with the incitement of Vere's generous contradictory address and the ignition of his kindly digital touch—neither Claggart nor Billy will emerge alive.

Further, in the scene of trial and sentencing, Vere succeeds by a similar tactic in getting the death sentence he wants against Billy. He foments a paranoid interspecularity between officers and crew, forcing his officers into an intensely projective fantasy of how the crew may be able, through their own projective fantasy, to read and interpret the officers' minds. In case of clemency, he asks,

> "how would they take it? Even could you explain to them—which our official position forbids—they, long molded by arbitrary discipline, have not that kind of intelligent responsiveness that might qualify them to comprehend and discriminate. . . . They would think that we flinch, that we are afraid of them—afraid of practicing a lawful rigor singularly demanded at this juncture, lest it should provoke new troubles. What shame to us such a conjecture on their part, and how deadly to discipline." (1416–17)

The reflexively structured mutiny panic aroused in these officers by one "not less their superior in mind than in naval rank" (1417) is, we are told,

13. Indeed, there is some suggestion that Vere's transcendent, "judicious" urbanity may be enabled by, or even indistinguishable from, a paranoid relation—"strong suspicion clogged by strange dubieties" (1402)—precisely to Claggart's relation to the crew. The same man who is rendered suspicious by Claggart's projective suggestion that Billy's "daisies" might conceal "a man trap" (1400) apprehends Claggart himself, in turn, as part of a gestalt of submerged dangers the very recognition of which could enmesh him the more fatally in their operations:

> [L]ong versed in everything pertaining to the complicated gun-deck life, which like every other form of life has its secret mines and dubious side, the side popularly disclaimed, Captain Vere did not permit himself to be unduly disturbed by the general tenor of his subordinate's report.
>
> Furthermore, if in view of recent events prompt action should be taken at the first palpable sign of recurring insubordination, for all that, not judicious would it be, he thought, to keep the idea of lingering disaffection alive by undue forwardness in crediting an informer. (1399)

the main thing that drives them to override their strong scruples of ethical and procedural propriety and to pass the death sentence Vere demands.

Majority/Minority; Impartiality/Partiality

The disciplinary triangle whose apex is the adjudicating eye, or the one capped by the exemplary object of discipline: these are only pseudo-alternative formations, to the degree that the same agent, Captain Vere, is in charge of the circulation of characters from one positioning to another. How steady his hand seems on this kaleidoscope—how consistent his desire! His hungers and his helmsmanship he wields together with a masterful economy. The desires of Captain Vere are desires of the eye:

> Now the Handsome Sailor as a signal figure among the crew had naturally enough attracted the captain's attention from the first. Though in general not very demonstrative to his officers, he had congratulated Lieutenant Ratcliffe upon his good fortune in lighting on such a fine specimen of the *genus homo*, who in the nude might have posed for a statue of young Adam before the Fall. . . . The foretopman's conduct, too, so far as it had fallen under the captain's notice, had confirmed the first happy augury, while the new recruit's qualities as a "sailor-man" seemed to be such that he had thought of recommending him to the executive officer for promotion to a place that would more frequently bring him under his own observation, namely, the captaincy of the mizzentop, replacing there in the starboard watch a man not so young whom partly for that reason he deemed less fitted for the post. (1400–1401)

The casting of sky-eyed Billy in the generic role of the "Handsome Sailor" has suggested from the beginning of the story his ocular consumability as a figure lofted high in the field of vision, "Aldebaran among the lesser lights of his constellation" (1353), "a superb figure, tossed up as by the horns of Taurus against the thunderous sky" (1354). When Claggart, unobserved, glimpses "belted Billy rolling along the upper gun deck," his repertoire of responses is circumscribed and ineffectual: "his eyes strangely suffused with incipient feverish tears" (1394), setting in motion again the embittering cycle of "pale ire, envy, and despair" (1475n.1384.14). Captain Vere, on the other hand, desires not to hold Billy but to behold him, for while Claggart "could even have loved Billy but for fate and ban" (1394), to Vere the "stripling" whom his instinctive fantasy is to (denude and) turn to marble must remain a mere "specimen" of "the right stuff" (1400–1401). In contrast to Claggart's toilsome enmeshments, Vere's eye sees in Billy a clean-cut stimulus to his executive aptitudes, the catalyst of a personnel-management project to get the magnificent torso hoisted up to "a place that would more frequently bring him under his own observation." If there are frustrations entailed in Vere's system of supplying his eye with sustenance, those have to do only with the contingency and mutability of particular, embodied flesh: unlike marble or the platonic abstraction *genus homo*, particular lads grow "not so young" and become "partly for that reason" unfitted to the prominent "watch."

Impossible not to admire the deftness with which Captain Vere succeeds in obviating his frustrations and assuring the fulfillment of his desire. Billy displayed, Billy aloft in "a place . . . under his own observation," Billy platonized, Billy the "pendant pearl" (1434), Billy who won't grow old. The last third of the novella, the shockingly quick forced-march of Billy to the mainyard gallows and his apotheosis there: wholly and purely the work of Captain Vere, these represent the perfect answer to a very particular hunger.

It is time to pause here, perhaps, and ask explicitly what it means to have found in Claggart the homosexual in this text, and in Vere its image of the normal. Just as the Uranian disciplinary justice of "Starry" Vere depends on the same paranoid policial clinch that it defines itself by transcending, Vere's supposedly impartial motivations toward Billy Budd are also founded on a Claggart-like partiality as against which, however, they as well are imperiously counterposed. Claggart's "partiality" and Vere's "impartiality": perhaps rather than being mutually external opposing entities, X versus non-X, desire versus non-desire, "partial" and "impartial" are meant to relate here instead as *part* to *whole*: Claggart's impotent constricted desire gnawing at his own viscera, Vere's potent systemic desire outspread through all the veins and fault lines of naval regulation. The most available term for Claggart's desire may be "private"; for Vere's, "public." But what do these designations mean?

Public/Private

The immense productiveness of the public/private crux in feminist thought has come, not from the confirmation of an original hypothesized homology that male:female::public:private, but from the wealth of its deconstructive deformations. Across the disciplines, from architecture to psychoanalysis, from the workplace and the welfare state to the ontologies of language and self, the public / private issue has sparked a series of founding feminist analyses, each in a new connection demonstrating the tendentiousness of a topos of pure *place* and an analytic structure of symmetrical opposition in any connection involving agency, power, or, indeed, narrative. One exemplary feminist flexion of that static homology might be Catherine MacKinnon's dictum: "Privacy is everything women as women have never been allowed to be or have; at the same time the private is everything women have been equated with and defined in terms of *men's* ability to have."[14]

On this subject, one of the most consequential intuitions of Melville's talent was how like the space of a sailing ship could be to that of the Shakespearean theatre. Each of these (all-male) venues made graphic the truth that the other architectural vernaculars of the nineteenth century, at any rate, conspired to cover over: that the difference between "public" and "private" could never be stably or intelligibly represented as a difference between two concrete classes of physical space. Instead, on shipboard as on the boards, the space for those acts whose performative efficacy depended on their being defined as either private or public had to be delineated and categorized anew for each. A model for this definition might be the rhetorical art of the actor, whose (for instance) relaxation of tone in the focal muscles of the eye can organize a sudden soliloquial space by which every other body on the stage is at once rendered invisible and *deaf.*

Many gorgeous effects in *Moby Dick* depend on the sweeping Shakespearean arrogation by the narrating consciousness itself of the power to define a particular swatch of upper- or below-deck, for a particular stretch of time, as private or public space. In *Billy Budd*, on the other hand, a more cross-grained local layering of enunciation means that a continuing struggle over the right to delineate shipboard space as public or private is a visible subject of the narrative. As it turns out, indeed, the barest setting of the stage (in this rhetorical sense) can be shown already to constitute both the plot of the drama and its range of meaning, so delicate is the calibration of social meaning organized around the incoherent register public / private.[15]

14. Catherine A. MacKinnon, "Feminism, Marxism, Method, and the State: Toward Feminist Jurisprudence," *Signs* 8, no. 4 (Summer 1983): 656–57.

15. And this is to say nothing of the other, never fully interdistinguishable systems of representation whose density and final unintelligibility innervate the space of the ship with equally fine webs of potential for meaning: most obviously, the anthropomorphic, as inalienable from as inadequate to the ship's body.

The grapplings of attention and knowledge, struggles of making as if anew the mise-en-scène, that have to be negotiated before the first word of any shipboard converse may be uttered! For only one example, the encounter between Claggart and Vere that finally turns into the novella's marathon of murder and judgment requires, in order to so much as get under way, three full paragraphs of the most intensive spatio-epistemological choreography:

> [T]he master-at-arms, ascending from his cavernous sphere, made his appearance cap in hand by the mainmast respectfully waiting the notice of Captain Vere, then solitary walking the weather side of the quarter-deck. . . . The spot where Claggart stood was the place allotted to men of lesser grades seeking some more particular interview either with the officer of the deck or the captain himself. But from the latter it was not often that a sailor or petty officer of those days would seek a hearing; only some exceptional cause would, according to established custom, have warranted that.
>
> Presently, just as the commander, absorbed in his reflections, was on the point of turning aft in his promenade, he became sensible of Claggart's presence, and saw the doffed cap held in deferential expectancy. . . .
>
> No sooner did the commander observe who it was that now deferentially stood awaiting his notice than a peculiar expression came over him. It was not unlike that which uncontrollably will flit across the countenance of one at unawares encountering a person who, though known to him indeed, has hardly been long enough known for thorough knowledge, but something in whose aspect nevertheless now for the first provokes a vaguely repellent distaste. But coming to a stand and resuming much of his wonted official manner, save that a sort of impatience lurked in the intonation of the opening word, he said "Well? What is it, Master-at-arms?" (1397)

Nor, once the demeaning interpellatory terms have been negotiated for Claggart's provisional entitlement to impinge on Vere's (much populated) "solitude," is the definition of their space appreciably stabilized. The audience Vere grants Claggart has itself an audience, or the more unsettling incipience of one:

> For although the few gun-room officers there at the time had, in due observance of naval etiquette, withdrawn to leeward the moment Captain Vere had begun his promenade on the deck's weather side; and though during the colloquy with Claggart they of course ventured not to diminish the distance; and though throughout the interview Captain Vere's voice was far from high, and Claggart's silvery and low; and the wind in the cordage and the wash of the sea helped the more to put them beyond earshot; nevertheless, the interview's continuance already had attracted

observation from some topmen aloft and other sailors in the waist or
further forward. (1402)

The carving-out of privacy for official work from the promiscuous public
space of individuals requires not only a large original investment of Vere's
authority but continually renewed draughts on it. And meanwhile the
very fact that even in this tightly organized and hierarchical little polis a
private space is at this moment what *official* work needs to occupy, while a
public space is seen as suited to the *individual*, suggests the irremediably
contradictory definitional field in which these struggles for meaning must
take place.

When Vere determines, therefore, that the measure required for the
continuance of this encounter "involve[s] a shifting of the scene, a transfer
to a place less exposed to observation" (1402), he is responding to a range
of difficult imperatives by manipulating a range of sensitive binarisms. In
addition to the discomfort of having to maintain by exertion of willpower
an impermeable interlocutory space within a physical space that is actually awash with people, he is also responding to the double bind constituted by the status of mutiny in his navy as an open secret:

> At first, indeed, he was naturally for summoning that substantiation of his
> allegations which Claggart said was at hand. But such a proceeding would
> result in the matter at once getting abroad, which in the present stage of it,
> he thought, might undesirably affect the ship's company. If Claggart was a
> false witness—that closed the affair. And therefore, before trying the
> accusation, he would first practically test the accuser; and he thought this
> could be done in a quiet undemonstrative way. (1402)

Along with stage-managing the physical space of the encounter over
the charged threshold from open-air to closed-door ("Go find [Budd]. It is
his watch off. Manage to tell him out of earshot that he is wanted aft.
Contrive it that he speaks to nobody. Keep him in talk yourself. And not
till you get well aft here, not till then let him know that the place where he
is wanted is my cabin. You understand. Go. —Master-at-arms, show
yourself on the decks below, and when you think it time for Albert to be
coming with his man, stand by quietly to follow the sailor in" [1403])—
along with ushering the physical space of the encounter over this threshold, and its informational space over the threshold from demonstrative to
secret, Vere has also activated yet another public/private threshold, the
threshold between acts done on the responsibility of the person and acts
done in the name of the state, between the official and the unofficial.

At whatever point in the story Vere may tacitly have decided on the fate he has in mind for Billy Budd, it is within an instant after the death of Claggart under these stressed and equivocal circumstances that he first utters aloud his declaration of purpose: "the angel must hang!" (1406). In accomplishing that project Vere can scarcely depend on the narrow channel of strict official procedure, since according to that, as the surgeon reflects, "The thing to do . . . was to place Billy Budd in confinement, and in a way dictated by usage, and postpone further action in so extraordinary a case to such time as they should rejoin the squadron, and then refer it to the admiral" (1406-7). For Vere, however (as indeed, it turns out, for his superiors), "martial duty" (1409), which refers to the overarching conjunction of his mutiny panic[16] with his visual desire, represents a higher law than the merely tactical facilities of official usage; and what "martial duty" dictates is a rhetorical tour de force by which the line between the official and the unofficial can be danced across back and forth, back and forth in a breathtakingly sustained choreography of the liminal, giving the authority of stern collective judgment and the common weal to what are, after all, the startlingly specific sensory hungers of a single man.

Thus, "reserving to himself . . . the right of maintaining a supervision of it, or formally or informally interposing at need," Vere "summarily" convenes a drumhead court, "he electing the individuals composing it" (1409). His desire in choosing them is to find men "altogether reliable in a moral dilemma involving aught of the tragic" (1409) — that is to say, men who can be persuaded from the beginning, as a matter of definition, that this is a story that *is* tragic: one that must inevitably end with death, and with a death of a certain exemplary altitude and gravity. In constructing that death as — against all the odds — inevitable, Captain Vere has to do not only the police but the judge, witness, defense, and D.A. in different voices. Always, however, from the same significant place in the room:

> Billy Budd was arraigned, Captain Vere necessarily appearing as the sole witness in the case, and as such temporarily sinking his rank, though singularly maintaining it in a matter apparently trivial, namely, that he testified from the ship's weather side, with that object having caused the court to sit on the lee side. (1410)

16. "Feeling that unless quick action was taken on it, the deed of the foretopman, so soon as it should be known on the gun decks, would tend to awaken any slumbering embers of the Nore among the crew, a sense of the urgency of the case overruled in Captain Vere every other consideration" (62-63).

If Captain Vere, as prosecution witness, happens to respond to testimony by the accused with the more than witnesslike affirmation "I believe you, my man," it will scarcely occasion surprise that Billy can address him only as "your honor" (1410). Billy's unwavering trust in him, on which the smoothness of the official proceedings also depends, comes, however, from viewing him in the wholly unofficial light of "his best helper and friend" (1411). As witness, as "coadjutor" (1414), as commanding officer, as best friend to the defendant, as chief prosecutor, as final judge, as consoler and explainer and visitant, and at the last as chief executioner and chief mourner, Vere contrives by his ceaseless crossing of these lines of oppositionality and of rank not to obscure such demarcations but to heighten them and, by doing so, to heighten the prestige of his own mastery in overruling them.

Sincerity/Sentimentality

Ann Douglas ends her jeremiad against "the feminization of American culture" with a climactic celebration of *Billy Budd*, choosing this particular text because *Billy Budd* represents in her argument the precise opposite of the category of the sentimental. Ann Douglas's *Billy Budd* is Captain Vere's *Billy Budd*: Vere is not only its "fair-minded" hero but its God. And in Douglas's account Captain Vere shares with the story itself a "remoteness" that only enhances the "essential fairness" of each; *his* virtue of a spacious judiciousness is *its* virtue of a spacious judiciousness.[17]

What most characterizes the exemplary nonsentimentality of the novella *Billy Budd* and of Captain Vere, according to Douglas, is the total scrupulousness with which each respects the boundaries between the public and the private. "Everything has its place," Douglas writes approvingly. "Melville respects his characters' privacy." Vere, analogously, operating "on the impersonal, even allegorical plane," is absolved of having any "personal" motivation for his sacrifice of Billy. And his divine stature is guaranteed by the complete impermeability that is said to obtain between his own public and private lives. "His action in condemning Budd is analogous to the Calvinist Deity's in sacrificing Christ. Vere suffers in private for the fact that he has pulled off a totally public gesture." Thus,

17. All the material quoted is from Ann Douglas, *The Feminization of American Culture* (New York: Alfred A. Knopf, 1977; rpt. ed., New York: Avon/Discus, 1978), pp. 391–95.

he and the story become, in Douglas's argument, the perfect antithesis to a century-long process of sentimental degradation of American culture, a process in the course of which public and private have become fatally confused.

Douglas's reading of Captain Vere is a powerful one in the sense that it records sharply an effect that Vere and his text do powerfully generate. It might be called the privacy effect: the illusion that a reader of *Billy Budd* has witnessed a struggle between private and public realms that are distinguished from one another with quite unusual starkness. Vere is the character who seems most identified with and responsible for the austerity of this definitional segregation, and as readers we habitually celebrate or deprecate Vere according to whether or not we approve of so scrupulous a segregation, or of so absolute a denegation of the private in favor of the public realm so demarcated.[18]

In agreeing to make this choice of approval or disapproval, however, we seem already to have allowed ourselves to be impressed into His Majesty's Service. Accepting that what we witness is a choice between public and private, we are in the position of the officers of Captain Vere's drumhead court, or of the sailors who make the audience for punishment on deck. Or, rather, we resanction their excruciatingly difficult position there, and often in terms far less skeptical than their own. Whatever, in these terms, we may "choose," nonetheless the angel must hang.

I hope I have already said enough about the incoherence of the public/ private duality aboard the *Bellipotent*, and about the sinuosity of Captain Vere's relation to it, to suggest that the creation by this text and this character of this intense a *privacy effect* is a stunning fictional achievement. How is the trick done? How, for instance, do readers come to be convinced that we know that "*Vere suffers in private*" for his "public" gesture?

For the most part, we receive this information in the same way the officers and crew receive it, which is why our conviction that we know "Vere suffers in private" is the thing that identifies many readers most haplessly with those disempowered men. We know "Vere suffers in pri-

---

18. Even Robert K. Martin, whose illuminating discussion of *Billy Budd* in the context of Melville's whole oeuvre overlaps at many points with my considerations here, tends to summarize Vere in terms of conflicts between the "man" and the "office" ("a reasonable man in the service of an unreasoning office"): "We are faced with a story that deals with a permanent political dilemma: Can the good person serve the state?" (*Hero, Captain, and Stranger*, p. 113).

vate" because Vere suffers in private in public. We know, furthermore, that Vere suffers in secret and in silence, by the operatic volubility and visibility with which he performs the starring role of Captain *agonistes*. Rather than seek out a private space for what may be his private suffering (as if there were private space aboard the *Bellipotent*—as if there were private space anywhere), Vere instead sets out to reorganize his immediate, populous community through a piece of theatre by which he himself may come to embody, in his speech and in his very physique, the site of definitional struggle between public and private. Through this act of daring, Vere is conclusively confirmed in his judicial authority by dramatizing, for a subjected audience, his own body as the suffering site of category division. "Sentimentality" can serve as a name for one side, the ejected side, of the category division embodied in him—and, at the same time, as a name for the overarching strategy that is here deployed around him.

We have already discussed Vere's words to some extent, but what about his body? This theatricality is, after all, the strategy that finally brings into congruence the two characteristic modes of Vere's scopic discipline: its apex positioning of a suffering male body as a visual object, and its apex positioning of Vere himself as a seeing and judging subject. When the countenance or body of "Starry" Vere becomes visible in *Billy Budd* as a physical site of conflict, that event is the more spectacular in that Vere has habitually been so disembodied a presence. Unlike Billy, whose epistemological simplicity and vulnerability are attested by the beefcake frontality with which the story evokes his physique, or Claggart, whose body is ceaselessly raked by the paranoid cross-fire of the view outward from within and the view inward from without,[19] Vere's introduction onto the narrative scene has been accompanied, in the place normally reserved for physical description, rather by a list of privileging privatives. "The most *un*demonstrative of men," "this gentleman *not* conspicuous by his stature and wearing *no* pronounced insignia" displays an "*un*obtrusiveness of demeanor [that] may have proceeded from a certain *un*affected modesty of manhood sometimes accompanying a resolute

19. E.g., "It served Claggart in his office that his eye could cast a tutoring glance. His brow was of the sort phrenologically associated with more than average intellect; silken jet curls partly clustering over it, making a foil to the pallor below, a pallor tinged with a faint shade of amber akin to the hue of time-tinted marbles of old. This complexion . . . though it was not exactly displeasing, nevertheless seemed to hint of something defective or abnormal in the constitution and blood" (1373).

nature" (1369, emphasis added). The reader's eye is not invited to the feast. Where Billy's flat blue eyes are meant to be gazed at, and Claggart's deep violet ones flash red (1394) or blur into a muddy purple (1403–4) with the double directionality of his glance of "serpent fascination" (but who's the serpent?), Vere's gray eyes, the only specifying detail of his corporeality, are for outcalls only—"gray eyes impatient and distrustful essaying to fathom to the bottom Claggart's calm violet ones" (1401), or desiring to keep Billy's welkin ones under direct observation.

Perhaps it is not surprising, then, that Vere has to hide his eyes in order to become most openly an object of view. Even then, what he becomes visible *as* is the dramatized site of internal division. After he and Billy have examined the inert form of the dead Claggart, for instance ("It was like handling a dead snake"):

> Regaining erectness, Captain Vere with one hand covering his face stood to all appearance as impassive as the object at his feet. Was he absorbed in taking in all the bearings of the event and what was best not only now at once to be done but also in the sequel? Slowly he uncovered his face; and the effect was as if the moon emerging from eclipse should reappear with quite another aspect than that which had gone into hiding. The father in him, manifested toward Billy thus far in the scene, was replaced by the military disciplinarian. (1405)

Again, to mark a turning point in the trial (the moment at which Billy leaves the cabin and at which Vere moves from "witness" to active prosecutor) he manifests himself as visible by turning his back. The officers

> exchanged looks of troubled indecision, yet feeling that decide they must and without long delay. For Captain Vere, he for the time stood, unconsciously with his back toward them, apparently in one of his absent fits gazing out from a sashed porthole to windward upon the monotonous blank of the twilight sea. But the court's silence continuing, broken only at moments by brief consultations in low earnest tones, this served to arouse him and energize him. Turning, he to-and-fro paced the cabin athwart; in the returning ascent to windward climbing the slant deck in the ship's lee roll, without knowing it symbolizing thus in his action a mind resolute to surmount difficulties even if against primitive instincts strong as the wind and sea. (1413)

Here the captain is again materialized, once more as erectness, and once more as a self embattled against itself. So it is too, all the more obviously, at the gallows moment when Billy's "consummation impended":

> Captain Vere, either through stoic self-control or a sort of momentary
> paralysis induced by emotional shock, stood erectly rigid as a musket in
> the ship-armorer's rack. (1426–27)

In describing Vere's "private" agony as something that, taking place in
"public," functions as theatre, I by no means wish to imply that it is
insincere. Such a charge would imply that somewhere behind the scenes of
the public performance of private agony there subsisted a quite different,
authentic space of privacy, whose inner drama could be a very different
one. Vere's own cabin, say — a bedchamber to which he could be imagined
as retiring from his agonistic public performance, only, once alone at last,
to hug himself in delight under the covers, getting off on the immutable
visual glory of the boy who "ascending, took the full rose of the dawn"
(1427). Who is to say that no such thing could happen? Yet if it could, not
even that would suffice to constitute as *private* the room in which, after all,
only hours before had been convened a court empowered to pass sentence
of death. Indeed, even lacking that, can a room be called private so long as
it is permeable to the discretions of a certain young Albert, "the captain's
hammock-boy, a sort of sea valet in whose discretion and fidelity his
master had much confidence" (1402)? A "privacy" populated by body-
servants is, as *Benito Cereno* might remind us, a space all the more
exquisitely innervated with the signifiers and for that matter the signifieds
of "public" power relations. A similar case can be made, too, from the
other direction: why assume that a genital sexuality would be, in Vere, the
mark of the private rather than of the public? The opposite assumption
might be more plausible: if Vere gets off at all, it seems to be on display,
whether of himself or another. The text is insistent, too, as we shall see, in
locating its masculine genital intensities not in the solitary or coupled
enjoyment or dissipation of erections but in the less messy economics of
their visible circulation.[20]

20. It may seem that this continued excursus on public and private male desire has
taken us out of the way of our present subject, the sentimental. After all, don't pro- and
anti-Vere readers of *Billy Budd* agree that Vere's heroism, or alternatively his crime, lies in
his willed expulsion from the rule of the *Bellipotent* of every energy associated with (along
with the private sphere) precisely *the sentimental*? And don't we, for that matter, recognize
the sentimental — whether we like it or not — by its substitutive association with women?
Vere makes the connection:

"let not warm hearts betray heads that should be cool. Ashore in a criminal case,
will an upright judge allow himself off the bench to be waylaid by some tender
kinswoman of the accused seeking to touch him with her tearful plea? Well, the
heart here, sometimes the feminine in man, is as that piteous woman, and hard
though it be, she must here be ruled out. . . . But something in your aspect seems to

Vere's performances before assemblies of officers or sailors are not, however, the only form given in *Billy Budd* to the sacrificial drama of a public privacy; the alibi of merely identifying with a corps de ballet of witnesses clustered on stage is liable to be withdrawn from readers, leaving us in a more exposed relation to our own avidities. The text constructs, after all, two moments of what could be called true privacy, one culminating in a kiss, the other in a hug, between men. The hug occurs in what is twice aptly referred to as "the closeted interview" (1419, 1423) in which Vere communicates to Billy the sentence of death. That is, it occurs or perhaps does not occur then, since the interview takes place not only in the closet of a small cabin but in the closet of a subjunctive grammar whose preteritive effect is to highlight the sacred/tabu importance of the single embrace by investing it with the maximally liminal ontological and epistemological standing:

> Beyond the communication of the sentence, what took place at this interview was never known. . . .

---

urge that it is not solely the heart that moves in you, but also the conscience, the private conscience. But tell me whether or not, occupying the position we do, private conscience should not yield to that imperial one formulated in the code under which alone we officially proceed?" (1415)

Vere indeed makes the connection—and with a neatness that one might, for that matter, find suspicious, though his friends, such as Ann Douglas, certainly take it straight, and even his enemies among the critics have treated it as reverently as if it were the holograph of a murderer's signed confession. Joseph Allen Boone, for instance: "For *as his amazingly explicit summary speech at Billy's trial indicates*, his hardness and rejection of mercy are directly linked to a fear of the 'feminine in man'" (emphasis added). Further: "Not only is the jury being told to rule out 'that piteous woman' in themselves, but they are implicitly being directed to 'rule out' Billy, who has come to represent the 'feminine in man,' the androgynous possibility and signifier of difference that must be expelled if the hierarchical supremacy of men is to be maintained in the world of which the Bellipotent is a microcosm" (*Tradition Counter Tradition*, p. 263). Or Robert K. Martin: "*Billy Budd* . . . is deeply aware of the need of male authority to suppress the female, just as masculine authority suppresses the feminine. Vere's execution of Billy is his final attempt to rid himself of anything that might be soft, gentle, and feminine; like Ahab's refusal of Starbuck's love, it is a final act that leads directly to his destruction, while at the same time creating for the reader a poignant awareness of the degree to which these men have come close to acknowledging a fundamental androgyny by daring to embrace another man" (*Hero, Captain, and Stranger*, p. 124). Insofar as this is an interpretation, I can scarcely disagree with it; I am worried, however, about the extent to which, not an interpretation but an almost verbatim reproduction of Vere's rhetoric, it serves his purpose by continuing to distract attention from the performative facts and effects of his and, concomitantly, the reader's rhetorical engagements. Vere's condemnation of Billy is scarcely the antithesis but, rather, the ground of their embrace, and certainly of its assumed poignancy for any reader. The figure of Vere himself, meanwhile, is erotized and glamorized for the reader by the very process of his "struggle" and "sacrifice," in ways that, rather than eradicating the ideal of a utopian androgyny, may be more efficiently repackaging it for symbolic circulation.

> It would have been in consonance with the spirit of Captain Vere
> should he on this occasion have concealed nothing. . . . On Billy's side it is
> not improbable that such a confession would have been received in much
> the same spirit that prompted it. . . . Nor, as to the sentence itself, could
> he have been insensible that . . . [e]ven more may have been. Captain Vere
> in end may have developed the passion sometimes latent under an exterior
> stoical or indifferent. He was old enough to have been Billy's father.[21] The
> austere devotee of military duty, letting himself melt back into what
> remains primeval in our formalized humanity, may in end have caught
> young Billy to his heart. (1418–19)

This strategy is called—incredibly—*privacy*; it is what Ann Douglas
means in saying Melville respects the privacy of his characters.

> But there is no telling the sacrament, seldom if in any case revealed to the
> gadding world, wherever under circumstances at all akin to those here
> attempted to be set forth two of great Nature's nobler order embrace.
> There is privacy at the time, inviolable to the survivor; and holy oblivion,
> the sequel to each diviner magnanimity, providentially covers all at last.
> (1419)

Not even this "closeted" interview fails to make its impression, through
the hyperexpressively resistant body of Captain Vere, on the ship's company: "The first to encounter Captain Vere in the act of leaving the
compartment was the senior lieutenant. The face he beheld, for the
moment one expressive of the agony of the strong, was to that officer,
though a man of fifty, a startling revelation" (1419). Still, its chief audience is the narratorial audience—though how delicately, and therefore
under what a steadily heightening pressure of narrative gloss and insistence, that audience is here in process of being forged should also be
evident. I am almost ready to call the effect simply prurient—that is to say,
simply sentimental—with the understanding that prurience and sentimentality are each in this usage the antithesis of simplicity and certainly
each the very opposite of easy to understand or analyze.

Suppose for the moment, however, that we are willing to accept the
definition implicit in Ann Douglas's work according to which sentimentality is the commingling of public and private realms, especially
through—let us add—any rhetoric that claims to differentiate them con-

---

21. Note that this is the only sentence that does not share the equivocal grammar of its
surround. Perhaps it doesn't need to: what sentence could be, in itself, more classically
equivocal (as prohibition, as invitation) than "I'm old enough to be your father"?

clusively. Under such a definition, Captain Vere is, as I hope I have demonstrated, consummately a sentimentalizing *subject*, an active wielder of the ruses of sentimentality for the satisfaction of needs that can be stably defined neither as public nor as private. But what then are we to say of the thoroughness with which Captain Vere is here narratively rendered, as well, in his embrace with Billy Budd as a sentimentalized *object*?

Health/Illness

For that matter, the rhetoric framing the "closeted interview" may remind us strangely of an earlier act of objectification, that of Claggart by the narrative.

> Beyond the communication of the sentence, what took place at this interview was never known. But in view of the character of the twain briefly closeted in that stateroom, each radically sharing in the rarer qualities of our nature—*so rare indeed as to be all but incredible to average minds however much cultivated*—some conjectures may be ventured. (1418; emphasis added)

The double message by which the reader is constituted here, her contemptible "average mind" (exemplar of the "gadding world") attested by the same gesture with which she is taunted or flattered into creating for herself the hallucination of being shown a scene of male embrace that is actually being withheld from her, is obviously less violent and less overtly sinister than the earlier interpellation of her "normal nature" as part of the creation of the homosexual Claggart. The sacralizing aura of the surrounding ethical designations may be the precise opposite of the odium attached to Claggart, but structurally the yoking of epistemological hyperstimulation ("all but incredible") with ontological inanition in this address also echoes that earlier one.

One would expect the construction of Vere's "paternal" embrace at this point to differ sharply from the construction of Claggart's homosexuality in that the introduction to Claggart began by framing him, demeaningly if fragmentarily, in the sight of "lawyers," "medical experts," "clerical proficients" (1475*n*.1384.3), expert witnesses from the plausible classes whose investment with taxonomic authority suits them for any public ritual involving custody. And, indeed, *while Claggart lives* Vere's relation to any diagnostic gaze is simply that he owns it. Still, for all the damaging heavy artillery of the *exceptional*, the *peculiar*, the *phenomenal*, as opposed to *the normal*, by which Claggart's male-directed desires are quarantined off and minoritized as against the male-directed desires of the men around him, and for all the narrator's empaneling against him of the newer forms of taxonomic expertise, it is an odd fact that, beginning immediately after the murder of Claggart, the specifically *medical* discourses in *Billy Budd* are actually the ones that most force on the reader's attention the congruence of Claggart's character with Vere's, thus offering the story's least complacent thematic view of the forms of knowledge by which minority and majority, illness and health, madness and sanity are to be distinguished. The diagnostic power of Vere's eyes may not distinguish him quite fully enough from the "mesmeric"-eyed Claggart, who can display "the measured step and calm collected air of an asylum physician approaching in the public hall some patient beginning to show indications of a coming paroxysm" (1403).[22] One of the definitive diagnostic passages on Claggart, after all, renders its diagnosis of "exception" squarely on the basis of a latent epistemological impasse:

> But the thing which in eminent instances signalizes so exceptional a nature is this: Though the man's even temper and discreet bearing would seem to intimate a mind peculiarly subject to the law of reason, not the less in heart he would seem to riot in complete exemption from that law, having apparently little to do with reason further than to employ it as an ambidexter implement for effecting the irrational. That is to say: Toward the accomplishment of an aim which in wantonness of atrocity would seem to partake of the insane, he will direct a cool judgment sagacious and sound. These men are madmen, and of the most dangerous sort, for their lunacy is not continuous, but occasional, evoked by some special object; it is protectively secretive, which is as much to say it is self-contained, so that when, moreover, most active it is to the average mind not distinguishable from sanity, and for the reason above suggested: that whatever its aims may be—and the aim is never declared—the method and the outward proceeding are always perfectly rational. (1383)

22. The distinction between them narratively suggested here is, of course, that while Vere's eyes are genuinely diagnostic ("something exceptional in the moral quality of Captain Vere made him, in earnest encounter with a fellow man, a veritable touchstone of that man's essential nature" [1401–2]), Claggart's regard is too productive or reproductive to have diagnostic value, the asylum doctor suspected of projecting his own passions "mesmerically" into the patient in whom he has actually induced the predicted paroxysms. (Compare the "look curious of the operation of his tactics" [1401] with which Claggart regards Vere—"curious," the double-edged Paterian adjective that characterizes the epistemological urgencies immanent in both things viewed and persons viewing them.) As we have already seen, however, Vere is even more expert than Claggart at inducing paroxysms in Billy Budd.

The description much later—in, as it happens, the paragraph in which Vere himself is killed in battle—of Vere as "the spirit that 'spite its philosophic austerity may yet have indulged in the most secret of all passions, ambition" (1432), does little more than activate the latent problem, confirming the impossibility of ever exempting anyone conclusively from this diagnosis of madness: the example of "ambition" demonstrates that the diagnosis's reliance on distinguishing reason from passion or head from heart is only a less fatal vulnerability than its reliance on distinguishing method from aim. The more obvious hypothesis about where to look in Vere for a motive of insanity—for "secretive" riot pellucidly manifested through "a cool judgment sagacious and sound"—must be in his hunger for a particular positioning of Billy Budd; but, as the narrator's analysis here suggests, the indistinguishability of *that* from Vere's professional *ambition* marks exactly the epistemological problem about madness and sanity.

Disarmingly, the question of Vere's sanity begins to be broached quite openly almost as soon as Claggart is killed. The ship's own medical expert is constrained by Vere's incoherence and his willful judgment to speculate, "Was he unhinged?" (1407), and the narrative itself ostentatiously suspends judgment on the question. And, predictably, the question of Vere's judicial impartiality can be raised only in terms of his possibly partialized or minoritized status as a potentially diagnosable madman.

When the surgeon wonders, "Was he unhinged?" and concludes that "assuming that he is, it is not so susceptible of proof," the effect of his recognizing the incoherence of one epistemological field is to force him to let his problem devolve onto another. Shall I obey this possible madman? Can I be made to do so?—these questions seem to offer a clearer set of alternatives couched in the language of state force whose claim to obedience, if not to moral authority, is more readily seen as natural:

> What then can the surgeon do? No more trying situation is conceivable than that of an officer subordinate under a captain whom he suspects to be. . . not quite unaffected in his intellects. To argue his order to him would be insolence. To resist him would be mutiny.
>
> In obedience to Captain Vere he communicated what had happened to the lieutenants and captain of marines, saying nothing as to the captain's state. (1407)

The medical discourse thus seems to have an oddly bifurcated status in *Billy Budd*. It is the only major discourse whose terms Vere does not succeed in mastering through his characteristic tactic of pseudo-transcendence—or, to put the same perception in another way, the irrepressibly "ambidexter instrument" of medical taxonomy allows, at Claggart's death, the opening-up of the only irreconcilable gap of perspective between Vere's consciousness and that of the narrative as such. In this sense it seems a peculiarly privileged discourse, the only tool in the text powerful enough to wrest itself out of the grasp of even the coolest single operative. At the same time, the abject lapse of the surgeon's diagnostic authority in the face of the captain's legal authority suggests that by a different measure of power, the elasticity of medical discourse must in any short term be subject to the sharper disjunctions of state definition and state discipline (as indeed it is also, the narrator sneers, subject to the crude contingencies of the fee [1407]). The characteristic Melvillean point that "military medicine" and, later in the story, "military religion" resemble "military music" and "military intelligence" in being irreducible oxymorons, however, is not the *last* word, insofar as oxymoron has become the site not simply of impasse but of the immense productive power of the strategically located, strategically maneuvered double bind.

To Vere, to the story, and to the little world of the *Bellipotent* two things are happening together, then, in the wake of the death of Claggart. First, Vere is increasingly impelled toward a strategy of dramaturgic embodiment. The uses he needs to make of the categories "public" and "private," and the increasing stress and visibility of his doing so, evoke in him a new, almost Nixonian verve and recklessness in exploiting and transgressing their boundaries. The fact that his resource for doing so is to organize a theatrical ritual around the liminal sufferings of not only Billy's body but his own, however, subjects him to a vulnerability entirely new to him. That is a vulnerability, not to the already accounted-for suffering or self-division he embodies, but to the exactions of embodiment itself. As an object of view—for his officers and men, but most of all for the narrative itself—the Nixonized Vere becomes subjected, in a way that he cannot, after all, bring under single-handed control, to the indignities of taxonomy, circulation, and ocular consumption. Nixonlike, he is most taxonomically vulnerable at the very moments when his strategy of embodiment is working most powerfully: competence and craziness, or discipline and desire, seem dangerously close to one another as they become manifest through the staged body.

The terms of Vere's taxonomy, circulation, consumption have been set by *the preexistence of a homosexual in the text*. Yet, until the death of the homosexual, those terms had seemed sufficiently stabilized by their attachment to that painstakingly minoritized, exploitable figure, and to the induced symmetries between him and the also objectified Billy. As soon as Billy has killed Claggart, however, the circuit of objectification gapes open to envelop Vere as well. This is perhaps clearest in the economy of erections to which I have alluded. The men in *Billy Budd*, rather than having erections, tend to turn into them, or to turn each other into them. Before his death, it is Claggart whose characteristic gesture is "bridling — erecting himself in virtuous self-assertion" (1401). Billy, too, in the mir- roring relation to Claggart enforced by the self-effacing Vere, can be helplessly rendered an "intent head and entire form straining forward" (1404) — the ambiguity of *active* and *passive* in this scenario suggested by the association of the phallicized body of Billy with "impotence" (1404) and with the object of a double sexual assault, "one impaled and gagged" (1403). When, at Billy's blow, Claggart is forever "tilted from erectness" (1404),[23] however, and Vere and Billy have bent down to ascertain that the man is indeed dead, it is the hitherto unremarked-upon body of *Vere* that on rising up again is described as "regaining erectness"; and it is exactly at this moment that, "with one hand covering his face" (1405), Vere takes on the complex project of an embodiment that, rendering his desire phallic, will by the same stroke render it finally vulnerable.

It is Vere and Billy, again, in a clustering of "phenomenal" effects at the scene of Billy's hanging, who seem each to take the place of the genitalia of the other, through the eyes, mouths, and ears of the crowd of witnesses. The first "phenomenal effect, not unenhanced by the rare personal beauty of the young sailor," is that Billy's "unobstructed" ejaculation, "God bless Captain Vere!" moves galvanically through the crowd ("without volition, as it were, as if indeed the ship's populace were but the vehicles of some vocal current electric") toward the captain whom it shocks into a visible rigor. The "momentary paralysis" of Vere's "erectly rigid" posture in turn comes — in the *nachträglichkeit* of the surgeon's and purser's post- mortem — to seem the supplement to a "phenomenal" *lack* in Billy of "mechanical spasm in the muscular system" — i.e., to the inexplicable absence of erection or orgasm at the moment of his death. At the same time, however — that is to say, in another wrinkle of the diachronic enfold- ments that surround the same climactic scene — the mainyard gallows and Billy's ascension and suspension there make the entire body of Billy Budd

23. To be referred to thereafter as "the prone one" (1405, 1412) or "the prostrate one" (1405).

an erection in its own right—Vere's erection—of which Billy's "pinioned figure" (1427) is both the rosy flesh and the nacreous ejaculate, "pendant pearl from the yardarm end" (1434). The prematurity of such an outcome (of course Billy can scarcely be more than nineteen) seems the verso side of Vere's indurated austerities. But to divide sexual attributions nicely between the two men, Vere's priapism, for instance, as against Billy's erethism, would belie how fully the two men perform and represent each for the other: how fully, that is, *Vere's* staging of the climactic sacrifice renders it reciprocal and sexual, precisely to the extent that it is public.

The expense of spirit, however, the expense of authority incurred by this masterful anthropomorphic staging of discipline and desire, is made graphic in a startling fact: the few minutes after Billy's death are the *only* time the possibility of rebellion by the crew of the *Bellipotent* is manifested as anything more than the defensive fantasy of the men charged with keeping order there. Demeaningly and, at least to the reader, visibly, Vere scurries—piping with "shrill" whistles, rearranging the customary time of the drum beat to quarters, creating transparent makework—against the oncoming of the now *de*anthropomorphized "freshet-wave of a torrent" (1428) of mutinous potential from the sailors. An embodied discipline is a vibrant but a vulnerable one; the fact has been proved on Claggart's body, and, Claggart gone, may now be visible in Vere's.

The sense of a dangerous sapping of Vere's authority and centrality through the very operation of his theatrical embodiment seems confirmed, too, if not by the fact of his death in the very next chapter then by the unceremonious anticlimax it makes in the story. Once Billy's apotheosis has been achieved, Vere, mortally wounded in battle, slips out of the story through the least sensational of the "ragged edges" (1431) of its plural ending. The question of whether his desire has been satisfied is so unarousing at this moment of *tristesse* and diminution that the narrative preterition almost leaves it unasked. Opiated and on his deathbed,

> he was heard to murmur words inexplicable to his attendant: "Billy Budd, Billy Budd." That these were not the accents of remorse would seem clear from what the attendant said to the *Bellipotent's* senior officer of marines, who, as the most reluctant to condemn of the members of the drumhead court, too well knew, though here he kept the knowledge to himself, who Billy Budd was. (1432)

What were the accents of, if not remorse? What, for that matter, did the attendant observe in the dying man to make so clear to him the impulse behind these words? But the possibility that Vere's final gesture toward Billy was the same "spasmodic movement" (1428) suppressed in Billy's own dying body is of no interest to the the the narrative here, which—no *Citizen Kane*—pauses not for inquiry but pans onward in its inexorable circuit.

Wholeness/Decadence; Utopia/Apocalypse

Repeatedly, the narrative fulcrum of *Billy Budd*, when the story is read as an account of the interplay between minoritizing and universalizing understandings of homo/heterosexual definition, has turned out to be the moment of the death of Claggart, the man through whom a minority definition becomes visible. What are we to make of so cruel a fact? *Billy Budd* is a document from the very moment of the emergence of a modern homosexual identity. But already inscribed in that emergent identity seems to be, not only the individual fatality that will metamorphose into the routine gay suicides and car crashes of the twentieth-century celluloid closet,[24] but something more awful: the fantasy trajectory toward a life *after the homosexual.*

> Now slides the silent meteor on, and leaves
> A shining furrow, as thy thoughts in me.[25]

The spatialized counterposition of characters we posed in the first half of our analysis should not obscure the narrative fact: the glamorized, phosphorescent romantic relations between Vere and the doomed Billy constitute the shining furrow of the disappearance of the homosexual. From the static tableau of Vere's discipline we moved on to look for temporality and change in Vere himself, in his ambitions, his strategies, his presentation, his fate—as, against a heaven already denuded of its minority constellation, Vere, like Billy, set his sights toward that greater majority, the dead, that Claggart had already joined.

From at least the biblical story of Sodom and Gomorrah, scenarios of same-sex desire would seem to have had a privileged, though by no means an exclusive, relation in Western culture to scenarios of both genocide

---

24. See Vito Russo, *The Celluloid Closet: Homosexuality in the Movies*, revised ed. (New York: Harper & Row, 1987), esp. the devastating "Necrology," pp. 347–49.

25. Alfred, Lord Tennyson, "The Princess," sec. 7, in Tennyson, *Poetical Works*, ed. Geoffrey Cumberledge (London: Oxford University Press, 1941), p. 197.

and omnicide. That sodomy, the name by which homosexual acts are known even today to the law of half of the United States and to the Supreme Court of all of them, should already be inscribed with the name of a site of mass extermination is the appropriate trace of a double history. In the first place there is a history of the mortal suppression, legal or subjudicial, of gay acts and gay people, through burning, hounding, physical and chemical castration, concentration camps, bashing — the array of sanctioned fatalities that Louis Crompton records under the name of gay genocide, and whose supposed eugenic motive becomes only the more colorable with the emergence of a distinct, naturalized minority identity in the nineteenth century. In the second place, though, there is the inveterate topos of associating gay acts or persons with fatalities vastly broader than their own extent: if it is ambiguous whether every denizen of the obliterated Sodom was a sodomite, clearly not every Roman of the late Empire can have been so, despite Gibbon's connecting the eclipse of the whole people to the habits of a few. Following both Gibbon and the Bible, moreover, with an impetus borrowed from Darwin, one of the few areas of agreement among modern Marxist, Nazi, and liberal capitalist ideologies is that there is a peculiarly close, though never precisely defined, affinity between same-sex desire and some historical condition of moribundity, called "decadence," to which not individuals or minorities but whole civilizations are subject. Bloodletting on a scale more massive by orders of magnitude than any gay minority presence in the culture is the "cure," if cure there be, to the mortal illness of decadence.

If a fantasy trajectory, utopian in its own terms, toward gay genocide has been endemic in Western culture from its origins, then, it may also have been true that the trajectory toward gay genocide was never clearly distinguishable from a broader, apocalyptic trajectory toward something approaching omnicide. The deadlock of the past century between minoritizing and universalizing understandings of homo/heterosexual definition can only have deepened this fatal bond in the heterosexist *imaginaire*. In our culture as in *Billy Budd*, the phobic narrative trajectory toward imagining a time *after the homosexual* is finally inseparable from that toward imagining a time *after the human*; in the wake of the homosexual, the wake incessantly produced since first there *were* homosexuals, every human relation is pulled into its shining representational furrow.

Fragments of visions of a time *after the homosexual* are, of course, currently in dizzying circulation in our culture. One of the many dangerous ways that AIDS discourse seems to ratify and amplify preinscribed homophobic mythologies is in its pseudo-evolutionary presentation of male homosexuality as a stage doomed to extinction (read, a phase the species is going through) on the enormous scale of whole populations.[26] The lineaments of openly genocidal malice behind this fantasy appear only occasionally in the respectable media, though they can be glimpsed even there behind the poker-face mask of our national experiment in laissez-faire medicine. A better, if still deodorized, whiff of that malice comes from the famous pronouncement of Pat Robertson: "AIDS is God's way of weeding his garden." The saccharine lustre this dictum gives to its vision of devastation, and the ruthless prurience with which it misattributes its own agency, cover a more fundamental contradiction: that, to rationalize complacent glee at a spectacle of what is imagined as genocide, a proto-Darwinian process of natural selection is being invoked—in the context of a Christian fundamentalism that is not only antievolutionist but recklessly oriented toward universal apocalypse. A similar phenomenon, also too terrible to be noted as a mere irony, is how evenly our culture's phobia about HIV-positive blood is kept pace with by its rage for keeping that dangerous blood in broad, continuous circulation. This is evidenced in projects for universal testing, and in the needle-sharing implicit in William Buckley's now ineradicable fantasy of tattooing HIV-positive persons. But most immediately and pervasively it is evidenced in the literal bloodbaths that seem to make the point of the AIDS-related resurgence in violent bashings of gays—which, unlike the gun violence otherwise ubiquitous in this culture, are characteristically done with two-by-fours, baseball bats, and fists, in the most literal-minded conceivable form of body-fluid contact.

It might be worth making explicit that the use of evolutionary thinking in the current wave of utopian/genocidal fantasy is, whatever else it may be, crazy. Unless one believes, first of all, that same-sex object-choice across history and across cultures is *one thing* with *one cause*, and, second, that its one cause is direct transmission through a nonrecessive genetic path—which would be, to put it gently, counter-intuitive—there is no warrant for imagining that gay populations, even of men, in post-AIDS generations will be in the slightest degree diminished. Exactly *to the degree* that AIDS is a gay disease, it's a tragedy confined to our generation;

26. These reflections were stimulated by an opportunity, for which I am grateful, to read Jeffrey Nunokawa's unpublished essay, "*In Memoriam* and the Extinction of the Homosexual."

the long-term demographic depredations of the disease will fall, to the contrary, on groups, many themselves direly endangered, that are reproduced by direct heterosexual transmission.

Unlike genocide directed against Jews, Native Americans, Africans, or other groups, then, gay genocide, the once-and-for-all eradication of gay populations, however potent and sustained as a project or fantasy of modern Western culture, is not possible short of the eradication of the whole human species. The impulse of the species toward its own eradication must not either, however, be underestimated. Neither must the profundity with which that omnicidal impulse is entangled with the modern problematic of the homosexual: the double bind of definition between the homosexual, say, as a distinct *risk group*, and the homosexual as a potential of representation within the universal.[27] As gay community and the solidarity and visibility of gays as a minority population are being consolidated and tempered in the forge of this specularized terror and suffering, how can it fail to be all the more necessary that the avenues of recognition, desire, and thought between minority potentials and universalizing ones be opened and opened and opened?

27. Richard Mohr, in "Policy, Ritual, Purity: Gays and Mandatory AIDS Testing," *Law, Medicine, and Health Care* (forthcoming), makes a related linkage, with a more settled hypothesis about the directionality of causation:

> AIDS social coercion has become a body accelerated under the gravitational pull of our anxieties over nuclear destruction. Doing anything significant to alleviate the prospects of the joint death of everything that can die is effectively out of the reach of any ordinary individual and indeed of any political group now in existence. So individuals transfer the focus of their anxieties from nuclear omnicide to AIDS, by which they feel equally and similarly threatened, but about which they think they can do something — at least through government. AIDS coercion is doing double duty as a source of sacred values and as a vent for universal anxieties over universal destruction.

3

Some Binarisms (II)
Wilde, Nietzsche, and the Sentimental Relations of the Male Body

For readers fond of the male body, the year 1891 makes an epoch. Chapter 1 of *Billy Budd* opens, as we have noted, with a discussion of the Handsome Sailor — "a superb figure, tossed up as by the horns of Taurus against the thunderous sky" (1354). As Chapter 1 of *The Picture of Dorian Gray* opens, "in the centre of the room, clamped to an upright easel, stood the full-length portrait of a young man of extraordinary personal beauty."[1] Like many Atget photographs, these two inaugural presentations of male beauty frame the human image high up in the field of vision, a singular apparition whose power to reorganize the visibility of more conventionally grounded figures is arresting and enigmatic.

For readers who hate the male body, the year 1891 is also an important one. At the end of *Dorian Gray* a dead, old, "loathsome" man lying on the floor is the moralizing gloss on the other thing the servants find in Dorian Gray's attic: "hanging upon the wall, a splendid portrait of their master as they had last seen him, in all the wonder of his exquisite youth and beauty" (248). The end of *Billy Budd* is similarly presided over by the undisfigured pendant: Billy noosed to the mainyard gallows "ascended, and, ascending, took the full rose of the dawn" (80). The exquisite portrait, the magnetic corpse swaying aloft: iconic as they are of a certain sexual visibility, their awful eminence also signalizes that the line between any male beauty that's articulated as such and any steaming offal strung up for purchase at the butcher's shop is, in the modern dispensation so much marked by this pair of texts, a brutally thin one.

In this chapter I am undertaking to consider some more of the modern relations over which this male body presides in formative texts of the late

1. Oscar Wilde, *The Picture of Dorian Gray* (Harmondsworth, Middlesex: Penguin, 1949), p. 7. Further citations are incorporated in parentheses in the text.

nineteenth century. Through a broader application of the same deconstructive procedure of isolating particular nodes in a web of interconnected binarisms, I move here from the last chapter's treatment of one 1891 text, *Billy Budd*, to treating a group of other texts dating from the 1880s and early 1890s, including the contemporaneous *Picture of Dorian Gray*. This chapter moves outward in two other principal ways, as well: from the sentimental / antisentimental relations around the displayed male figure toward, on the one hand, the modernist crisis of individual identity and figuration itself; toward, on the other, the intersections of sexual definition with relatively new problematics of kitsch, of camp, and of nationalist and imperialist definition.

The two, roughly contemporaneous figures whom I will treat as representing and overarching this process are Wilde and Nietzsche, perhaps an odd yoking of the most obvious with the least likely suspect. Wilde is the obvious one because he seems the very embodiment of, at the same time, (1) a new turn-of-the-century homosexual identity and fate, (2) a modernist antisentimentality, and (3) a late-Victorian sentimentality. Interestingly, the invocation of Nietzsche's name has become a minor commonplace in Wilde criticism, though certainly not vice versa. It has served as a way, essentially, of legitimating Wilde's seriousness as a philosopher of the modern—in the face of his philosophically embarrassing, because narratively so compelling, biographical entanglements with the most mangling as well as the most influential of the modern machineries of male sexual definition. Needless to say, however, the opposite project interests me as much here: the project of looking at Nietzsche through a Wildean optic. That, too, however, to the very degree that it does seem to promise access to the truths of twentieth-century culture, involves the built-in danger of a spurious sense of familiarity, given what the received figure "Nietzsche" has in common with certain received topoi of homosexuality and of sentimentality or kitsch: namely, that all three are famous for occasioning unresolved but highly popular and exciting "questions"—insinuations—about the underpinnings of twentieth-century fascism. To avoid the scapegoating momentum that appears to be built into the structure of sentimental attribution and of homosexual attribution in the culture of our century will require care.

This project involves, among other things, a binocular displacement of time and space between Germany of the 1880s (for my focus will be on Nietzsche's last several texts) and England of the 1890s. It also embodies the distance between a new, openly problematical German national identity and an "immemorial," very naturalized English one, though, as we shall see, one none the less under definitional stress for that. German unification under Prussian leadership, culminating with the proclamation of the Second Reich in 1871, led newly to the criminalization of homosexual offenses for the entire Reich—a process that coincided, as James Steakley points out, with "the escalating estimates of the actual number of homosexuals" in Germany, from .002 percent of the population in 1864, to 1.4 percent in 1869, to 2.2 percent in 1903. "These estimates," Steakley says, "appear astonishingly low in light of modern studies, but they nonetheless document the end of homosexual invisibility." The same period encompassed the first formation—in Germany—of organized homosexual emancipation movements.[2]

It seems patent that many of Nietzsche's most effective intensities of both life and writing were directed toward other men and toward the male body; it's at least arguable, though not necessary for my present argument, that almost all of them were. Given that, and especially given all the thought recently devoted to the position of women in Nietzsche's writing, it is striking how difficult it seems to have been to focus on the often far more cathected position of men there. There are reasons for this even beyond the academic prudishness, homophobia, and heterosexist obtuseness that always seem to obtain: Nietzsche offers writing of an open, Whitmanlike seductiveness, some of the loveliest there is, about the joining of men with men, but he does so in the stubborn, perhaps even studied absence of any explicit generalizations, celebrations, analyses, reifications of these bonds as specifically same-sex ones. Accordingly, he has been important for a male-erotic-centered anarchist tradition, extending from Adolf Brand and Benedict Friedländer through Gilles Deleuze and Félix Guattari, that has a principled resistance to any minoritizing model of homosexual identity. (Friedländer, for instance, ridiculed those with an exclusively hetero- or homosexual orientation as *Kümmerlinge* [atrophied or puny beings].)[3] But the harder fact to deal with is that Nietzsche's writing is full and overfull of what were just in the process of becoming, for people like Wilde, for their enemies, and for the institutions that regulated and defined them, the most pointed and contested signifiers of precisely a minoritized, taxonomic male homosexual identity.

---

2. Steakley, *The Homosexual Emancipation Movement in Germany*, pp. 14, 33.
3. On Brand and Friedländer, see Steakley, *The Homosexual Emancipation Movement in Germany*, pp. 43–69; on *Kümmerlinge*, pp. 46–47.

At the same time it is also full and overfull of the signifiers that had long marked the nominally superseded but effectually unvacated prohibitions against sodomitic acts.

A phrase index to Nietzsche could easily be confused with a concordance to, shall we say, Proust's *Sodome et Gomorrhe*, featuring as it would "inversion," "contrary instincts," the *contra naturam*, the effeminate, the "hard," the sick, the hyper-virile, the "*décadent*," the neuter, the "intermediate type" — and I won't even mention the "gay." Nietzsche's writing never makes these very differently valued, often contradictory signifiers coextensive with any totality of male-male desire; in many usages they seem to have nothing to do with it at all. This is because, to repeat, he never posits same-sex desire or sexuality as one subject. Instead, these signifiers — old markers for, among other things, same-sex acts and relations; incipient markers for, among other things, same-sex-loving identities — cut in Nietzsche's writing across and across particular instances or evocations of it. But they do it so repetitiously, so suggestively as to contribute, and precisely *in* their contradictoriness, to the weaving of a fatefully impacted definitional fabric already under way.

Just one example of the newly emerging problematics of male homosexuality across which Nietzsche's desire flung its stinging shuttle. The question of how same-sex desire could be interpreted in terms of *gender* was bitterly embattled almost from the beginnings of male homosexual taxonomy: already by 1902, the new German gay rights movement, the first in the world, was to split over whether a man who desired men should be considered feminized (as in the proto-modern English "molly-house" culture and the emerging inversion model) or, to the contrary, virilized (as in the Greek pederastic or initiation model) by his choice of object. The energy Nietzsche devotes to detecting and excoriating male effeminacy, and in terms that had been stereotypical for at least a century in anti-sodomitic usage, suggests that this issue is a crucial one for him; any reader of Nietzsche who inherits, as most Euro-American readers must, the by now endemic linkage of effeminacy with this path of desire will find their store of homophobic energies refreshed and indeed electrified by reading him. But far from explicitly making male same-sex desire coextensive with that effeminacy, Nietzsche instead associates instance after instance of homoerotic desire, though never named as such, with the precious virility of Dionysiac initiates or of ancient warrior classes. Thus, his rhetoric charges with new spikes of power some of the most conventional lines of prohibition, even while preserving another space of careful de-definition in which certain objects of this prohibition may arbitrarily be invited to shelter.

An even more elegant example is the insistence with which he bases his defense of sexuality on its connection with "the actual road to life, procreation."[4] "Where is innocence? Where there is a will to procreate."[5] He execrates antisexuality as a resistance to procreation, "*ressentiment against* life in its foundations," which "threw *filth* on the beginning, on the prerequisite of our life" (*Twilight*, 110). In the definitional stress he places on *this* defense of sexuality and in the venom he reserves for non-procreative acts and impulses, if anywhere, one might imagine oneself, according to discourses ranging from the biblical to the nineteenth-century medical, to be close to the essence of an almost transhistorical prohibition of a homosexuality itself thereby rendered almost trans-historical. But, oddly, what Nietzsche, with the secret reserves of elasticity that always characterized his relation to the biological metaphor, framed most persistently within the halo of this imperative to procreate was scenes of impregnation of men (including himself: "The term of eighteen months might suggest, at least to Buddhists, that I am really a female elephant")[6] or of abstractions that could be figured as male.[7] The space

---

4. Friedrich Nietzsche, *Twilight of the Idols / The Anti-Christ*, trans. J. R. Hollingdale (New York: Viking Penguin, 1968), p. 110. Further quotations from this edition will cite it as *Twilight* or *Anti* in the text.

5. Friedrich Nietzsche, *Thus Spoke Zarathustra*, trans. Walter Kaufmann (New York: Viking Compass, 1966), p. 123. Further quotations from this edition will cite it as *Zarathustra* in the text.

6. Friedrich Nietzsche, *Ecce Homo*, trans. R. J. Hollingdale (New York: Penguin, 1979), p. 99. Further quotations from this edition will cite it as *Ecce* in the text.

7. One example that may stand for many (Friedrich Nietzsche, *Beyond Good and Evil*, trans. R. J. Hollingdale [New York: Viking Penguin, 1973], p. 161, sec. 248; further quotations from this edition will cite it as *Beyond* in the text):

> There are two kinds of genius: the kind which above all begets and wants to beget, and the kind which likes to be fructified and to give birth. And likewise there are among peoples of genius those upon whom has fallen the woman's problem of pregnancy and the secret task of forming, maturing, perfecting—the Greeks, for example, were a people of this kind, and so were the French—; and others who have to fructify and become the cause of new orders of life—like the Jews, the Romans and, to ask it in all modesty, the Germans?—peoples tormented and enraptured by unknown fevers and irresistibly driven outside themselves, enamoured of and lusting after foreign races (after those which "want to be fructified") and at the same time hungry for dominion.

To ask who is *self* and who is *other* in these dramas of pregnancy is as vain as anywhere else in Nietzsche. The relation to Zarathustra may be taken as emblematic:

> That I may one day be ready and ripe in the great noon: as ready and ripe as

cleared by this move for a sexy thematics of ripeness, fructification, mess, ecstatic rupture, penetration, between men was bought dearly, however, in the sense of being excruciatingly vulnerable to any increased definitional pressure from the angry impulsions that Nietzsche's own celebrations fed: the virulence, only a couple of decades later, of a D. H. Lawrence against a realm of desire that was by then *precisely* circumscribed as coextensive with "the homosexual," even with all the self-contradictions of that definition intact, borrowed wholesale from Nietzsche the rhetorical energies for anathematizing the desire that was Nietzsche's own, not to say Lawrence's own.

Greek/Christian

For Nietzsche as for Wilde, a conceptual and historical interface between Classical and Christian cultures became a surface suffused with meanings about the male body. In both German and English culture, the Romantic rediscovery of ancient Greece cleared out — as much as recreated — for the nineteenth century a prestigious, historically underfurnished imaginative space in which relations to and among human bodies might be newly a subject of utopian speculation. Synecdochically represented as it tended to be by statues of nude young men, the Victorian cult of Greece gently, unpointedly, and unexclusively positioned male flesh and muscle as the indicative instances of "the" body, of a body whose surfaces, features, and abilities might be the subject or object of unphobic enjoyment. The Christian tradition, by contrast, had tended both to condense "the flesh" (insofar as it represented or incorporated pleasure) as the *female* body and to surround its attractiveness with an aura of maximum anxiety and prohibition. Thus two significant differences from Christianity were conflated or conflatable in thought and rhetoric about "the Greeks": an imagined dissolving of the bar of prohibition against the enjoyed body, and its new gendering as indicatively male.

Dorian Gray, appearing in *The Picture of Dorian Gray* first as artist's model, seems to make the proffer of this liberatory vision — at least he

---

glowing bronze, clouds pregnant with lightning, and swelling milk udders — ready for myself and my most hidden will: a bow lusting for its arrow, an arrow lusting for its star — a star ready and ripe in its noon, glowing, pierced, enraptured by annihilating sun arrows — a sun itself and an inexorable solar will, ready to annihilate in victory! (*Zarathustra*, 214–15)

evokes formulations of its ideology from his two admirers. The artist Basil Hallward says of him, "Unconsciously he defines for me the lines of a fresh school, a school that is to have in it all the passion of the romantic spirit, all the perfection of the spirit that is Greek. The harmony of soul and body—how much that is! We in our madness have separated the two, and have invented a realism that is vulgar, an ideality that is void" (16–17). And Lord Henry Wotton addresses the immobilized sitter with a Paterian invocation:

"The aim of life is self-development. To realize one's nature perfectly— that's what each of us is here for. People are afraid of themselves, nowadays. . . . And yet . . . I believe that if one man were to live out his life fully and completely, were to give form to every feeling, expression to every thought, reality to every dream—I believe that the world would gain such a fresh impulse of joy that we would forget all the maladies of medievalism, and return to the Hellenic ideal—to something finer, richer, than the Hellenic ideal, it may be. But the bravest man among us is afraid of himself. The mutilation of the savage has a tragic survival in the self-denial that mars our lives. We are punished for our refusals." (25)

The context of each of these formulations, however, immediately makes clear that the conceptual divisions and ethical bars instituted by, or attributed to, Christianity are easier to condemn than to undo, or perhaps even wish to undo. The painter's manifesto for Dorian's ability to reinstitute a modern "harmony of soul and body," for instance, is part of his extorted confession—and confession is the appropriate word—to Lord Henry concerning "this curious artistic idolatry, of which, of course, I have never cared to speak to [Dorian]. He knows nothing about it. He shall never know anything about it. But the world might guess it; and I will not bare my soul to their shallow prying eyes" (17). To delineate and dramatize a space of *the secret* also emerges as the project of Lord Henry's manifesto, an address whose performative aim is after all less persuasion than seduction. Like Basil, Lord Henry constructs *the secret* in terms that depend on (unnameable) prohibitions attached specifically to the beautiful male body; and like Basil's, Lord Henry's manifesto for the Hellenic unity of soul and body derives its seductive rhetorical force from a culmination that depends on their irreparable divorce through shame and prohibition.

"We are punished for our refusals. . . . The only way to get rid of a temptation is to yield to it. Resist it, and your soul grows sick with longing for the things it has forbidden to itself, with desire for what its monstrous laws have made monstrous and unlawful. . . . You, Mr Gray, you yourself, with your rose-red youth and your rose-white boyhood, you have had passions that have made you afraid, thoughts that have filled you with terror, day-dreams and sleeping dreams whose mere memory might stain your cheek with shame—"

"Stop!" faltered Dorian Gray, "stop! you bewilder me. I don't know what to say. There is some answer to you, but I cannot find it." (25–26)

The crystallization of desire as "temptation," of the young body as the always initiatory encroachment of rose-red on rose-white, gives the game of wholeness away in advance. Each of these enunciations shows that the "Hellenic ideal," insofar as its reintegrative power is supposed to involve a healing of the culturewide ruptures involved in male homosexual panic, necessarily has that panic so deeply at the heart of its occasions, frameworks, demands, and evocations that it becomes not only inextricable from but even a propellant of the cognitive and ethical compartmentalizations of homophobic prohibition. That it is *these* in turn that become exemplary propellants of homosexual desire seems an inevitable consequence.

In *The Victorians and Ancient Greece*, Richard Jenkyns points out that precisely a visible incipience or necessity of this phobic fall was read back into Greek selves and Greek culture *as* the charm of their wholeness, a charm defined by the eschatological narrative it appeared to defy or defer.[8] And this seems a good characterization of Nietzsche's classicism, as well, with its insistent pushing-backward of the always-already date of a fall into decadent moral prohibition defined as Christian, which, however deplored, makes the enabling condition for rhetorical force.

For example, consider, in the blush-stained light of Lord Henry's manifesto, the double scene of seduction staged in these sentences from the Preface to *Beyond Good and Evil*:

To be sure, to speak of spirit and the good as Plato did meant standing truth on her head and denying *perspective* itself, the basic condition of all life; indeed, one may ask as a physician: "how could such a malady attack this loveliest product of antiquity, Plato? did the wicked Socrates corrupt him after all? could Socrates have been a corrupter of youth after all? and have deserved his hemlock?"—But the struggle against Plato, or, to express it more plainly and for "the people," the struggle against the

8. Richard Jenkyns, *The Victorians and Ancient Greece* (Cambridge: Harvard University Press, 1980), e.g., pp. 220–21.

Christian-ecclesiastical pressure of millennia—for Christianity is Platonism for "the people"—has created in Europe a magnificent tension of the spirit such as has never existed on earth before: with so tense a bow one can now shoot for the most distant targets. (*Beyond*, 14)

With his characteristically Socratic flirtatiousness ("as a physician"!), Nietzsche frames the proto-Christian fall into metaphysics as an incident of classroom sexual harassment among the ancients. The seduction at which his own language aims, however, and which seems to mirror the first one at the same time as repudiate it by "worldly" trivialization, is the seduction of the reader. His tactics are those of the narrator of *Billy Budd*, mixing, under pressure of a very difficult style and argument, the threat of contempt for those who don't understand or *merely* understand ("the people") with a far more than Melvillean balm of flattery, hilarity, and futurity promised to those who can surrender themselves to his nameless projectile uses. Nietzsche makes almost explicit—what no character in *Dorian Gray* does more than demonstrate—that the philosophic and erotic potential lodged in this modern pedagogic-pederastic speech situation comes not from some untainted mine of "Hellenic" potency that could be directly tapped but, rather, from the shocking magnetism exerted by such a fantasy across (i.e., because of) the not-to-be-undone bar of Christian prohibitive categorization. Modern homosexual panic represents, it seems, not a temporally imprisoning obstacle to philosophy and culture but, rather, the latent energy that can hurtle them far beyond their own present place of knowledge.[9]

9. To evidence the mix of eroticism and prohibition that characterizes this bent bow, I quote from "Epode" (*Beyond*, 203–4)—a prothalamion in the garden with Zarathustra. The speaker's prospective union with Zarathustra has made him an object of unspeakable horror to his other friends:

A *wicked* huntsman is what I have become! See how bent my bow! He who drew that bow, surely he was the mightiest of men—: but the arrow, alas—ah, *no* arrow is dangerous as *that* arrow is dangerous—away! be gone! For your own preservation!. . . What once united us, the bond of *one* hope—who still can read the signs love once inscribed therein, now faint and faded? It is like a parchment—discoloured, scorched—from which the hand *shrinks back*.

And, supposing the "wide-spanned rhythm" to refer to the same bent-bow sensation:

The concept of revelation, in the sense that something suddenly, with unspeakable certainty and subtlety, becomes *visible*, audible, something that shakes and overturns one to the depths, simply describes the fact. One hears, one does not seek; one takes, one does not ask who gives; a thought flashes up like lightning, with necessity, unfalteringly formed—I have never had any choice. An ecstasy whose tremendous tension sometimes discharges itself in a flood of tears, while one's steps

The assumption I have been making so far, that the main impact of Christianity on men's desire for the male body—and the main stimulus it offers to that desire—is prohibitive, is an influential assumption far beyond Wilde and Nietzsche. It is also an assumption that even (or especially) those who hold and wield it, including both Wilde (who was never far from the threshold of Rome) and Nietzsche (who, at the last, subscribed himself as "The Crucified"), know is not true. Christianity may be near-ubiquitous in modern European culture as a figure of phobic prohibition, but it makes a strange figure for that indeed. Catholicism in particular is famous for giving countless gay and proto-gay children the shock of the possibility of adults who don't marry, of men in dresses, of passionate theatre, of introspective investment, of lives filled with what could, ideally without diminution, be called the work of the fetish. Even for the many whose own achieved gay identity may at last include none of these features or may be defined as against them, the encounter with them is likely to have a more or other than prohibitive impact. And presiding over all are the images of Jesus. These have, indeed, a unique position in modern culture as images of the unclothed or unclothable male body, often in extremis and/or in ecstasy, prescriptively meant to be gazed at and adored. The scandal of such a figure within a homophobic economy of the male gaze doesn't seem to abate: efforts to disembody this body, for instance by attenuating, Europeanizing, or feminizing it, only entangle it the more compromisingly among various modern figurations of the homosexual.

The nominal terms of the Greek/Christian contrast, as if between permission and prohibition or unity and dichotomy, questionable as (we have seen) they may be in themselves, have even less purchase on this aspect of Christianity by which, nonetheless, they are inevitably inflected. Both in Nietzsche and in Wilde—and, partly through them, across

---

now involuntarily rush along, now involuntarily lag; a complete being outside of oneself with the distinct consciousness of a multitude of subtle shudders and trickles down to one's toes . . . an instinct for rhythmical relationships which spans forms of wide extent—length, the need for a *wide-spanned* rhythm is almost the measure of the force of inspiration, a kind of compensation for its pressure and tension. . . . Everything is in the highest degree involuntary but takes place as in a tempest of a feeling of freedom, of absoluteness, of power, of divinity. . . . It really does seem, to allude to a saying of Zarathustra's, as if the things themselves approached and offered themselves as metaphors (— "here all things come caressingly to your discourse and flatter you: for they want to ride upon your back . . ."). (*Ecce*, 102–3)

twentieth-century culture — this image is, I believe, one of the places where the extremely difficult and important problematic of sentimentality is centered. Let me take a little time to explore why it is so difficult to get hold of analytically and so telling for the twentieth century, on the way back to a discussion of its pivotal place in the homo/heterosexual definitional struggles of Wilde and Nietzsche.

Sentimental/Antisentimental

One night in Ithaca in the mid-seventies, I happened to tune into a country music station in the middle of a song I had never heard before. An incredibly pretty male voice that I half recognized as Willie Nelson's was singing:

> And he walks with me, and he talks with me,
> And he tells me I am his own.
> And the joy we share, as we tarry there,
> None other has ever known.
>
> He speaks; and the sound of his voice
> Is so sweet the birds hush their singing.
> And the melody that he gave to me
> Within my heart is ringing.
>
> And he walks with me, and he talks with me,
> And he tells me I am his own.
> And the joy we share, as we tarry there,
> None other has ever known.
>
> I'd stay in the garden with him
> Though the night around me be falling,
> But he bids me go through the voice of woe,
> His voice to me is calling...

This blew me away. I had already listened to a lot of Willie Nelson's songs about Waylon Jennings, which I always interpreted as love songs, but I never thought I was meant to; and nothing had prepared me for a song in which the love and sensuality between two men could be expressed with such a pellucid candor, on AM shit-kicker radio or maybe anywhere.

A decade later, I noted an article by J. M. Cameron in the *New York Review* about religious kitsch, which, he says, "presents us with a serious theological problem and stands, far beyond the formal bounds of theology, for something amiss in our culture":[10]

---

10. J. M. Cameron, reply to a letter in response to the review quoted below, in *New York Review of Books* 33 (May 29, 1986): 56–57.

Kitsch must include more than the golden-haired Madonnas, the epicene statues of Jesus, the twee pictures of the infant Jesus. . . . It must also include music, and the words of the liturgy, and hymns as well. . . . [An] example is:

> I come to the garden alone,
> While the dew is still on the roses.
> And the voice I hear,
> Falling on my ear,
> The Son of God discloses.
> And He walks with me and He talks with me,
> And He tells me I am his own.
> And the joys we share, as we tarry there,
> None other has ever known.[11]

Cameron considers it important not only to

> describe . . . this as sentimental . . . but . . . discuss it as what it surely is, a terrible degradation of religion not simply as a purveyor of the false and the unworthy but as a kind of nastily flavored religious jello, a fouling of the sources of religious feeling. It is as though the image of Jesus is caught in a cracked, discolored distorting mirror in a fun house.[12]

Let me remark on two possible sources for Cameron's ostentatious disgust here, one topical, regarding the *subject* of sentimentality, and the other grammatical, regarding its *relations*. Topically, I have to wonder if a certain erotic foregrounding of the male body, what made the song so exciting to me, may not be tied to the stigmatization of these verses as sentimental and kitsch. I have mentioned the difficult kind of cynosure that proliferating images of Jesus, what Cameron refers to as the "epicene statues," create within a homophobic economy of the male gaze. This scandal might account for the discomfort of a J. M. Cameron with the hymn, but it does leave us with questions about the local specifications of the sentimental, and in particular about its gender: if the sentimental, as we have been taught, coincides topically with the feminine, with the place of women, then why should the foregrounded *male* physique be in an indicative relation to it?

If indeed, however, as I want to hypothesize, the embodied male figure *is* a distinctive, thematic marker for the potent and devalued categories of

11. J. M. Cameron, "The Historical Jesus" (a review of Jaroslav Pelikan, *Jesus through the Centuries: His Place in the History of Culture*), *New York Review of Books* 33 (February 13, 1986): 21.

12. Cameron, "The Historical Jesus," p. 22.

kitsch and the sentimental in this century, then it is only the equivocal use of the first person ("And he tells me I am his own") — the first person that could be your grandmother but could be Willie Nelson, too, or even a distinguished professor of religion at the University of Toronto — that lends such a nasty flavor to the gender-slippage of this morsel of religious "jello" down the befouled and violated gullet of Mr. J. M. Cameron. The gender-equivocal first person, or the impossible first person — such as the first person of someone dead or in process of dying — are common and, at least to me, peculiarly potent sentimental markers: my goose bumps, at any rate, are always poised for erection at "She walks these hills in a long black veil, / Visits my grave when the night winds wail," and my water-works are always primed for "Rocky, I've never had to die before," or letters to Dear Abby purporting to be from seventeen-year-olds who were too young to die in that after-school car crash. Arguably, indeed, the locus classicus of this tonally and generically unsettling, ingenuous-disingenuous first-person mode, other versions of which can be found in any high school literary magazine, is the ballad that ends *Billy Budd*:

> No pipe to those halyards. — But aren't it all sham?
> A blur's in my eyes; it is dreaming that I am.
> A hatchet to my hawser? All adrift to go?
> The drum roll to grog, and Billy never know?
> But Donald he has promised to stand by the plank;
> So I'll shake a friendly hand ere I sink.
> But — no! It is dead then I'll be, come to think.
> I remember Taff the Welshman when he sank.
> And his cheek it was like the budding pink.
> But me they'll lash in hammock, drop me deep.
> Fathoms down, fathoms down, how I'll dream fast asleep.
> I feel it stealing now. Sentry, are you there?
> Just ease these darbies at the wrist,
> And roll me over fair!
> I am sleepy, and the oozy weeds about me twist.
>
> (1435)

These knowing activations of the ambiguities always latent in grammatical person as such, at any rate, point to the range of meanings of sentimentality that identify it, not as a thematic or a particular subject matter, but as a structure of relation, typically one involving the author- or audience-relations of spectacle; most often, where the epithet "sentimental" itself is brought onto the scene, a discreditable or devalued one — the sentimental as the *insincere*, the *manipulative*, the *vicarious*, the *morbid*, the *knowing*, the *kitschy*, the *arch*.

To begin with the question of thematic content. In recent feminist criticism, particularly that involving nineteenth-century American women's fiction, a conscious rehabilitation of the category of "the sentimental" has taken place, insofar as "the sentimental" is seen as a derogatory code name for female bodies and the female domestic and "reproductive" preoccupations of birth, socialization, illness, and death.[13] The devaluation of "the sentimental," it is argued, has been of a piece with the devaluation of many aspects of women's characteristic experience and culture: in this view "the sentimental," like the very lives of many women, is typically located in the private or domestic realm, has only a tacit or indirect connection with the economic facts of industrial marketplace production, is most visibly tied instead to the "reproductive" preoccupations of birth, socialization, illness, and death, and is intensively occupied with relational and emotional labor and expression. Since one influential project of recent popular feminist thought has been to reverse the negative valuation attached to these experiences, emphases, and skills by both high culture and marketplace ideology, an attempted reversal of the negative charge attached to "the sentimental" has been a natural corollary.

It would make sense to see a somewhat similar rehabilitation of "the sentimental" as an important gay male project as well—indeed, one that has been in progress for close to a century under different names, including that of "camp." This gay male rehabilitation of the sentimental obviously occurs on rather different grounds from the feminist one, springing as it does from different experiences. The kid in Ohio who recognizes in "Somewhere Over the Rainbow" the national anthem of a native country, his own, whose name he's never heard spoken is constructing a new family romance on new terms; and for the adult he becomes, the sense of value attaching to a "private" realm, or indeed to expressive and relational skills, is likely to have to do with a specific history of secrecy, threat, and escape as well as with domesticity. A very specific association of gay male sexuality with tragic early death is recent, but the structure of its articulation is densely grounded in centuries of homoerotic and homophobic intertextuality;[14] the underpinnings here have long been in place

13. For example, Jane P. Tompkins, *Sensational Designs: The Cultural Work of American Fiction, 1790–1860* (New York: Oxford University Press, 1985).

14. One might look, for instance, to Achilles and Patroclos, to Virgilian shepherds, to David and Jonathan, to the iconography of St. Sebastian, to elegiac poetry by Milton, Tennyson, Whitman, and Housman, as well as to the Necrology of Vito Russo's *Celluloid Closet*...

for both a gay male sentimentality and, even more, a sentimental appropriation by the larger culture of male homosexuality as spectacle.

I have been arguing that constructions of modern Western gay male identity tend to be, not in the first place "essentially gay," but instead (or at least also) in a very intimately responsive and expressive, though always oblique, relation to incoherences implicit in modern male *hetero*sexuality. Much might be said, then, following this clue, about the production and deployment, especially in contemporary U.S. society, of an extraordinarily high level of self-pity in nongay men.[15] Its effects on our national politics, and international ideology and intervention, have been pervasive. (Snapshot, here, of the tear-welling eyes of Oliver North.) In more intimate manifestations this straight male self-pity is often currently referred to (though it appears to exceed) the cultural effects of feminism, and is associated with, or appealed to in justification of, acts of violence, especially against women. For instance, the astonishing proportion of male violence done on separated wives, ex-wives, and ex-girlfriends, women just at the threshold of establishing a separate personal space, seems sanctioned and guided as much as reflected by the flood of books and movies in which such violence seems an expression not of the macho personality but of the maudlin. (One reason women get nervous when straight men claim to have received from feminism the gift of "permission to cry.") Although compulsively illustrated for public consumption (see, on this, the *New York Times*'s "About Men," passim, or for that matter any newspaper's sports pages, or western novels, male country music, the dying-father-and-his-son stories in *The New Yorker*, or any other form of genre writing aimed at men), this vast national wash of masculine self-pity is essentially never named or discussed as a cultural and political fact; machismo and competitiveness, or a putative gentleness, take its place as subjects of nomination and analysis. Poised between shame and shamelessness, this regime of heterosexual male self-pity has the projective potency of an open secret. It would scarcely be surprising if gay men, like all women, were a main target of its scapegoating projections — viciously sentimental attributions of a vitiated sentimentality.

The sacred tears of the heterosexual man: rare and precious liquor

---

15. It was Neil Hertz, especially in some discussions of responses to his essay "Medusa's Head: Male Hysteria under Political Pressure" (now included in *The End of the Line: Essays on Psychoanalysis and the Sublime* [New York: Columbia University Press, 1985]), who alerted me to the importance of this phenomenon.

whose properties, we are led to believe, are rivaled only by the *lacrimae Christi* whose secretion is such a specialty of religious kitsch. What charm, compared to this chrism of the gratuitous, can reside in the all too predictable tears of women, of gay men, of people with something to cry about? Nietzsche asks scornfully: "Of what account is the pity of those who suffer!" But, he explains, "a man who can do something, carry out a decision, remain true to an idea, hold on to a woman, punish and put down insolence . . . in short a man who is by nature a *master*—when such a man has pity, well! *that* pity has value!" (*Beyond*, 198). Both the mass and the high culture of our century ratify this judgment, by no means stopping short at such a man's pity for himself. Cry-y-yin'—lonely teardrops, teardrops cryin' in the rain, blue velvet through the tracks of my tears, the tears of a clown, maybe Cathy's clown, the Red Skelton clown by whose tears every show of lowbrow art must be baptized, the Norman Mailer or Harold Bloom buffoon by whose tears . . .

If these modern images borrow some of their lasting power from the mid-nineteenth-century association of sentimentality with the place of women, what their persistence and proliferation dramatize is something new: a change of gears, occupying the period from the 1880s through the First World War, by which the exemplary instance of the sentimental ceases to be a woman per se, but instead becomes the body of a man who, like Captain Vere, physically dramatizes, *embodies* for an audience that both desires and cathartically identifies with him, a struggle of masculine identity with emotions or physical stigmata stereotyped as feminine. Nietzsche says, "With hard men, intimacy is a thing of shame—and" (by implication: therefore) "something precious" (*Beyond*, 87). This male body is not itself named as the place or topos of sentimentality, the way the home, the female body, and female reproductive labor had been in the mid-nineteenth century. Rather, the relations of figuration and perception that circulate around it, including antisentimentality, might instead be said to enact sentimentality as a trope.

How, then, through the issue of sentimentality can we bring to Nietzsche questions that Wilde and the reading of Wilde may teach us to ask? Gore Vidal begins a recent essay on Wilde: "Must one have a heart of stone to read *The Ballad of Reading Gaol* without laughing?"[16] The opening points in only too many directions. Between it and the same

---

16. Gore Vidal, "A Good Man and a Perfect Play" (review of Richard Ellmann, *Oscar Wilde*), *Times Literary Supplement* (October 2–8, 1987): 1063.

remark made by Wilde himself, a century earlier, about the death of Little
Nell, where to look for the wit-enabling relation? One story to tell is the
historical/thematic one just sketched: that whereas in the nineteenth
century it was images of women in relation to domestic suffering and
death that occupied the most potent, symptomatic, and, perhaps, friable
or volatile place in the sentimental *imaginaire* of middle-class culture, for
the succeeding century—the century inaugurated by Wilde among others—it has been images of agonistic male self-constitution. Thus the
careful composition of *The Ballad of Reading Gaol*, where Wilde frames
his own image between, or even as, those of a woman-murdering man and
the Crucified, sets in motion every conceivable mechanism by which most
readers know how to enter into the circuit of the sentimental:

> Alas! it is a fearful thing
>   To feel another's guilt!
> For, right, within, the Sword of Sin
>   Pierced to its poisoned hilt,
> And as molten lead were the tears we shed
>   For the blood we had not spilt.
> . . . .
>
> And as one sees most fearful things
>   In the crystal of a dream,
> We saw the greasy hempen rope
>   Hooked to the blackened beam,
> And heard the prayer the hangman's snare
>   Strangled into a scream.
>
> And all the woe that moved him so
>   That he gave that bitter cry,
> And the wild regrets, and the bloody sweats,
>   None knew so well as I:
> For he who lives more lives than one
>   More deaths than one must die.[17]

Think of the cognate, ravishing lines of Cowper—

> We perished, each alone,
> But I beneath a rougher sea
> And whelmed in deeper gulfs than he[18]

---

17. *The Complete Works of Oscar Wilde* (Twickenham, Middlesex: Hamlyn, 1963),
pp. 732, 735. Further quotations from this edition will cite it as *Complete* in the text.
  18. William Cowper, "The Castaway," lines 64–66, in the *Complete Poetical Works of
William Cowper*, ed. H. S. Milford (Oxford: Humphrey Milford, 1913), p. 652.

—and the cognate sentimental markers (the vicariousness, the uncanny shifting first person of after death, the heroic self-pity) that give them their awful appropriateness, their appropriability, to the narrow, imperious, incessant self-reconstitution of, say, Virginia Woolf's paterfamilias Mr. Ramsay. Yet the author of *Reading Gaol* is also the creator of "Ernest in town and Jack in the country" and of Mr. Bunbury, of men whose penchant for living more lives than one, and even dying more deaths, not to speak of having more christenings, seems on the contrary to give them a fine insouciance about such identity issues as the name of the father—which his sons, who have forgotten it, have to look up in the Army Lists. "Lady Bracknell, I hate to seem inquisitive, but would you kindly inform me who I am?" (*Earnest*, in *Complete*, 181). At the same time, the precise grammatical matrix of even the most anarchic Wildean wit still tends toward the male first-person singular in the mode of descriptive self-definition. "None of us are perfect. I myself am peculiarly susceptible to draughts." "I can resist anything except temptation." "I have nothing to declare except my genius." The project of constructing the male figure is not made any the less central by being rendered as nonsense; in fact, one might say that it's the candor with which Wilde is often capable of centering this male project in the field of vision that enables him to operate so explosively on it.

The squeam-inducing power of texts like *De Profundis* and *Reading Gaol*—and I don't mean to suggest that they are a bit the less powerful for often making the flesh crawl—may be said to coincide with a thematic choice made in each of them: that the framing and display of the male body be placed in the explicit context of the displayed body of Jesus. One way of reading *The Picture of Dorian Gray* would tell the same story, since the fall of that novel from sublime free play into sentimental potency comes with the framing and hanging of the beautiful male body as a visual index of vicarious expiation.

That the circumference of sentimental danger in Wilde's writing should have at its center the image of a crucified man would have been no surprise to Nietzsche. Nietzsche oriented, after all, his own narrative of the world-historical vitiation of the species around the fulcrum point of the same displayed male body; appropriately his meditations concerned, not the inherent meaning of the crucifixion or the qualities of the man crucified, but instead the seemingly irreversible relations of pity, desire, vicariousness, and mendacity instituted in the mass response to that image.

Evidently Nietzsche's ability to describe the relations around the cross from a new perspective depends on an Odyssean trick: blindfolding himself against a visual fixation on the focal figure aloft, deaf to the aural penetration of his distant appeal, Nietzsche (like the jello-phobic J. M. Cameron) gives himself over, in his discussions of Christianity, to the other three senses—taste, touch, smell, those that least accommodate distance, the ones that French designates by the verb *sentir*—and in the first place to the nose. "I was the first to sense—*smell*—the lie as a lie. . . . My genius is in my nostrils" (*Ecce*, 126). Possessing "a perfectly uncanny sensitivity of the instinct for cleanliness, so that I perceive physiologically—*smell*—the proximity or—what am I saying?—the innermost parts, the 'entrails,' of every soul" (*Ecce*, 48–49), Nietzsche is alive to "the complete lack of psychological cleanliness in the priest" (*Anti*, 169), is able "to *smell* what dirty fellows had [with Christianity] come out on top" (*Anti*, 183). He gags most on the proximity into which this spectacle of suffering draws the men who respond to it: "pity instantly smells of mob" (*Ecce*, 44). And in this phenomenon he finds the origin of virtually every feature of the world he inhabits. "One who smells not only with his nose but also with his eyes and ears will notice everywhere these days an air as of a lunatic asylum or sanatorium . . . so paltry, so stealthy, so dishonest, so sickly-sweet! Here . . . the air stinks of secretiveness and pent-up emotion."[19]

Nietzsche, then, is the psychologist who put the scent back into sentimentality. And he did it by the same gesture with which he put the rank and the rancid back into rancor. The most durably productive of Nietzsche's psychological judgments was to place the invidious, mendacious mechanism rather mysteriously called *ressentiment*—re-sniffing, one might say as much as "resentment," or re-tonguing, re-palpating—at the center of his account of such ordinary anno Domini virtues as love, goodwill, justice, fellow-feeling, egalitarianism, modesty, compassion. *Ressentiment* was for Nietzsche the essence of Christianity and hence of all modern psychology ("there never was but one psychology, that of the priest");[20] and the genius of his nostrils repeatedly reveals these appar-

---

19. "What noble eloquence flows from the lips of these ill-begotten creatures! What sugary, slimy, humble submissiveness swims in their eyes!" Friedrich Nietzsche, *The Birth of Tragedy and The Genealogy of Morals*, trans. Francis Golffing (New York: Doubleday Anchor, 1956), pp. 258–59. Further citations are given in the text as *Birth* or *Genealogy*.

20. Paraphrased in Gilles Deleuze and Félix Guattari, *Anti-Oedipus: Capitalism and Schizophrenia*, trans. Robert Hurley, Mark Seem, and Helen R. Lane (New York: Viking, 1977), p. 110.

ently simple and transparent impulses as complex, unstable laminates of self-aggrandizement and delectation with self-contempt and abnegation, fermented to a sort of compost under the pressure of time, of internal contradiction, and of deconstructive work like Nietzsche's own. The *re*-prefix of *ressentiment* marks a space of degeneration and vicariousness: the nonsingularity of these laminates as *re*doublings of one's own motives, and their nonoriginality as *re*flexes of the impulses of others. Thus the sentimental misnaming, in the aftermath of the crucifixion, of its observers' sensuality and will-to-power as *pity* becomes the model for the whole class of emotions and bonds of which Nietzsche was the privileged analyst:

> At first sight, this problem of pity and the ethics of pity (I am strongly opposed to our modern sentimentality in these matters) may seem very special, a marginal issue. But whoever sticks with it and learns how to ask questions will have the same experience that I had: a vast new panorama will open up before him; strange and vertiginous possibilities will invade him; every variety of suspicion, distrust, fear will come to the surface; his belief in ethics of any kind will begin to be shaken. (*Genealogy*, 154)

Sentimentality, insofar as it overlaps with *ressentiment* in a structure we would not be the first to call ressentimentality, represents modern emotion itself in Nietzsche's thought: modern emotion as vicariousness and misrepresentation, but also as sensation brought to the quick with an insulting closeness.

Direct/Vicarious; Art/Kitsch

It would be hard to overestimate the importance of vicariousness in defining the sentimental. The strange career of "sentimentality," from the later eighteenth century when it was a term of high ethical and aesthetic praise, to the twentieth when it can be used to connote, beyond pathetic weakness, an actual principle of evil—and from its origins when it circulated freely between genders, through the feminocentric Victorian version, to the twentieth-century one with its complex and distinctive relation to the male body—is a career that displays few easily articulable consistencies; and those few are not, as we have seen, consistencies of subject matter. Rather, they seem to inhere in the nature of the investment by a viewer *in* a subject matter. The sacralizing contagion of tears was the much reenacted primal scene of the sentimental in the eighteenth century.

If its early celebrants found it relatively (only relatively) easy to take for granted the disinterestedness and beneficence of the process by which a viewer "sympathized" with the sufferings of a person viewed, however, every psychological and philosophic project of the same period gave new facilities for questioning or even discrediting that increasingly unsimple-looking bond.[21] Most obviously, the position of sentimental spectatorship seemed to offer coverture for differences in material wealth (the bourgeois weeping over the spectacle of poverty) or sexual entitlement (the man swooning over the spectacle of female virtue under siege) — material or sexual exploitations that might even be perpetuated or accelerated by the nonaccountable viewer satisfactions that made the point of their rehearsal. The tacitness and consequent nonaccountability of the identification between sufferer and sentimental spectator, at any rate, seems to be the fulcrum point between the most honorific and the most damning senses of "sentimental." For a spectator to misrepresent the quality or locus of her or his implicit participation in a scene — to misrepresent, for example, desire as pity, *Schadenfreude* as sympathy, envy as disapproval — would be to enact defining instances of the worst meaning of the epithet; the defining instances, increasingly, of the epithet itself. The prurient; the morbid; the wishful; the snobbish;[22] the knowing; the arch: these denote subcategories of the sentimental, to the extent that each involves a covert reason for, or extent or direction of, identification through a spectatorial route. As Nietzsche says of Renan (with whom he has so much in common), "I can think of nothing as nauseating as such an 'objective' armchair, such a perfumed epicure of history, half priest, half satyr. . . . [S]uch 'spectators' embitter me against the spectacle more than the spectacle itself" (*Genealogy*, 294).

It follows from this that the description of scenes, or even texts, as intrinsically "sentimental" (or prurient, morbid, etc.) is extremely prob-

---

21. On this, see David Marshall, *The Surprising Effects of Sympathy: Marivaux, Diderot, Rousseau, and Mary Shelley* (Chicago: University of Chicago Press, 1989); and Jay Caplan, *Framed Narratives: Diderot's Genealogy of the Beholder* (Minneapolis: University of Minnesota Press, 1986).

22. I mean "snobbish," of course, not in the sense of a mere preference for social altitude, but in the fuller sense explicated by Girard, the one whose foundational principle is Groucho Marx's "I wouldn't belong to any club that would have me as a member": it is the tacit evacuation of the position of self that makes snob relations such a useful model for understanding sentimental relations. See René Girard, *Deceit, Desire, and the Novel: Self and Other in Literary Structure*, trans. Yvonne Freccero (Baltimore: Johns Hopkins University Press, 1965), esp. pp. 53–82, 216–28.

lematical, not least because such descriptions tend to carry an unappeal-able authority: the epithet "sentimental" is *always* stamped in indelible ink. "Sentimental" with its quiverful of subcategories: don't they work less as static grids of analysis against which texts can be flatly mapped than as projectiles whose bearing depends utterly on the angle and impetus of their discharge? In the last chapter, we discussed "worldliness" as an attribution whose force depended, not on its being attached firmly to a particular person or text, but on its ability to delineate a chain of attributive angles of increasing privilege and tacitness; a "worldly" per-son, for instance, is one whose cognitive privilege over a world is being attested, but the person who can attest it implicitly claims an even broader angle of cognitive privilege out of which the "worldly" angle can be carved, while a silent proffer to the reader or auditor of a broader angle yet can form, as we discussed, the basis for powerful interpellations. "The sentimental" and its damning subcategories work in an analogous way. Themselves descriptions of relations of vicariousness, the attributive career of each of these adjectives is again a vicariating one. For instance, it is well known that in Proust the snobbish characters are easy to recognize because they are the only ones who are able to recognize snobbism in others — hence, the only ones who really disapprove of it. Snobbism, as René Girard points out, can be discussed and attributed only by snobs, who are always right about it except in their own disclaimers of it.[23] The same is true of the phenomenon of "the sentimental" as a whole and of its other manifestations such as prurience and morbidity. *Honi soit qui mal y pense* is both the watchword and the structural principle of sentimen-tality-attribution. What chain of attribution is being extended, under pretense of being cut short, when Nietzsche exclaims, "O you sentimental hypocrites, you lechers! You lack innocence in your desire and therefore you slander all desire" (*Zarathustra*, 122–23)? What tacit relations of prurient complicity are compounded under the prurience-attribution of Nietzsche's discussion of the *Law-Book of Manu*:

> One sees immediately that it has a real philosophy behind it, *in* it... —it gives even the most fastidious psychologist something to bite on.... All the things upon which Christianity vents its abysmal vulgarity, procrea-tion for example, women, marriage, are here treated seriously, with reverence, with love and trust. How can one actually put into the hands of women and children a book containing the low-minded saying: "To

23. Girard, *Deceit, Desire, and the Novel*, pp. 72–73.

avoid fornication let every man have his own wife, and let every woman have her own husband . . . for it is better to marry than burn"? And is it *allowable* to be a Christian as long as the origin of man is Christianized, that is to say *dirtied*, with the concept of the *immaculata conceptio*? . . . I know of no book in which so many tender and kind remarks are addressed to woman as in the Law-Book of Manu; these old graybeards and saints have a way of being polite to women which has perhaps never been surpassed. "A woman's mouth" — it says in one place — "a girl's breast, a child's prayer, the smoke of a sacrifice are always pure." Another passage: "There is nothing purer than the light of the sun, the shadow of a cow, air, water, fire and a girl's breath." A final passage — perhaps also a holy lie — : "All the openings of the body above the navel are pure, all below impure. Only in the case of a girl is the whole body pure." (*Anti*, 176)

Vidal's score off Wilde, "Must one have a heart of stone . . . ?", seems to depend on the same structure. If the joke were that the Wilde who took advantage of the enormous rhetorical charge to be gained from hurling at Dickens the aspersion of sentimentality also at another time, perhaps later in his life when the hideous engines of state punishment had done their work of destroying the truth and gaiety of his sensibility, developed a proneness to the same awful failing, that would be one thing. Perhaps, though, the point is that there isn't a differentiation to be *made* between sentimentality and its denunciation. But then we are dealing with a joke that can only be on Gore Vidal himself, whose hypervigilance for lapses in the tough-mindedness of others can then only suggest that he in turn must be, as they say, insecure about his own. It may be only those who are themselves prone to these vicariating impulses who are equipped to detect them in the writing or being of others; but it is also they who for several reasons tend therefore to be perturbed in their presence.

By "they" here I definitionally mean "we." In order to dispense with the further abysmal structuring of this bit of argument through an infinity of insinuating readings of "other" writers, let me try to break with the tradition of personal disclaimer and touch ground myself with a rapid but none the less genuine guilty plea to possessing the attributes, in a high degree, of at the very least sentimentality, prurience, and morbidity. (On the infinitesimally small chance that any skepticism could greet this confession, I can offer as evidence of liability — or, one might say, of expert qualification — the pathos injected into the paraphrase of *Esther*, in Chapter 1, which I loved composing but which is rendered both creepy and, perhaps, rhetorically efficacious by a certain obliquity in my own trail of identifications. As a friend who disliked those paragraphs put it acidly, it's not me risking the coming out, but it's all too visibly me having the salvational fantasies.)

Clearly, this understanding of "sentimentality" makes problems for a project, whether feminist- or gay-centered, of rehabilitating the sentimental. The problem is not just that the range of discrediting names available for these forms of attention and expression is too subtle, searching, descriptively useful, and rhetorically powerful to be simply jettisoned, though that is true enough. A worse problem is that since antisentimentality itself becomes, in this structure, the very engine and expression of modern sentimental relations, to enter into the discourse of sentimentality at any point or with any purpose is almost inevitably to be caught up in a momentum of essentially scapegoating attribution.

The attempt to construct versions of the present argument has offered, I might as well say, startlingly clear evidence of the force of this momentum. Given a desire to raise the questions I'm raising here, it's all too easy to visualize the path of least resistance of such an argument. The ballistic force of the attribution of "sentimentality" is so intense today that I've found it amazingly difficult to think about any analytic or revaluative project involving it that wouldn't culminate its rehabilitative readings with some yet more damning unmasking of the "true," and far more dangerous, sentimentality of an author not previously associated with the term. This would be congruent with a certain difficult-to-avoid trajectory of universalizing understandings of homo/heterosexual definition — Irigaray's writing about the "hom(m)osexual" is the locus classicus of this trajectory, although feminist thought has no monopoly on it — according to which authoritarian regimes or homophobic masculinist culture may be damned on the grounds of being *even more homosexual* than gay male culture.[24] And each of these trajectories of argument leads straight to terrible commonplaces about fascism. In the case of Nietzsche and Wilde, the most readily available — the almost irresistibly available — path of argument would have been to use the manifestly gay Wilde as a figure for the necessity and truth of a "good" version of sentimentality, then to prove that the ostensibly heterosexual and antisentimental Nietzsche was, like Wilde, maybe even more actively than Wilde because unacknowledgedly,

24. Craig Owens discusses this argument in "Outlaws: Gay Men in Feminism," in Alice Jardine and Paul Smith, eds., *Men in Feminism* (New York: Methuen, 1987), pp. 219–32.

and in ways that could be shown to have implications for his writing and thought, "really" homosexual, and at the same time "really" sentimental.

Why should it be so hard to think about these issues without following an argumentative path that must lead to the exposure of a supposed fascist precursor as the *true* homosexual, or especially as the *true* sentimentalist? I have tried to avoid that path of exposure, for four reasons. First, of course, Nietzsche, like Whitman, is a cunning and elusive writer on whose self-ignorance one never does well to bet the mortgage money. Second, though, such a trajectory of argument presupposes that one has somewhere in reserve a stable and intelligible definition for both what is "really homosexual" and what is "really sentimental," while our historical argument is exactly the opposite: that those definitions are neither historically stable in this period nor internally coherent. Third, obviously, that argument necessarily depends for its rhetorical if not its analytic force on the extreme modern cultural devaluations of both categories, the homosexual and the sentimental—a dependence that had better provoke discomfort, however much Nietzsche's own writing may sometimes be complicit in those fatal devaluations. And finally, the most productive questions we can ask about these definitional issues must be, I think, not "What is the true meaning, the accurate assignment of these labels?" but, rather, "What are the relations instituted by the giving of these labels?" In that case, any enabling analytic distance we might have would be vitiated to the degree that our argument was so aimed as to climax with this act of naming.

The categories "kitsch" and "camp" suggest, perhaps, something about how the formation of modern gay identities has intervened to reimagine these potent audience relations. Kitsch is a classification that redoubles the aggressive power of the epithet "sentimental" by, on the one hand, claiming to exempt the speaker of the epithet from the contagion of the kitsch object, and, on the other, positing the existence of a true *kitsch consumer* or, in Hermann Broch's influential phrase, "kitsch-man."[25] Kitsch-man is never the person who uses the word "kitsch"; kitsch-man's ability to be manipulated by the kitsch object and the kitsch creator is imagined to be seamless and completely uncritical. Kitsch-man is seen

---

25. Hermann Broch, *Einer Bemerkungen zum Problem des Kitsches*, in *Dichten und Erkennen*, vol. 1 (Zurich: Rhein-Verlag, 1955), p. 295; popularized by, among others, Gillo Dorfles, in *Kitsch: The World of Bad Taste* (New York: Universe Books, 1969).

either as the exact double of the equally unenlightened producer of kitsch or as the unresistant dupe of his cynical manipulation: that is to say, the imagined kitsch-producer is *either* at the abjectly low consciousness level of kitsch-man *or* at the transcendent, and potentially abusive, high consciousness level of the man who can recognize kitsch when he sees it. In the highly contestative world of kitsch and kitsch-recognition there is no mediating level of consciousness; so it is necessarily true that the structure of contagion whereby *it takes one to know one*, and whereby *any* object about which the question "Is it kitsch?" can be asked immediately *becomes* kitsch, remains, under the system of kitsch-attribution, a major scandal, one that can induce self-exemption or cynicism but nothing much more interesting than that.

Camp, on the other hand, seems to involve a gayer and more spacious angle of view. I think it may be true that, as Robert Dawidoff suggests, the typifying gesture of camp is really something amazingly simple: the moment at which a consumer of culture makes the wild surmise, "What if whoever made this was gay too?"[26] Unlike kitsch-attribution, then, camp-recognition doesn't ask, "What kind of debased creature could possibly be the right audience for this spectacle?" Instead, it says *what if*: What if the right audience for this were exactly *me*? What if, for instance, the resistant, oblique, tangential investments of attention and attraction that I am able to bring to this spectacle are actually uncannily responsive to the resistant, oblique, tangential investments of the person, or of some of the people, who created it? And what if, furthermore, others whom I don't know or recognize can see it from the same "perverse" angle? Unlike kitsch-*attribution*, the sensibility of camp-*recognition* always sees that it is dealing in reader relations and in projective fantasy (projective though not infrequently true) about the spaces and practices of cultural production. Generous because it acknowledges (unlike kitsch) that its perceptions are necessarily also creations,[27] it's little wonder that camp can encompass effects of great delicacy and power in our highly sentimental-attributive culture.

26. Personal communication, 1986. Of course, discussions of camp have proliferated since Susan Sontag's "Notes on 'Camp,'" in *Against Interpretation and Other Essays* (New York: Farrar, Straus & Giroux, 1966). One of the discussions that resonates most with this book's emphasis on the open secret is Philip Core, *Camp: The Lie That Tells the Truth* (New York: Delilah Books, 1984).

27. "CAMP depends on where you pitch it. . . . CAMP is in the eyes of the beholder, especially if the beholder is camp." Core, "CAMP RULES," *Camp*, p. 7.

Neither rehabilitation nor rubbishing, wholesale, is a possible thing to do, then, with these representational meanings of "sentimental," "antisentimental," or even "ressentimental"; they stand for rhetorical—that is to say, for relational—figures, figures of concealment, obliquity, vicariousness, and renaming, and their ethical bearings can thus be discussed only in the multiple contexts of their writing and reading. Though each could be called a form of bad faith, each can also be seen as a figure of irrepressible desire and creativity—if only the sheer, never to be acknowledged zest of finding a way to frame and reproduce the pain or the pleasure of another. "Good," Nietzsche remarks, but his affect here may be rather enigmatic, "is no longer good when your neighbour takes it into his mouth" (*Beyond*, 53).

Same/Different; Homo/Hetero

If sentimentality, antisentimentality, and ressentimentality are figures of vicariated desire, however, how is one to know whose desire it is that is thus figured? By whom can it be so figured? More: if we hypothesize that a central misrepresentation of Christian-era ressentimentality is the back-and-forth misrepresentation that incessantly occurs between the concepts "same" and "different," do we risk generalizing our topic out of existence? Of course we do; nothing, in Western thought, isn't categorizable and deconstructible under "same" and "different." Suppose we move to the Greek translation, then, and make the same hypothesis about ressentimentality as the mutual misrepresentation between *homo* and *hetero*: haven't we then already overspecified our topic fatally? Yet this is the overlapping field of double-binding binarisms into which we are indeed plunged by, not the scandalous, sentimental vicariety of Christian psychology itself, nor the desire in itself of many men for other men, but the late-nineteenth-century juxtaposition of these two things in the concepts homo- and heterosexuality.

Since Foucault, it has been common to distinguish a modern concept of "homosexuality"—delineating a continuous *identity*—from a supposedly premodern (though persistent) concept of "sodomy," which delineated discrete *acts*. More recent research has, however, been demonstrating that even within the minoritizing, taxonomic identity-discourses instituted in the late nineteenth century, there was an incalculably consequential divergence between terms Foucault had treated as virtually interchangeable: homosexuality and sexual inversion. As George Chauncey argues, "Sexual inversion, the term used most commonly in the nineteenth century, did not denote the same conceptual phenomenon as homosexuality. 'Sexual inversion' referred to an inversion in a broad range of deviant gender behavior"—the phenomenon of female "masculinity" or male "femininity," condensed in formulations such as Karl Heinrich Ulrichs' famous self-description as *anima muliebris virili corpore inclusa*, a woman's soul trapped in a man's body—"while 'homosexuality' focused on the narrower issue of sexual object choice."[28] According to David Halperin, "That sexual object-choice might be wholly independent of such 'secondary' characteristics as masculinity or femininity never seems to have entered anyone's head until Havelock Ellis waged a campaign to isolate object-choice from role-playing and Freud . . . clearly distinguished in the case of the libido between the sexual 'object' and the sexual 'aim.'"[29]

Halperin describes some consequences of this shift:

> The conceptual isolation of sexuality *per se* from questions of masculinity and femininity made possible a new taxonomy of sexual behaviors and psychologies based entirely on the anatomical sex of the persons engaged in a sexual act (same sex vs. different sex); it thereby obliterated a number of distinctions that had traditionally operated within earlier discourses pertaining to same-sex sexual contacts and that had radically differentiated active from passive sexual partners, normal from abnormal (or conventional from unconventional) sexual roles, masculine from feminine styes, and paederasty from lesbianism: all such behaviors were now to be classed alike and placed under the same heading. Sexual identity was thus polarized around a central opposition rigidly defined by the binary play of sameness and difference in the sexes of the sexual partners; people belonged henceforward to one or the other of two exclusive categories. . . . Founded on positive, ascertainable, and objective behavioral phenomena—on the facts of who had sex with whom—the new sexual taxonomy could lay claim to a descriptive, trans-historical validity. And so it crossed the "threshold of scientificity" and was enshrined as a working concept in the social and physical sciences.[30]

It is startling to realize that the aspect of "homosexuality" that now seems in many ways most immutably to fix it—its dependence on a defining *sameness* between partners—is of so recent crystallization.[31] That process

28. Chauncey, "From Sexual Inversion to Homosexuality," p. 124.
29. Halperin, *One Hundred Years of Homosexuality*, p. 16.
30. Halperin, *One Hundred Years of Homosexuality*, p. 16.
31. Indeed, though the two etymological roots of the coinage "*homo-sexual*ity" may originally have been meant to refer to relations (of an unspecified kind) between persons of the *same sex*, I believe the word is now almost universally heard as referring to relations of

is also, one might add, still radically incomplete.[32] The potential for defamiliarization implicit in this historical perception is only beginning to be apparent.

The *homo-* in the emerging concept of the homosexual seems to have the potential to perform a definitive de-differentiation—setting up a permanent avenue of potential slippage—between two sets of relations that had previously been seen as relatively distinct: identification and desire.[33] It is with *homo*-style homosexuality, and *not* with inversion, pederasty, or sodomy (least of all, of course, with cross-gender sexuality) that an erotic language, an erotic discourse comes into existence that makes available a continuing possibility for symbolizing slippages between identification and desire. It concomitantly makes available new possibilities for the camouflage and concealment, or the very selective or pointed display, of proscribed or resisted erotic relation and avowal through chains of vicariation—through the mechanisms that, I argue, cluster under the stigmatizing name "sentimentality."

Let me make it clear what I am and am not saying here. I do not, myself, believe same-sex relationships are much more likely to be based on similarity than are cross-sex relationships. That is, I do not believe that identification and desire are necessarily more closely linked in same-sex than in cross-sex relationships, or in gay than in nongay persons. I assume them to be closely linked in many or most relationships and persons, in fact. I certainly do not believe that any given man must be assumed to have more in common with any other given man than he can possibly have in common with any given woman. Yet these *are* the assumptions that underlie, and are in turn underwritten by, the definitional invention of "homosexuality."[34]

---

sexuality between persons who are, because of their sex, more flatly and globally categorized as *the same.*

32. For instance, many Mediterranean and Latin American cultures distinguish sharply between insertive and receptive sexual roles, in assessing the masculinity / femininity of men involved in male-male sex; the concept of homosexual identity per se tends not to make sense readily in these cultural contexts, or tends to make sense to self-identified *jotos* or *pasivos* but not *machos* or *activos*. And these are, along with the Anglo-European and others, among the cultures that are also U.S. cultures. See, for instance, Ana Maria Alonso and Maria Teresa Koreck, "Silences: 'Hispanics,' AIDS, and Sexual Practices," *Differences* 1 (Winter 1989): 101–24.

33. On this, see Chapter 1 of *Between Men.*

34. At the same time, the fact that "homosexuality," being—unlike its predecessor terms—posited on definitional similarity, was the first modern piece of sexual definition that simply took as nugatory the distinction between relations of identification and relations of desire, meant that it posed a radical question to cross-gender relations and, in

How does a man's love of *other* men become a love of the *same?* The process is graphic in *Dorian Gray,* in the way the plot of the novel facilitates the translation back and forth between "men's desire for men" and something that looks a lot like what a tradition will soon call "narcissism." The novel takes a plot that is distinctively one of male-male desire, the competition between Basil Hallward and Lord Henry Wotton for Dorian Gray's love, and condenses it into the plot of the mysterious bond of figural likeness and figural expiation between Dorian Gray and his own portrait. The suppression of the original defining *differences between* Dorian and his male admirers — differences of age and initiatedness, in the first place — in favor of the problematic of Dorian's *similarity to* the painted male image that is and isn't himself does several things. To begin with, the similarity trope does not, I believe, constitute itself strongly here as against an "inversion" model, in which Wilde seldom seemed particularly interested and whose rhetoric is virtually absent from *Dorian Gray.* Rather, this plot of the novel seems to replicate the discursive eclipse in this period of the Classically based, *pederastic* assumption that male-male bonds of any duration must be structured around some diacritical difference — old/young, for example, or active/passive — whose binarizing cultural power would be at least comparable to that of gender. Initiating, along with the stigma of narcissism, the utopic modern vision of a strictly egalitarian bond guaranteed by the exclusion of any consequential difference, the new calculus of homo/hetero, embodied in the portrait plot, owes its sleekly utilitarian feel to the linguistically unappealable classification of anyone who shares one's gender as being "the same" as oneself, and anyone who does not share one's gender as being one's Other.

It served, however, an additional purpose. For Wilde, in 1891 a young man with a very great deal to lose who was trying to embody his own talents and desires in a self-contradictory male-homosocial terrain where too much was not enough but, at the same time, anything at all might always be too much, the collapse of homo/hetero with self/other must

---

turn, to gender definition itself. For the first time since at least the Renaissance, there existed the potential for a discourse in which a man's desire for a woman could not guarantee his difference from her — in which it might even, rather, suggest his likeness to her. That such a possibility is a clear contradiction of the *homo/hetero* gender definitions of which it is nonetheless also the clear consequence made a conceptual knot whose undoing may be said to have been the determinative project, continuously frustrated but continuously productive, of psychoanalytic theory from Freud to the present.

also have been attractive for the protective/expressive camouflage it offered to distinctively gay content. Not everyone has a lover of their own sex, but everyone, after all, has a self of their own sex.[35] (This camouflage, by the way, continues to be effective in institutions that connive with it: in a class I taught at Amherst College, fully half the students said they had studied *Dorian Gray* in previous classes, but not one had ever discussed the book in terms of any homosexual content: all of them knew it could be explained in terms of either the Theme of the Double—"The Divided"—or else the Problem of Mimesis—"Life and Art.")

For Wilde, the progression from *homo* to same to self resulted at least briefly, as we shall see, in a newly articulated modernist "self"-reflexiveness and antifigurality, antirepresentationism, iconophobia that struggles in the antisentimental entanglements of *Dorian Gray* and collapses in the sentimental mobilizations of *Reading Gaol*.[36] Nietzsche's use of the nascent accommodations of the new concept are oddly simpler, for all that you would have to describe him as the man who tried to put the hetero back into *Ecce Homo*. Freud in his discussion of Dr. Schreber gives the following list of the possible eroto-grammatical transformations that can be generated in contradiction of the sentence, unspeakable under a homophobic regime of utterance, "*I* (a man) *love him* (a man)." First, "I do not *love* him—I *hate* him"; second, "I do not love *him*, I love *her*"; third, "*I* do not love him; *she* loves him"; and finally, "I do not love him; I do not love any one."[37] None of these translations is exactly foreign to Nietzsche; in fact, one could imagine a Nietzsche life-and-works whose table of contents simply rotated the four sentences in continual reprise. But his

35. If, at any rate, under this new definitional possibility, that which I *am* and that which I *desire* may no longer be assumed to be distinct, then each one of those terms can be subjected to the operations of slippage. We have seen how both Wilde and Nietzsche camouflage what seem to be the male objects of male desire as, "ultimately," mere reflections of a divided "self." But it can work in the other direction: the *homo*- construction also makes a language in which a man who desires may claim to take on some of the lovable attributes of the man desired. In Nietzsche, for example, the unimaginable distance between the valetudinarian philosopher who desires, and the bounding "masters of the earth" whom he desires, is dissolved so resolutely by the force of his rhetoric that it is startling to be reminded that "Homer would not have created Achilles, nor Goethe Faust, if Homer had been an Achilles, or Goethe a Faust" (*Genealogy*, 235). And, as we shall see, Wilde presents a similar double profile.

36. For Nietzsche, whose literary impulses aren't in that sense modernist, the desired male figure never ceases to be visible as a male figure, except, as we've noted, in those instances where the sense of sight is willfully suppressed.

37. "Psycho-analytic Notes upon an Autobiographical Account of a Case of Paranoia (Dementia Paranoides)," in *Three Case Histories*, ed. Philip Rieff (New York: Macmillan/Collier, 1963), pp. 165–68.

own most characteristic and invested grammar for this prohibited sentence is a different one, one that underlies Freud's project so intimately that it does not occur to Freud to make it explicit, and far closer to the bone of the emergent "homo-" reading of what it means for man to desire man: "I do not *love* him, I *am* him."

I do not desire, let us say, Wagner; I *am* Wagner. In the loving panegyric of *Wagner in Bayreuth*, "I am the only person referred to—one may ruthlessly insert my name . . . wherever the text gives the word Wagner" (*Ecce*, 82). (Or: "Supposing I had baptized my Zarathustra with another name, for example with the name of Richard Wagner, the perspicuity of two millennia would not have sufficed to divine that the author of 'Human, All Too Human' is the visionary of Zarathustra" [*Ecce*, 59].) It was not "one of my friends, the excellent Dr. Paul Ree, whom [in *Human, All Too Human*] I bathed in world-historic glory"; that was merely how, "with my instinctive cunning, I here too avoided the little word 'I'" (*Ecce*, 94). I do not desire Zarathustra, though "we celebrate the feast of feasts; friend *Zarathustra* has come, the guest of guests! Now the world is laughing, the dread curtain is rent, the wedding day has come for light and darkness" (*Beyond*, 204)—rather, at the moments of definitional stress, I *am* Zarathustra. I do not desire Dionysus, for all the gorgeous eroticism surrounding

> that great hidden one, the tempter god . . . whose voice knows how to descend into the underworld of every soul, who says no word and gives no glance in which there lies no touch of enticement . . . the genius of the heart . . . who divines the hidden and forgotten treasure, the drop of goodness and sweet spirituality under thick and opaque ice, and is a divining-rod for every grain of gold . . . the genius of the heart from whose touch everyone goes away . . . newer to himself than before, broken open, blown upon and sounded out by a thawing wind, more uncertain perhaps, more delicate, more fragile, more broken, but full of hopes that as yet have no names, full of new will and current, full of new ill will and counter-current. . . . Dionysus, that great ambiguous and tempter god (*Beyond*, 199–200)

—no, in the last analysis, I *am* Dionysus. (The dedicatory phrases, for instance, that begin the "Dionysus" section of *The Will to Power*, "*To him that has turned out well*, who does my heart good, carved from wood that is hard, gentle, and fragrant—in whom even the nose takes pleasure," turn up almost verbatim in the "Why I am so Wise" section of *Ecce Homo*, with the notation, "I have just described *myself.*")[38] Indeed, "What is disagreeable and offends my modesty is that at bottom I am every name in history."[39] And, as with Dr. Schreber, the whole elaborated syntax of the contraries of *these* propositions emerges in turn: Nietzsche as the *contra* Wagner ("we are antipodes");[40] "*Dionysus against the Crucified*" (the last words of *Ecce Homo*); Nietzsche, in perhaps the most central turn, as the Anti-Christ.

Abstraction/Figuration

To point to the paranoid structure of these male investments is not, in the framework I hope I have created, to pathologize or marginalize them but, rather, to redeploy their admitted centrality. "Madness is something rare in individuals—but in groups, parties, peoples, ages it is the rule" (*Beyond*, 85). To the degree that Nietzsche is here engaged in a projective heroics of embodiment already characteristic of post-Romantic projects, he provides an exemplar for the Gothic-marked view of the nineteenth century as the Age of Frankenstein, an age philosophically and tropologically marked by the wildly dichotomous play around solipsism and intersubjectivity of a male paranoid plot—one that always ends in the tableau of two men chasing one another across a landscape evacuated of alternative life or interest, toward a climax that tends to condense the amorous with the murderous in a representation of male rape.[41] What is anomalous about Nietzsche in this context is scarcely the hold this plot has on him, but indeed the flexuous sweetness with which sometimes he uniquely invests it:

> You who with your spear of fire
> Melt the river of my soul,
> So that, freed from ice, it rushes

38. *The Will to Power*, trans. Walter Kaufmann (New York: Vintage, 1968), p. 520 (hereafter cited in the text as *Will*); *Ecce*, 40–41.

39. From his letter to Jacob Burckhardt, dated January 6, 1889; *The Portable Nietzsche*, ed. and trans. Walter Kaufmann (New York: Viking Penguin, 1976), p. 686.

40. *Nietzsche Contra Wagner*, in *The Portable Nietzsche*, p. 662 (further citations are given as *Contra* in the text). "What respect can I have for the Germans when even my friends cannot discriminate between me and a liar like Richard Wagner?" (cancelled paragraphs for *Ecce*, in *Basic Writings of Nietzsche*, trans. Walter Kaufmann [New York: Modern Library, 1968], p. 798).

41. On this, see *Between Men*, Chapters 5, 6, 9, and 10.

Toward the ocean of its goal:
Brighter still and still more healthy,
Free in most desired constraint —
Thus your miracle it praises,
January, lovely saint![42]

The overtly Gothic *Dorian Gray*, insofar as its plot devolves, as we've seen, from a worldly one of complex intersubjective rivalries to a hermetic one of the Double *tout court*, drinks as deeply and much more conventionally of this nineteenth-century current by which the energies of a male-male desire by now complexly prohibited but still rather inchoately defined could be at once circulated, channeled, extended, and occluded. Chapter 4, on the historical creation and manipulation of male homosexual panic per se, will discuss these mechanisms more fully. What makes *Dorian Gray* so distinctively modern(ist) a book, however, is not the degree to which it partakes of the paranoid-associated homophobic alibi "I do not *love* him; I *am* him." It is a different though intimately related alibi that the *modernism* of *Dorian Gray* performs: the alibi of abstraction.

Across the turn of the century, as we know, through a process that became most visible in, but antedated and extended far beyond, the trials of Oscar Wilde, the discourse related to male homosexuality itself became for the first time extremely public and highly ramified through medical, psychiatric, penal, literary, and other social institutions. With a new public discourse concerning male homosexuality that was at the same time increasingly discriminant, increasingly punitive, and increasingly trivializing or marginalizing, the recuperative rhetoric that emerged had an oddly oblique shape. I would describe it as the occluded intersection between a minority rhetoric of the "open secret" or glass closet and a subsumptive public rhetoric of the "empty secret."

The term "open secret" designates here a very particular secret, a homosexual secret. As I explain in Chapter 1, I use it as a condensed way of describing the phenomenon of the "glass closet," the swirls of totalizing knowledge-power that circulate so violently around any but the most openly acknowledged gay male identity. The lavender button I bought the other day at the Oscar Wilde Memorial Bookstore, that laconically says, "I KNOW YOU KNOW," represents a playful and seductive version of the

---

42. The translation is Hollingdale's (*Ecce*, 98). The poem appears as the epigraph to Book Four of *The Gay Science* and is translated by Walter Kaufmann in his edition of that book (New York: Random House / Vintage, 1974), p. 221.

Glass Closet. Hitchcock's recently re-released Gothic film *Rope* is a good example of the murderous version. It opens with two men, clearly lovers, strangling a third man in a darkened penthouse; then pulling back the curtains from the skylight with orgasmic relief— "Pity we couldn't have done it with the curtains open, in bright sunlight. Well, we can't have everything, can we? We did do it in daytime"—they put their friend's dead body in a large box which they place in the middle of the living room and use as the buffet table and centerpiece for a party, the guests to which include the fiancée, the father, the aunt, the best friend, and the prep-school ex-housemaster of the murdered man. Needless to say, the two lovers manage to make sure that the existence of A Secret, and the location of that secret in the big box in the middle of the room, does not remain A Secret for long.

The public rhetoric of the "empty secret," on the other hand, the cluster of aperçus and intuitions that seems distinctively to signify "modernism" (at least, male high modernism), delineates a space bounded by hollowness, a self-reference that refers back to—though it differs from—nineteenth-century paranoid solipsism, and a split between content or thematics on the one hand and structure on the other that is stressed in favor of structure and at the expense of thematics. I will argue in the next chapter that this rhetoric of male modernism serves a purpose of universalizing, naturalizing, and thus substantively voiding—depriving of content—elements of a specifically and historically male homosexual rhetoric. But just as the gay male rhetoric is itself already marked and structured and indeed necessitated and propelled by the historical shapes of homophobia, for instance by the contingencies and geographies of the highly permeable closet, so it is also true that homophobic male modernism bears the structuring fossil-marks of and in fact spreads and reproduces the specificity of desire that it exists to deny.

The Picture of Dorian Gray occupies an especially symptomatic place in this process. Published four years before Wilde's "exposure" as a sodomite, it is in a sense a perfect rhetorical distillation of the open secret, the glass closet, shaped by the conjunction of an extravagance of deniability and an extravagance of flamboyant display. It perfectly represents the glass closet, too, because it is in so many ways *out* of the purposeful control of its author. Reading *Dorian Gray* from our twentieth-century vantage point where the name Oscar Wilde virtually *means* "homosexual," it is worth reemphasizing how thoroughly the elements of even this novel can be read doubly or equivocally, can be read either as having a thematically empty "modernist" meaning or as having a thematically full "homosexual" meaning. And from the empty "modernist" point of view, this full meaning — *any* full meaning, but, in some exemplary representative relation to that, *this* very particular full meaning — *this* insistence on narrative content, which means the insistence on *this* narrative content, comes to look like kitsch.

Basil Hallward perfectly captures the immobilizing panic that underlies this imperfect transformation of the open secret into the empty secret. He had been able, in decent comfort, to treat artistically of his infatuation with Dorian so long as he had framed it anachronistically, Classically — even while knowing that "in such mad worships there is peril" (128) — but

> Then came a new development. I had drawn you as Paris in dainty armour, and as Adonis with huntsman's cloak and polished boat-spear. . . . And it had all been what art should be — unconscious, ideal, and remote. One day, a fatal day I sometimes think, I determined to paint a wonderful portrait of you as you actually are, not in the costume of dead ages, but in your own dress and your own time. Whether it was the Realism of the method, or the mere wonder of your own personality, thus directly presented to me without mist or veil, I cannot tell. But I know that as I worked at it, every flake and film of colour seemed to me to reveal my secret. I grew afraid that others would know of my idolatry. I felt, Dorian, that I had told too much, that I had put too much of myself into it. . . . Well, after a few days the thing left my studio, and as soon as I had got rid of the intolerable fascination of its presence it seemed to me that I had been foolish in imagining that I had seen anything in it, more than that you were extremely good-looking, and that I could paint. Even now I cannot help feeling that it is a mistake to think that the passion one feels in creation is ever really shown in the work one creates. Art is always more abstract than we fancy. Form and colour tell us of form and colour — that is all. (128–29)

Or, as Basil has put it earlier, interrupting his own confession of love and desire for Dorian: "He is never more present in my work than when no image of him is there. He is a suggestion, as I have said, of a new manner. I find him in the curves of certain lines, in the loveliness and subtleties of certain colours. That is all." (17)

Passages like these, as well as some of the important antinarrative projects that seem to shape the early parts of *Dorian Gray*, suggest the prefiguring manifesto of a modernist aesthetic according to which sentimentality inheres less in the object figured than in a prurient vulgarity associated with figuration itself. Postmodernism, in this view, the strenuous rematch between the reigning champ, modernist abstraction, and the deposed challenger, figuration, would thus *necessarily* have kitsch and sentimentality as its main spaces of contestation. But insofar as there is a case to be made that the modernist impulse toward abstraction in the first place owes an incalculable part of its energy precisely to turn-of-the-century male homo/heterosexual definitional panic—and such a case is certainly there for the making, in at any rate literary history from Wilde to Hopkins to James to Proust to Conrad to Eliot to Pound to Joyce to Hemingway to Faulkner to Stevens—to that extent the "figuration" that had to be abjected from modernist self-reflexive abstraction was not the figuration of just *any* body, the figuration of figurality itself, but, rather, that represented in a very particular body, the desired male body. So as kitsch or sentimentality came to mean representation itself, what represented "representation itself" came at the same time signally to be a very particular, masculine object and subject of erotic desire.

Invention/Recognition; Wholeness/Decadence

An antifiguralist modernism per se never seems to have formed any part of Nietzsche's program. It seems, however, that after the revulsion against his love for Wagner, opera functioned for Nietzsche rather as figuration itself did for Wilde; it stood, that is, for a fascinating, near-irresistible impulse barely transcended if transcended at all, but against which a scouring polemic might none the less productively and revealingly be mounted. Thematically and rhetorically, as well, Nietzsche's treatment of opera is similar to Wilde's treatment of mimesis—writing in 1886 about his major Wagnerian work of fifteen years before:

> To say it once more: today I find [*The Birth of Tragedy*] an impossible book: I consider it badly written, ponderous, embarrassing, image-mad and image-confused, sentimental, in places saccharine to the point of effeminacy, uneven in tempo, without the will to logical cleanliness . . . a book for initiates, "music" for those dedicated to music, those who are closely related to begin with on the basis of common and rare aesthetic experiences, "music" meant as a sign of recognition for close relatives *in artibus*. . . . Still, the effect of the book proved and proves that it had a knack for seeking out fellow-rhapsodizers and for luring them on to new secret paths and dancing places. What found expression here was any-way—this was admitted with as much curiosity as antipathy—a *strange* voice, the disciple of a still "unknown God." . . . Here was a spirit with strange, still nameless needs.[43]

43. From "Attempt at Self-Criticism," 1886 introduction to a reissue of *The Birth of Tragedy*, in *Basic*, pp. 19–20.

Nietzsche calls the "image-mad" relations around Wagner "sentimen-tal" in the specific sense that they involved his "confounding of myself with what I was not" (*Ecce*, 93); as for "the Wagnerian" more generally, "I have 'experienced' three generations of them, from the late Brendel, who confused Wagner with Hegel, to the 'idealists' of the Bayreuther Blätter, who confuse Wagner with themselves" (*Ecce*, 90). The promiscuously vicariating impulse triggered by Wagner, while entailing all the "un-cleanliness" attributed to its Christian original ("I put on gloves when I read the score of *Tristan*" [*Will*, 555]), also performs, however, another function that Nietzsche finds more difficult to repudiate: a function of community-building through the mechanism of mutual recognition en-abled by this slippage, among "initiates," between desire and identifica-tion. The very stress on the "secret," "curious," "strange," "unknown," and "nameless," terms that flamboyantly condense the open secret with the empty one, dares such recognitions.

One of the most Wildean functions that the opera serves in Nietzsche is to anchor a rhetoric of decadence. Wagner was a perfect foil for Nietzsche's erotic grammars here: himself certifiable as heterosexually active, if not hyperactive, he nonetheless, like Nietzsche, crystallized a hypersaturated solution of what were and were about to become homo-sexual signifiers. Set up under the notorious aegis of Ludwig II, the Wagnerian opera represented a cultural lodestar for what Max Nordau, in *Degeneration*, refers to as "the abnormals"; the tireless taxonomist Krafft-Ebing quotes a homosexual patient who is "an enthusiastic par-tisan of Richard Wagner, for whom I have remarked a predilection in most of us [sufferers from "contrary-sexual-feeling"]; I find that this music accords so very much with our nature."[44] Thus when Nietzsche refers to Wagner's "incredibly pathological sexuality" (*Will*, 555), he can charac-teristically tap into and refresh the energies of emergent tropes for homo-sexuality without ever taking a reified homosexuality itself as a subject. From the late twentieth-century retrospect there is, as we have mentioned, almost only one out of the panoply of nineteenth-century sexualities that represents *the* pathological (just as the phrase "sexual orientation" now refers quite exclusively to gender of object-choice); the reading of

44. Nordau, *Degeneration*, trans. from the 2d ed. of the German work, 6th ed. (New York: D. Appleton, 1895), p. 452; Krafft-Ebing, quoted by Nordau, p. 452*n*, from Richard von Krafft-Ebing, *Neue Forschungen auf dem Gebiet der Psychopathia sexualis* (Stuttgart: F. Enke, 1891), p. 128.

Nietzsche through these tendentiously filtered lenses certainly represents a violence to his meaning, but a violence in which he is anything but unimplicated.

The thematics as well as argumentation of decadence in Nietzsche are close to those of ressentimentality: loosening of the laminated integument, as in the "over-ripe, manifold and much-indulged conscience" of Christianity (*Beyond*, 57), a palpable gaping, crawling, or fermentation where firmness ought to be, like the Overture to *Meistersinger*, which has "the loose yellow skin of fruits which ripen too late" (*Beyond*, 151). Although the negative valuation attached to *ressentiment* per se — *ressentiment* under its own name — is one of the most consistent of Nietzsche's ethical judgments, it's nonetheless clear that his acuity as a psychologist of ressentimentality requires that he as well undergo subjection to its processes. It is an easy task for anyone instructed by Nietzsche to demonstrate the infusion of his most powerful thought with *ressentiment*, given both the absence in Nietzsche of any comparably psychologized alternative account of human emotion, and the implication in the very terminology of *ressentiment* that the supposed activity of emotion and the supposed passivity of perception are indistinguishable from one another, the degradation of *re-* already implicit in every sense of *sentiment*. But Nietzsche makes explicit about *décadence* what he leaves to be inferred about *ressentiment* — how absolutely its recognition, whether to celebrate or deprecate it, is implicated in the interminable logic of, among other things, homosexual attribution whereby *it takes one to know one*:

> If one is to be fair to [*The Wagner Case*] one has to suffer from the destiny of music as from an open wound. — *What* is it I suffer from when I suffer from the destiny of music? From this . . . that it is *décadence* music and no longer the flute of Dionysos. . . . Supposing, however, that one in this way feels the cause of music to be *one's own* cause, to be the history of *one's own* suffering, one will find this writing full of consideration and mild beyond measure. . . . — I have loved Wagner. — Ultimately this is an attack on a subtle "unknown" who could not easily be detected by another, in the sense and direction of my task. (*Ecce*, 119)

His aptitude for perceiving decadence is traced directly to his affinity with it; correspondingly, the ability of others to suspect it in him is traced to their own.

> I have a subtler sense for signs of ascent and decline than any man has ever had, I am the teacher *par excellence* in this matter — I know both, I am

> both. —My father died at the age of 36: he was delicate, lovable and morbid. . . . A doctor who treated me for some time as a nervous case said at last: "No! there is nothing wrong with your nerves, it is only I who am nervous.". . . —Convalescence means with me a long, all too long succession of years—it also unfortunately means relapse, deterioration, periods of *décadence*. Do I need to say that in questions of *décadence* I am *experienced*? I have spelled it out forwards and backwards. (*Ecce*, 38–39)

> What is strangest is this: after [the ordeal of a long sickness] one has a different taste—a *second* taste. Out of such abysses, also out of the abyss of great suspicion, one returns newborn, having shed one's skin, more ticklish and sarcastic, with a more delicate taste for joy, with a more tender tongue for all good things. . . more childlike and yet a hundred times more subtle than one has ever been before. (*Contra*, 681)

The relatively relaxed openness with which this epistemological structure is acknowledged means that decadence, unlike the *ressentiment* to which it otherwise seems so closely to correspond, can often be discussed in Nietzsche without mobilizing the fierce, accusatory machinery of projective denial:

> We Europeans of the day after tomorrow, we first-born of the twentieth century—with all our dangerous curiosity, our multiplicity and art of disguise, our mellow and as it were sugared cruelty in spirit and senses—*if* we are to have virtues we shall presumably have only such virtues as have learned to get along with our most secret and heartfelt inclinations, with our most fervent needs: very well, let us look for them within our labyrinths! (*Beyond*, 128)

Perhaps, indeed, the most exquisite erotic meditation of the nineteenth century lies spread out in this subcutaneous fermentation of the *décadent*, the "multitude of subtle shudders and trickles down to one's toes" (*Ecce*, 102–3) radiating around the point of a penetration whose object is both oneself and not. Where, for instance, to locate the boundary between self and other in Nietzsche's encounter with his own book *Daybreak*?

> Even now, when I chance to light on this book every sentence becomes for me a spike with which I again draw something incomparable out of the depths: its entire skin trembles with tender shudders of recollection. (*Ecce*, 95)

As Nietzsche says of his own ideal, "It is impossible for the Dionysian man not to understand any suggestion of whatever kind, he ignores no signal from the emotions. . . . He enters into every skin" (*Twilight*, 73).

Voluntarity/Addiction; Cosmopolitan/National

Richard Gilman's important book *Decadence* suggests that a lot of the powerful illusion of meaning that clings to the notion of "decadence"—a notion whose absolute conceptual inanition he demonstrates—seems to have to do with something more thematic, a useful and frightening suppleness in its relation to the visualized outline of the individual organism. "As an adjective," Gilman writes, for example,

> ["decadent"] functions now like a coating, a sleek enameled skin applied to the "unhealthy" but not fully sinful; as a noun it exists as a disturbing substance with shifting, blobby outlines, like some animated and threatening gel from a science-fiction horror film.[45]

In fact, although Gilman's book is not interested in pursuing such an inquiry it shows that "decadence" is a centrally symptomatic laboratory-word for any exploration of the consequences of the irreducible immanence of the anthropomorphic within theory itself. Certainly this would be true in Nietzsche. And although, as we have seen, Nietzsche's tropism toward a thematics of the organ of the skin—its fit, its integrity, its concealments, its breachableness, the surface it offers or doesn't offer for vicarious relations—although that doesn't by any means *necessarily* entail a stance of paranoid defensive exclusion, the all but built-in potential in such a metaphorics for such a stance will inevitably ramify into the political career of these metaphorics, as well.

Some of the most important headings under which the work of decadence-attribution fatefully entangled, in Nietzsche's thought as in the ambient culture, other definitional nexuses themselves under stress include the relations of natural to artificial, of health to illness, of voluntarity to addiction, of Jew to anti-Semite, of nationality to cosmopolitanism. Nietzsche's habitual association of Wagner's sentimentality with drugs and addiction, for instance, of Wagner's "narcotic art" (*Ecce*, 92) with the "poison" (*Ecce*, 61) of a "hashish world" of "strange, heavy, enveloping vapors" (*Will*, 555), comes out of the late nineteenth-century reclassification of opiate-related ingestion behaviors that had previously been at worst considered bad habits, under the new medicalizing aegis of *addictions* and the corresponding new social entity of drug subcultures—

---

45. Richard Gilman, *Decadence: The Strange Life of an Epithet* (New York: Farrar, Straus & Giroux, 1979), p. 175.

developments that both paralleled and entangled the new developments in homo/heterosexual definition.[46] So Nietzsche says of the "total aberration of the instinct" that can attract young German men to Wagner's art, "one piece of anti-nature downright *compels* a second" (*Ecce*, 91–92). In *The Picture of Dorian Gray* as in, for instance, *Dr. Jekyll and Mr. Hyde*, drug addiction is both a camouflage and an expression for the dynamics of same-sex desire and its prohibition: both books begin by looking like stories of erotic tensions between men, and end up as cautionary tales of solitary substance abusers. The two new taxonomies of the addict and the homosexual condense many of the same issues for late nineteenth-century culture: the old antisodomitic opposition between something called nature and that which is *contra naturam* blends with a treacherous apparent seamlessness into a new opposition between substances that are *natural* (e.g., "food") and those that are *artificial* (e.g., "drugs"); and hence into the characteristic twentieth-century way of problematizing almost every issue of will, dividing desires themselves between the natural, called "needs," and the artificial, called "addictions." It seems as though the reifying classification of certain particular, palpable substances as unnatural in their (artificially stimulating) relation to "natural" desire must necessarily throw into question the naturalness of any desire (Wilde: "Anything becomes a pleasure if one does it too often"),[47] so that Nietzsche's hypostatization of Will "itself," for example, would necessarily be part of the same historical process as the nineteenth-century isolation of addiction "itself."[48] Inexorably, from this grid of overlapping classifications — a purported taxonomic system that in fact does no more than chisel a historically specific point of stress into the unresolved issue of voluntarity — almost no individual practice in our culture by now remains exempt. The development of recent thought related to food is a good example: the concept of addiction to food led necessarily to that of addiction to dieting and in turn to that of addiction to exercise: each assertion of *will* made voluntarity itself appear problematical in a new area, with the consequence that that assertion of will itself came to appear

46. On this see Virginia Berridge and Griffith Edwards, *Opium and the People: Opiate Use in Nineteenth-Century England* (New Haven: Yale University Press, 1987), e.g., pp. 229–69.

47. *Dorian Gray*, p. 236.

48. This discussion of will and addiction, and what follows on opium as a figure for imperialist relations, builds on the discussion in Chapter 10 of *Between Men*, "Up the Postern Stair: *Edwin Drood* and the Homophobia of Empire," pp. 180–200.

addictive. (In fact, there has recently been a spate of journalism asserting that antiaddiction programs such as Alcoholics Anonymous and others modeled on it are addictive.) Some of the current self-help literature is explicit by now in saying that every extant form of behavior, desire, relationship, and consumption in our culture can accurately be described as addictive. Such a formulation does not, however, seem to lead these analysts to the perception that "addiction" names a counter-structure always internal to the ethicizing hypostatization of "voluntarity"; instead, it drives ever more blindly their compulsion to isolate some new space of the purely voluntary.

The "decadence" of drug addiction, in these late nineteenth-century texts, intersects with two kinds of bodily definition, each itself suffused with the homo/heterosexual problematic. The first of these is the national economic body; the second is the medical body. From the Opium Wars of the mid-nineteenth century up to the current details of U.S. relations with Turkey, Colombia, Panama, Peru, and the Nicaraguan Contras, the drama of "foreign substances" and the drama of the new imperialisms and the new nationalisms have been quite inextricable. The integrity of (new and contested) national borders, the reifications of national will and vitality, were readily organized around these narratives of introjection. From as far back as Mandeville, moreover, the opium product—the highly condensed, portable, expensive, commerce-intensive substance seen as having a unique ability to pry the trajectory of demand conclusively and increasingly apart from the homeostasis of biological need—was spectacularly available to serve as a representation for emerging intuitions about commodity fetishism. The commodity-based orientalism of *Dorian Gray*, for instance, radiates outward from "a green paste, waxy in lustre, the odour curiously heavy and persistent" that represents an ultimate recourse for Dorian—outward through its repository, "a small Chinese box of black and gold-dust lacquer, elaborately wrought, the sides patterned with curved waves, and the silken cords hung with round crystals and tasselled inplaited metal threads"—outward through the "Florentine cabinet, made out of ebony, and inlaid with ivory and blue lapis," from whose triangular secret drawer his fingers move "instinctively" to extract the box (201–2). Like Wagnerian opera, *Dorian Gray* accomplished for its period the performative work of enabling a European community of gay mutual recognition and self-constitution at least partly by popularizing a consumerism that already derived an economic model from the traffic in drugs.

Take an example from the prodigally extravagant guide to lifestyle, interior decoration, and textiles offered in *Dorian Gray*'s aptly titled Chapter 11. A whole set of epistemological compactions around desire, identification, and the responsive, all but paranoid mutuality attributed to gay recognition are condensed in the almost compulsive evocation there, even more than elsewhere in the novel, of the drug-tinged adjectives "curious" and "subtle," two of the Paterian epithets that trace in *Dorian Gray* the homosexual-homophobic path of simultaneous epistemological heightening and ontological evacuation. Unlike the cognate labels attached so nearly inalienably to Claggart in *Billy Budd*, these adjectives float freely through the text: "some curious dream" (8), "this curious artistic idolatry" (17), "throbbing to curious pulses" (26), "a subtle magic" (26), "his subtle smile" (27), "a curious charm" (28), "a subtle fluid or a strange perfume" (44), "so curious a chance" (44), "women . . . are curious" (55), "a mad curiosity" (57), "a curious influence" (61), "some curious romance" (63), "a subtle sense of pleasure" (64), "poisons so subtle" (66), "the curious hard logic of passion" (66), "some curious race-instinct" (77), "curious Renaissance tapestries" (102), "pleasures subtle and secret" (119), "the curious secret of his life" (136), "curious unpictured sins whose very mystery lent them their subtlety and their charm" (137), "metaphors as monstrous as orchids, and as subtle in colour" (140), "subtle symphonic arrangements of exotic flowers" (144), "that curious indifference that is not incompatible with a real ardour of temperament" (147), "their subtle fascination" (148), "a curious pleasure" (148), "a curious delight" (150), and so on apparently endlessly. Besides being almost violently piquant and uninformative, "curious" shares with "subtle" a built-in epistemological indecision or doubling. Each of them can describe, as the *OED* puts it, "an object of interest": among the *OED* meanings for this sense of "curious" are "made with care or art, delicate, *recherché*, elaborate, unduly minute, abstruse, subtle, exquisite, exciting curiosity . . . queer. (The ordinary current objective sense)." At the same time, however, each adjective also describes, and in almost the same terms, the quality of the perception brought by the attentive subject *to* such an object: for "curious" "as a subjective quality of persons," the *OED* lists, e.g., "careful, attentive, anxious, cautious, inquisitive, prying, subtle." The thing known is a reflection of the impulse toward knowing it, then, and each describable only as the excess, "wrought" intensiveness of that knowledge-situation.

In their usage in the fetish-wrought Chapter 11, the epithets record, on the one hand, the hungrily inventive raptness of the curious or subtle perceiving eye or brain; and, on the other, the more than answering intricacy of the curious or subtle objects perceived—imported or plundered artifacts, in these typifying cases, whose astonishing density of jewels and "wrought" work such as embroidery testify, more than to taste, to the overt atrocities they sometimes depict, and most of all to the "monstrous," "strange," "terrible" (I use the Wildean terms) exactions of booty in precious minerals, tedious labor, and sheer wastage of (typically female) eyesight, levied on the Orient by the nations of Europe. "Yet, after some time, he wearied of them, and would sit in his box at the Opera, either alone or with Lord Henry, listening in rapt pleasure to 'Tannhauser'" (150).

Still, it would be reductive to confine the national question embodied in the sexuality of *Dorian Gray* to an exercise in orientalism. Indeed, the very patency of Wilde's gay-affirming and gay-occluding orientalism renders it difficult to turn back and see the outlines of the sexual body and the national body sketched by his *occidentalism*. With orientalism so ready-to-hand a rubric for the relation to the Other, it is difficult (Wilde seems to want to make it difficult) to resist seeing the desired English body as simply the domestic Same. Yet the sameness of this Same—or put another way, the *homo-* nature of this sexuality—is no less open to question than the self-identicalness of the national borders of the domestic. After all, the question of the national in Wilde's own life only secondarily—though profoundly—involved the question of overseas empire in relation to European *patria*. To the contrary: Wilde, as an ambitious Irish man, and the son, intimate, and protégé of a celebrated Irish nationalist poet, can only have had as a fundamental element of his own sense of self an exquisitely exacerbated sensitivity to how by turns porous, brittle, elastic, chafing, embracing, exclusive, murderous, in every way contestable and contested were the membranes of "domestic" national definition signified by the ductile and elusive terms England, Britain, Ireland. Indeed, the consciousness of foundational and/or incipient national *difference* already internal to national *definition* must have been part of what Wilde literally embodied, in the expressive, specularized, and symptomatic relation in which he avowedly stood to his age. As a magus in the worship of the "slim rose-gilt soul"—the individual or generic figure of the "slim thing, gold-haired like an angel" that stood at the same time for a sexuality, a sensibility, a class, and a narrowly English national type—Wilde, whose own physical make was of an opposite sort and (in that context) an infinitely less appetizing, desirable, and placeable one, showed his usual uncanny courage ("his usual uncanny courage," *anglice* chutzpah) in foregrounding his own body so insistently as an index to such erotic and political meanings. Wilde's alienizing physical heritage of unboundable bulk from his Irish nationalist mother, of a louche swarthiness from his Celticizing father, underlined with every self-foregrounding gesture of his person and *persona* the fragility, unlikelihood, and strangeness — at the same time, the transformative reperceptualizing power — of the new "*homo-*" homosexual imagining of male-male desire. By the same pressure, it dramatized the uncouth nonequivalence of an English national body with a British with an Irish, as domestic grounds from which to launch a stable understanding of national/imperial relations.

For Nietzsche, more explicitly antinationalist than Wilde, virulently anti-German, and by the later 1880s virulently anti–anti-Semitic (which is hardly to say he was not anti-Semitic), the conjunction of the drug topic with the national also evokes a dangerous rhetoric of the double-edged. He writes retrospectively, for instance:

> If one wants to get free from an unendurable pressure one needs hashish. Very well, I needed Wagner. Wagner is the counter-poison to everything German *par excellence* — still poison, I do not dispute it. . . . To become healthier — that is *retrogression* in the case of a nature such as Wagner. . . . The world is poor for him who has never been sick enough for this "voluptuousness of hell.". . . I think I know better than anyone what tremendous things Wagner was capable of, the fifty worlds of strange delights to which no one but he had wings; and as I am strong enough to turn even the most questionable and perilous things to my own advantage and thus to become stronger, I call Wagner the great benefactor of my life. (*Ecce*, 61)[49]

A characteristic gesture in Nietzsche is to summon up the spectre of an addiction, but at the same time to make an assertion of transcendent or instrumental will that might be paraphrased as "but as for me, I can take it or leave it." The ability to *use* a potentially addictive stimulus without surrendering to it is attributed to a laudable strength. Thus, for instance, "Grand passion uses and uses up convictions, it does not submit to

49. Or of the English, "To finer nostrils even this English Christianity possesses a true English by-scent of the spleen and alcoholic excess against which it is with good reason employed as an antidote — the subtler poison against the coarser: and indeed a subtle poisoning is in the case of coarse peoples already a certain progress" (*Beyond*, 165).

them—it knows itself sovereign" (*Anti*, 172). *Zarathustra* says that sex is "only for the wilted, a sweet poison; for the lion-willed, however, the great invigoration of the heart and the reverently reserved wine of wines" (*Zarathustra*, 188).[50] The equivocal way Nietzsche describes the relation of Judaism to decadence has the same structure as the way he describes his own relation to the potentially addictive:

> Considered psychologically, the Jewish nation is a nation of the toughest vital energy which, placed in impossible circumstances, voluntarily, from the profoundest shrewdness in self-preservation, took the side of all *décadence* instincts—*not* as being dominated by them but because it divined in them a power by means of which one can prevail *against* "the world." The Jews are the counterparts of *décadents*: they have been compelled to *act* as *décadents* to the point of illusion. . . . For the kind of man who desires to attain power through Judaism and Christianity, the *priestly* kind, *décadence* is only a *means*. (*Anti*, 135)

And any danger posed by nineteenth-century Jews to nineteenth-century Europe occurs because "that which is called a 'nation' in Europe today and is actually more of a *res facta* than *nata* (indeed sometimes positively resembles a *res ficta et picta*—) is in any case something growing, young, easily disruptable, not yet a race, let alone such an *aere perennius* as the Jewish" (*Beyond*, 163).

As always in Nietzsche, his implacable resistance to giving stable figuration to even the possibility of a minoritizing homosexual identity makes one hesitate to read into these passages what one might look for in, say, Proust. But nor is the figuration so very stable in Proust. For Proust, whose plots of Dreyfusism and of gay recognition are the organizing principles for one another as they are for the volumes through which they ramify, the numinous identification of male homosexuality with a *pre*-national, premodern dynastic cosmopolitanism, through the figure of Charlus as much as through the Jews, is no more than haunted by the spectre of a sort of gay Zionism or pan-Germanism, a normalizing politics on the nominally ethnic model that would bring homosexual identity itself under the sway of what Nietzsche called "that *névrose nationale* with which Europe is sick" (*Ecce*, 121). Each of these writers, at any rate, seems to use an erotics of decadence to denaturalize the body of

---

50. More: a section of *The Genealogy of Morals* juxtaposes, without confronting, the "drugged tranquillity" of the "impotent and oppressed" with the healthy "power of oblivion" of "strong, rich temperaments" (*Genealogy*, 172–73).

the national per se. But, as Nietzsche's pseudo-psychiatric diagnostic stance in this memorable formulation may already suggest, the standpoint from which that denaturalization proceeds may itself present new problems.

Health/Illness

The most fateful aspect of Nietzsche's understanding of decadence is his philosophical reliance on a medical model of the human body. As we have seen, the thematics of decadence does not, of itself, entail for him any *necessarily* phobic ethical valuation—and this is true even as that thematics is crossed and recrossed by what had been and what were becoming the main signifiers of male-male-loving acts and identities. Indeed, Nietzsche's writing is rich in what amount to—in some cases, what explicitly present themselves as—avowals of identification with and desire for the signifieds of decadence. Such avowals barely loosen, however, the horrifyingly potent knot of accusatory decadence-attribution, so long as authority over that process is vested, as the anthropomorphizing logic of the metaphor historically required that it be, in an embattled and expansive expert science of health and hygiene.

It can be argued, after all, that Nietzsche made only one disastrously mistaken wager with his culture: the wager that the progress he had painfully made in wrestling the explicit bases of his thought inch by inch away from the gravely magnetic axis of good/evil could be most durably guaranteed by battening them to the apparently alternative, scientifically guaranteed axis of health/illness or vitality/morbidity. ("Whoever does not agree with me on this point I consider *infected*" [*Ecce*, 97].) The genocidal potential in his thought seems to have been retroactivated only through a cultural development that, however predictable it might have seemed to others, completely blindsided him. That is the indefatigably sinister hide-and-seek that ethicizing impulses have played in this century behind the mask of the human and life sciences. The hide-and-seek has depended, in turn, on the invisible elasticity by which, in the developments toward eugenic thought around and after the turn of the century, reifications such as "the strong," "the weak," "the nation," "civilization," particular classes, "the race," and even "life" itself have assumed the vitalized anthropomorphic outlines of the individual male body and object of medical expertise. For instance:

To refrain from mutual injury, mutual violence, mutual exploitation, to equate one's own will with that of another: this may in a certain rough sense become good manners between individuals if the conditions for it are present (namely if their strength and value standards are in fact similar and they both belong to *one* body). As soon as there is a desire to take this principle further, however, and if possible even as the *fundamental principle of society*, it at once reveals itself for what it is: as the will to the *denial* of life, as the principle of dissolution and decay. One has to think this matter thoroughly through to the bottom and resist all sentimental weakness: life itself is *essentially* appropriation, injury, overpowering of the strange and weaker, suppression, severity, imposition of one's own forms, incorporation and, at the least and mildest, exploitation—but why should one always have to employ precisely those words which have from of old been stamped with a slanderous intention? Even that body within which, as was previously assumed, individuals treat one another as equals—this happens in every healthy aristocracy—must, if it is a living and not a decaying body, itself do all that to other bodies which the individuals within it refrain from doing to one another: it will have to be the will to power incarnate, it will want to grow, expand, draw to itself, gain ascendancy—not out of any morality or immorality, but because it *lives*, and because life *is* will to power. On no point, however, is the common European consciousness more reluctant to learn than it is here; everywhere one enthuses, even under scientific disguises, about coming states of society in which there will be "no more exploitation"—that sounds to my ears like promising a life in which there will be no organic functions. "Exploitation" does not pertain to a corrupt or imperfect or primitive society: it pertains to the *essence* of the living thing as a fundamental organic function, it is a consequence of the intrinsic will to power which is precisely the will of life. (*Beyond*, 174–75)

From the body of the "individual" to the body of the "healthy aristocracy" to "the will of life" itself: these invocations are no unproblematical metonymies, but anthropomorphic pseudo-equivalencies whose slippery scientism conceals the very violence it purports to celebrate.

Thus when Nietzsche comes, in a late book, to offer a description of the actual body of Christ, the terms he chooses are both tellingly congruent with his own decadent self-descriptions and at the same time tellingly distanced through the figuration and narrative implicit in the medical model in its most dangerously elastic incarnations.

To make a *hero* of Jesus! —And what a worse misunderstanding is the word "genius"! To speak with the precision of the physiologist a quite different word would rather be in place here: the word idiot. We recognize a condition of morbid susceptibility of the *sense of touch* which makes it shrink back in horror from every contact, every grasping of a firm object. Translate such a physiological *habitus* into its ultimate logic—an instinctive hatred of *every* reality. . . .

I call it a sublime further evolution of hedonism on a thoroughly morbid basis. (*Anti*, 141–42)

The word "idiot" here points in the direction of the blank male cynosure of erotic flux and surplus: "One has to regret that no Dostoyevsky lived in the neighbourhood of this most interesting *décadent*; I mean someone who could feel the thrilling fascination of such a combination of the sublime, the sick and the childish" (*Anti*, 143). Nothing in Nietzsche has licensed one to read this as merely a sneer; indeed, nothing has quite licensed one to read it as not about Nietzsche himself. The word "idiot" points as well, however, by the same gesture toward the taxonomic and ultimately eugenic sciences of the "morbid"—the sciences that move imperceptibly back and forth from delineating the outlines and describing the prognosis of the individual body to enforcing an ethics of collective hygiene, on an infinitely elastic scale, in response to a chimera of demographic degeneration and a fatally tacit swarm of phylogenetic fantasies. It points to the genocidal space of slippage, in a single page of *Beyond Good and Evil*, among the individual man, the "corruption of *the European race*," and "the will to make of *man* a sublime *abortion*" (*Beyond*, 70–71; emphasis added).

It may be, then, that much of the heritage that today sets "sentimentality" and its ever more elusive, indeed, ever more impossible Other at the defining center of so many judgments, political as well as aesthetic, impinging so today on every issue of national identity, postcolonial populism, religious fundamentalism, high versus mass culture, relations among races, to children, to other species, and to the earth, as well as most obviously between and within genders and sexualities—it may be that the structuring of so much cultural work and apperception around this impossible criterion represents a kind of residue or remainder of erotic relations to the male body, relations excluded from but sucked into supplementarity to the tacitly ethicized medical anthropomorphizations that have wielded so much power over our century.

That antisentimentality can never be an adequate Other for "the sentimental," but only a propellant for its contagious scissions and figurations, means that the sources of courage or comfort for our homophobically galvanized century will remain peculiarly vulnerable to the impossibility of the male first person, the unexpected bathos of the anthropomorphic—for those who wish, in the words W. H. Auden wrote in 1933,

> That later we, though parted then,
> May still recall these evenings when
> Fear gave his watch no look;
> The lion griefs loped from the shade
> And on our knees their muzzles laid
> And death put down his book.[51]

51. From "Out on the lawn I lie in bed" (1933), pp. 29–32, *W. H. Auden: Selected Poems*, ed. Edward Mendelson (New York: Random House/Vintage, 1979); lines quoted are from p. 30. I encountered these lines, not reading Auden, but in the obituary listings in the *New York Times*, July 23, 1988, where someone had purchased space to reproduce them as an unsigned memorial to a man, who had died the previous day, named Nick Knowlden.

4

The Beast in the Closet
James and the Writing of Homosexual Panic

Historicizing Male Homosexual Panic

At the age of twenty-five, D. H. Lawrence was excited about the work of James M. Barrie. He felt it helped him understand himself and explain himself. "*Do* read Barrie's *Sentimental Tommy* and *Tommy and Grizel*," he wrote Jessie Chambers. "They'll help you understand how it is with me. I'm in exactly the same predicament."[1]

Fourteen years later, though, Lawrence placed Barrie among a group of writers whom he considered appropriate objects of authorial violence. "What's the good of being hopeless, so long as one has a hob-nailed boot to kick [them] with? *Down with the Poor in Spirit!* A war! But the Subtlest, most intimate warfare. Smashing the face of what one *knows* is rotten."[2]

It was not only in the intimate warfares of one writer that the years 1910 to 1924 marked changes. But Lawrence's lurch toward a brutal, virilizing disavowal of his early identification with Barrie's sexually irresolute characters reflects two rather different trajectories: first, of course, changes in the historical and intellectual context within which British literature could be read; but second, a hatingly crystallized literalization, as *between* men, of what had been in Barrie's influential novels portrayed as exactly "the Subtlest, most intimate warfare" *within* a man. Barrie's novel sequence was also interested, as Lawrence was not, in the mutilating effects of this masculine civil war on women.

The previous two chapters have attempted to suggest, in as great a variety of ways as possible, how pervasively the issues of male homo/heterosexual definition could—or, properly, *must*—be read through the ramified interstitial relations that have constituted modern Euro-

1. Lawrence to Jessie Chambers, August 1910, *The Collected Letters of D. H. Lawrence*, ed. Harry T. Moore (London: W. H. Heinemann, 1962), 1: 63.
2. Lawrence to Rolf Gardiner, August 9, 1924, in *The Collected Letters*, 2: 801.

American culture. In this chapter (which represents genetically, as it happens, the inaugurating investigation of the present study), I argue that the Barrie to whom Lawrence reacted with such volatility and finally with such virulence was writing out of a post-Romantic tradition of fictional meditations on the subject quite specifically of male homosexual panic. The writers whose work I will adduce here include—besides Barrie—Thackeray, George Du Maurier, and James: an odd mix of big and little names. The cheapnesses and compromises of this tradition will, however, turn out to be as important as its freshest angularities, since one of the functions of a tradition *is* to create a path of least resistance (or at the last resort, a pathology of least resistance) for the expression of previously inchoate material.

An additional problem: this tradition was an infusing rather than a generically distinct one in British letters, and it is thus difficult to discriminate it with confidence or to circumscribe it within the larger stream of nineteenth- and early twentieth-century fictional writing. But the tradition is worth tracing partly on that very account, as well: the difficult questions of generic and thematic embodiment resonate so piercingly with another set of difficult questions, those precisely of sexual definition and embodiment. The supposed oppositions that characteristically structure this writing—the respectable "versus" the bohemian, the cynical "versus" the sentimental, the provincial "versus" the cosmopolitan, the anesthetized "versus" the sexual—seem to be, among other things, recastings and explorations of another pseudo-opposition that had come by the middle of the nineteenth century to be cripplingly knotted into the guts of British men and, through them, into the lives of women. The name of this pseudo-opposition, when it came to have a name, was, as we have seen, homosexual "versus" heterosexual.

Recent sexual historiography by, for instance, Alan Bray in his *Homosexuality in Renaissance England* suggests that until about the time of the Restoration, homophobia in England, while intense, was for the most part highly theologized, was anathematic in tone and structure, and had little cognitive bite as a way for people to perceive and experience their own and their neighbors' actual activities.[3] Homosexuality "was not conceived as part of the created order at all," Bray writes, but as "part of its dissolution. And as such it was not a sexuality in its own right, but

---

3. Bray, *Homosexuality*, chapters 1–3. Note the especially striking example on pp. 68–69, 76–77.

existed as a potential for confusion and disorder in one undivided sexuality."[4] If sodomy was the most characteristic expression of antinature or the Anti-Christ itself, it was nevertheless, or perhaps for that very reason, not an explanation that sprang easily to mind for those sounds from the bed next to one's own—or even for the pleasures of one's own bed. Before the end of the eighteenth century, however, Bray shows, with the beginnings of a crystallized male homosexual role and male homosexual culture, a much sharper-eyed and acutely psychologized secular homophobia was current.

I argued in *Between Men* that this development was important not only for the persecutory regulation of a nascent minority population of distinctly homosexual men but also for the regulation of the male homosocial bonds that structure *all* culture—at any rate, all public or heterosexual culture.[5] This argument follows Lévi-Strauss in defining culture itself, like marriage, in terms of a "total relationship of exchange . . . not established between a man and a woman, but between two groups of men, [in which] the woman figures only as one of the objects in the exchange, not as one of the partners";[6] or follows Heidi Hartmann in defining patriarchy itself as "*relations between men*, which have a material base, and which, though hierarchical, establish or create interdependence and solidarity among men that enable them to dominate women."[7] To this extent, it makes sense that a newly active concept, a secular, psychologized homophobia, that seemed to offer a new proscriptive or descriptive purchase on the whole continuum of male homosocial bonds would be a pivotal and embattled concept indeed.

Bray describes the earliest legal persecutions of the post-Restoration gay male subculture, centered in gathering places called "molly houses," as being random and, in his word, "pogrom"-like in structure.[8] I would emphasize the specifically terroristic or exemplary workings of this structure: because a given homosexual man could not know whether or not to

4. Bray, *Homosexuality*, p. 25.

5. *Between Men*, pp. 83–96.

6. Claude Lévi-Strauss, *The Elementary Structures of Kinship* (Boston: Beacon Press, 1969), p. 115; also quoted and well discussed in Rubin, "The Traffic in Women," pp. 157–210.

7. Heidi Hartmann, "The Unhappy Marriage of Marxism and Feminism: Towards a More Progressive Union," in Lydia Sargent, ed., *Women and Revolution: A Discussion of the Unhappy Marriage of Marxism and Feminism* (Boston: South End Press, 1981), p. 14; emphasis added.

8. Bray, *Homosexuality*, chapter 4.

expect to be an object of legal violence, the legal enforcement had a disproportionately wide effect. At the same time, however, an opening was made for a subtler strategy in response, a kind of ideological pincers-movement that would extend manyfold the impact of this theatrical enforcement. As *Between Men* argues, under this strategy (or, perhaps better put, in this space of strategic potential),

> not only must homosexual men be unable to ascertain whether they are to be the objects of "random" homophobic violence, but no man must be able to ascertain that he is not (that his bonds are not) homosexual. In this way, a relatively small exertion of physical or legal compulsion potentially rules great reaches of behavior and filiation. . . .
>
> So-called "homosexual panic" is the most private, psychologized form in which many . . . western men experience their vulnerability to the social pressure of homophobic blackmail.[9]

Thus, at least since the eighteenth century in England and America, the continuum of male homosocial bonds has been brutally structured by a secularized and psychologized homophobia, which has excluded certain shiftingly and more or less arbitrarily defined segments of the continuum from participating in the overarching male entitlement—in the complex web of male power over the production, reproduction, and exchange of goods, persons, and meanings. I argue that the historically shifting, and precisely the arbitrary and self-contradictory, nature of the way *homosexuality* (along with its predecessor terms) has been defined in relation to the rest of the male homosocial spectrum has been an exceedingly potent and embattled locus of power over the entire range of male bonds, and perhaps especially over those that define themselves, not *as* homosexual, but *as against* the homosexual. Because the paths of male entitlement, especially in the nineteenth century, required certain intense male bonds that were not readily distinguishable from the most reprobated bonds, an endemic and ineradicable state of what I am calling male homosexual panic became the normal condition of male heterosexual entitlement.

Some consequences of this approach to male relationships should perhaps be made more explicit. To begin with, as I have suggested earlier, the approach is not founded on an essential differentiation between "basically homosexual" and "basically heterosexual" men, aside from the

9. *Between Men*, pp. 88–89.

historically small group of consciously and self-acceptingly homosexual
men, who are no longer susceptible to homosexual panic as I define it
here. If such compulsory relationships as male friendship, mentorship,
admiring identification, bureaucratic subordination, and heterosexual
rivalry all involve forms of investment that force men into the arbitrarily
mapped, self-contradictory, and anathema-riddled quicksands of the
middle distance of male homosocial desire, then it appears that men enter
into adult masculine entitlement only through acceding to the permanent
threat that the small space they have cleared for themselves on this terrain
may always, just as arbitrarily and with just as much justification, be
foreclosed.

The result of men's accession to this double bind is, first, the acute
manipulability, through the fear of one's own "homosexuality," of accultu-
rated men; and second, a reservoir of potential for *violence* caused by the
self-ignorance that this regime constitutively enforces. The historical
emphasis on enforcement of homophobic rules in the armed services in,
for instance, England and the United States supports this analysis. In
these institutions, where both men's manipulability and their potential for
violence are at the highest possible premium, the *pre*scription of the most
intimate male bonding and the *pro*scription of (the remarkably cognate)
"homosexuality" are both stronger than in civilian society—are, in fact,
close to absolute.

My specification of widespread, endemic male homosexual panic as a
post-Romantic phenomenon, rather than as coeval with the beginnings,
under homophobic pressure, of a distinctive male homosexual culture a
century or so earlier, has to do with (what I read as) the centrality of the
paranoid Gothic[10] as the literary genre in which homophobia found its
most apt and ramified embodiment. Homophobia found in the paranoid
Gothic a genre of its own, not because the genre provided a platform for
expounding an already formed homophobic ideology—of course, it did
no such thing—but through a more active, polylogic engagement of
"private" with "public" discourses, as in the wildly dichotomous play
around solipsism and intersubjectivity of a male paranoid plot like that of

10. By "paranoid Gothic" I mean Romantic novels in which a male hero is in a close,
usually murderous relation to another male figure, in some respects his "double," to whom
he seems to be mentally transparent. Examples of the paranoid Gothic include, besides
Frankenstein, Ann Radcliffe's *The Italian*, William Godwin's *Caleb Williams*, and James
Hogg's *Confessions of a Justified Sinner*. This tradition is discussed more fully in my
Between Men, chapters 5 and 6.

Frankenstein. The transmutability of the intrapsychic with the intersubjective in these plots where one man's mind could be read by that of the feared and desired other; the urgency and violence with which these plots reformed large, straggly, economically miscellaneous families such as the Frankensteins in the ideologically hypostatized image of the tight oedipal family; and then the extra efflorescence of violence with which the remaining female term in these triangular families was elided, leaving, as in *Frankenstein*, a residue of two potent male figures locked in an epistemologically indissoluble clench of will and desire—through these means, the paranoid Gothic powerfully signified, at the very moment of crystallization of the modern, capitalism-marked oedipal family, the inextricability from that formation of a strangling double bind in male homosocial constitution. Put another way, the usefulness of Freud's formulation, in the case of Dr. Schreber, that paranoia in men results from the repression of their homosexual desire,[11] has nothing to do with a classification of the paranoid Gothic in terms of "latent" or "overt" "homosexual" "types," but everything to do with the foregrounding, under the specific, foundational historic conditions of the early Gothic, of intense male homosocial desire as at once the most compulsory and the most prohibited of social bonds.

To inscribe that vulgar classification supposedly derived from Freud on what was arguably the founding moment of the worldview and social constitution that he codified would hardly be enlightening. Still, the newly formulated and stressed "universal" imperative/prohibition attached to male homosocial desire, even given that its claim for universality already excluded (the female) half of the population, nevertheless required, of course, further embodiment and specification in new taxonomies of personality and character. These taxonomies would mediate between the supposedly classless, "personal" entities of the ideological fictions and the particular, class-specified, economically inscribed lives that they influenced; and at the same time, the plethoric and apparently comprehensive pluralism of the taxonomies occluded, through the illusion of choice, the overarching existence of the double bind that structured them all.

Recent gay male historiography, influenced by Foucault, has been especially good at unpacking and interpreting those parts of the nineteenth-century systems of classification that clustered most closely around

11. Freud, "Psycho-Analytic Notes upon an Autobiographical Account of a Case of Paranoia."

what current taxonomies construe as "the homosexual." The "sodomite," the "invert," the "homosexual," the "heterosexual" himself, all are objects of historically and institutionally explicable construction. In the discussion of male homosexual *panic*, however — the treacherous middle stretch of the modern homosocial continuum, and the terrain from whose wasting rigors *only* the homosexual-identified man is at all exempt — a different and less distinctly sexualized range of categories needs to be opened up. Again, however, it bears repeating that the object of doing that is not to arrive at a more accurate or up-to-date assignment of "diagnostic" categories, but to understand better the broad field of forces within which masculinity — and thus, *at least* for men, humanity itself — could (can) at a particular moment construct itself.

I want to suggest here that with Thackeray and other early and mid-Victorians a character classification of "the bachelor" came into currency, a type that for some men both narrowed the venue, and at the same time startlingly desexualized the question, of male sexual choice.[12] Later in the century, when a medical and social-science model of "the homosexual man" had institutionalized this classification for a few men, the broader issue of endemic male homosexual panic was again up for grabs in a way that was newly redetached from character taxonomy and was more apt to be described narratively, as a decisive moment of choice in the developmental labyrinth of the generic individual (male). As the unmarried Gothic hero had once been, the bachelor became once again the representative man: James wrote in his 1881 *Notebook*, "I take [London] as an artist and as a bachelor; as one who has the passion of observation and whose business is the study of human life."[13] In the work of such writers as Du Maurier, Barrie, and James, among others, male homosexual panic was acted out as a sometimes agonized sexual anesthesia that was damaging to both its male subjects and its female non-objects. The paranoid Gothic itself, a generic structure that seemed to have been domesticated in the development of the bachelor taxonomy, returned in some of these works as a formally intrusive and incongruous, but notably persistent, literary element.[14]

12. For more on bachelors see Fredric Jameson, *Wyndham Lewis: Fables of Aggression* (Berkeley and Los Angeles: University of California Press, 1979), chapter 2; also, cited in Jameson, Jean Borie, *Le Célibataire français* (Paris: Le Sagittaire, 1976); and Edward Said, *Beginnings* (New York: Basic Books, 1975), pp. 137–52.

13. Henry James, *The Notebooks of Henry James*, ed. F. O. Matthiessen and Kenneth B. Murdock (New York: Oxford University Press, 1947), p. 28.

14. Bachelor literature in which the paranoid Gothic — or, more broadly, the supernatural — makes a reappearance includes, besides Du Maurier's *Trilby* and numerous

Meet Mr. Batchelor

"Batchelor, my elderly Tiresias, are you turned into a lovely
young lady *par hasard*?"
"Get along, you absurd Trumperian professor!" say I.
Thackeray, *Lovel the Widower*

In Victorian fiction it is perhaps the figure of the urban bachelor, especially as popularized by Thackeray, who personifies the most deflation-
ary tonal contrast to the eschatological harrowings and epistemological
doublings of the paranoid Gothic. Where the Gothic hero had been
solipsistic, the bachelor hero is selfish. Where the Gothic hero had raged,
the bachelor hero bitches. Where the Gothic hero had been suicidally
inclined, the bachelor hero is a hypochondriac. The Gothic hero ranges
from euphoria to despondency; the bachelor hero, from the eupeptic to
the dyspeptic.

Structurally, moreover, whereas the Gothic hero had personified the
concerns and tones of an entire genre, the bachelor is a distinctly circumscribed and often a marginalized figure in the books he inhabits. Sometimes, like Archie Clavering, Major Pendennis, and Jos Sedley, he is simply
a minor character; but even when he is putatively the main character, like
Surtees's hero "Soapey" Sponge, he more often functions as a clotheshorse
or comic place-marker in a discursive plot.[15] The bachelor hero can only
be mock-heroic; not merely diminished and parodic himself, he sym-
bolizes the diminution and undermining of certain heroic and totalizing
possibilities of generic embodiment. The novel of which the absurd Jos
Sedley is not the hero is a novel *without* a hero.

It makes sense, I think, to see the development of this odd character the
bachelor, and his dissolutive relation to romantic genre, as, among other
things, a move toward the recuperation as character taxonomy of the
endemic double bind of male homosexual panic that had been acted out
in the paranoid Gothic as plot and structure. This recuperation is perhaps
best described as, in several senses, a domestication. Most obviously, in
the increasingly stressed nineteenth-century bourgeois dichotomy between domestic female space and extrafamilial, political and economic
male space, the bachelor is at least partly feminized by his attention to and

---

James stories such as "The Jolly Corner," George Eliot's *The Lifted Veil*, Robert Louis
Stevenson's *Dr. Jekyll and Mr. Hyde*, and Kipling stories such as "In the Same Boat."
    15. In, respectively, Trollope's *The Claverings* and Thackeray's *Pendennis* and *Vanity
Fair*; "Soapey" Sponge is in R. S. Surtees's *Mr. Sponge's Sporting Tour*.

interest in domestic concerns. (At the same time, though, his intimacy with clubland and bohemia gives him a special passport to the world of men, as well.) Then, too, the disruptive and self-ignorant potential for violence in the Gothic hero is replaced in the bachelor hero by physical timidity and, often, by a high value on introspection and by (at least partial) self-knowledge. Finally, the bachelor is housebroken by the severing of his connections with a discourse of genital sexuality.

The first-person narrators of much of Thackeray's later fiction are good examples of the urban bachelor in his major key. Even though the Pendennis who narrates *The Newcomes* and *Philip* is supposedly married, his voice, personality, and tastes are strikingly similar to those of the archetypal Thackeray bachelor, the narrator of his novella *Lovel the Widower* (1859) — a man called, by no coincidence at all, Mr. Batchelor. (Of course, Thackeray's own ambiguous marital status — married, but to a permanently sanitarium-bound, psychotically depressed woman — facilitated this slippage in the narrators whom Thackeray seemed to model on himself.) Mr. Batchelor is, as James says of Olive Chancellor, unmarried by every implication of his being. He is compulsively garrulous about marital prospects, his own (past and present) among others, but always in a tone that points, in one way or another, to the absurdity of the thought. For instance, his hyperbolic treatment of an early romantic disappointment is used both to mock and undermine the importance to him of that incident and, at the same time, by invidious comparison, to discredit in advance the seriousness of any later involvement:

> Some people have the small-pox twice; *I do not*. In my case, if a heart is broke, it's broke: if a flower is withered, it's withered. If I choose to put my grief in a ridiculous light, why not? why do you suppose I am going to make a tragedy of such an old, used-up, battered, stale, vulgar, trivial every-day subject as a jilt who plays with a man's passion, and laughs at him, and leaves him? Tragedy indeed! Oh, yes! poison — black-edged note-paper — Waterloo Bridge — one more unfortunate, and so forth! No: if she goes, let her go! — *si celeres quatit pennas*, I puff the what-d'ye-call-it away![16]

The plot of *Lovel* — slight enough — is an odd local station on the subway from *Liber Amoris* to Proust. Mr. Batchelor, when he lived in lodgings,

---

16. *Lovel the Widower*, in *Works of Thackeray*, vol. 1 (New York: National Library, n.d.), chapter 2. Subsequent references to this novel are to this edition and are cited parenthetically in the text by chapter number.

had had a slightly tender friendship with his landlady's daughter Bessy, who at that time helped support her family by dancing in a music hall. A few years later, he gets her installed as governess in the home of his friend Lovel, the widower. Several men in the vicinity are rivals for Bessy's affections: the local doctor, the shrewd autodidact butler, and, halfheartedly, Batchelor himself. When a visiting bounder attacks Bessy's reputation and her person, Batchelor, who is eavesdropping on the scene, fatally hesitates in coming to her defense, suddenly full of doubts about her sexual purity ("Fiends and anguish! he had known her before" [chapter 5]) and his own eagerness for marriage. Finally it is the autodidact butler who rescues her, and Lovel himself who marries her.

If the treatment of the romantic possibilities that are supposedly at the heart of *Lovel* has a tendency to dematerialize them almost before they present themselves, the treatment of certain other physical pleasures is given an immediacy that seems correspondingly heightened. In fact, the substantiality of physical pleasure is explicitly linked to the state of bachelorhood.

> To lie on that comfortable, cool bachelor's bed. . . . Once at Shrublands I heard steps pacing overhead at night, and the feeble but continued wail of an infant. I wakened from my sleep, was sulky, but turned and slept again. Biddlecombe the barrister I knew was the occupant of the upper chamber. He came down the next morning looking wretchedly yellow about the cheeks, and livid round the eyes. His teething infant had kept him on the march all night. . . . He munched a shred of toast, and was off by the omnibus to chambers. I chipped a second egg; I may have tried one or two other nice little things on the table (Strasbourg pâté I know I never can resist, and am convinced it is perfectly wholesome). I could see my own sweet face in the mirror opposite, and my gills were as rosy as any broiled salmon. (chapter 3)

Unlike its sacramental, community-building function in Dickens, food in Thackeray, even good food, is most apt to signify the bitterness of dependency or inequality.[17] The exchange value of food and drink, its expensiveness or cheapness relative to the status and expectations of those who partake, the ostentation or stinginess with which it is doled out, or the meanness with which it is cadged, mark out for it a shifty and invidious path through each of Thackeray's books, including this one.

17. On this, see Barbara Hardy, *The Exposure of Luxury: Radical Themes in Thackeray* (London: Owen, 1972), pp. 118–60.

The rounded Pickwickian self-complacency of the rosy-gilled bachelor at breakfast is, then, all the more striking by contrast. In Thackeray's bitchy art where, as in James's, the volatility of the perspective regularly corrodes both the object and the subject of perception, there are moments when the bachelor hero, exactly through his celibacy and selfishness, can seem the only human particle atomized enough to plump through unscathed.

Sometimes unscathed; never unscathing. Of course one of the main pleasures of reading this part of Thackeray's oeuvre is precisely its feline gratuitousness of aggression. At odd moments one is apt to find kitty's unsheathed claws a millimeter from one's own eyes. "Nothing, dear friend, escapes your penetration: if a joke is made in your company, you are down upon it instanter, and your smile rewards the wag who amuses you: so you knew at once..." (chapter 1). When one bachelor consults another bachelor about a third bachelor, nothing is left but ears and whiskers:

> During my visit to London, I had chanced to meet my friend Captain Fitzb — dle, who belongs to a dozen clubs, and knows something of every man in London. "Know anything of Clarence Baker?" "Of course I do," says Fitz; "and if you want any *renseignement*, my dear fellow, I have the honor to inform you that a blacker little sheep does not trot the London *pavé*... know anything of Clarence Baker! My dear fellow, enough to make your hair turn white, unless (as I sometimes fondly imagine) nature has already performed that process, when of course I can't pretend to act upon mere hair-dye." (The whiskers of the individual who addressed me, innocent, stared me in the face as he spoke, and were dyed of the most unblushing purple.)...." From the garrison towns where he has been quartered, he has carried away not only the hearts of the milliners, but their gloves, haberdashery, and perfumery." (chapter 4)

If, as I am suggesting, Thackeray's bachelors created or reinscribed as a personality type one possible path of response to the strangulation of homosexual panic, their basic strategy is easy enough to trace: a preference of atomized male individualism to the nuclear family (and a corresponding demonization of women, especially mothers); a garrulous and visible refusal of anything that could be interpreted as genital sexuality, toward objects male or female; a corresponding emphasis on the pleasures of the other senses; and a well-defended social facility that freights with a good deal of magnetism its proneness to parody and to unpredictable sadism.

I must say that this does not strike me as a portrait of an exclusively

Victorian human type. To refuse sexual choice, in a society where sexual choice for men is both compulsory and always self-contradictory, seems, at least for educated men, still often to involve invoking the precedent of this nineteenth-century persona—not Mr. Batchelor himself perhaps, but, generically, the self-centered and at the same time self-marginalizing bachelor he represents. Nevertheless, this persona *is* highly specified as a figure of the nineteenth-century metropolis. He has close ties with the *flâneurs* of Poe, Baudelaire, Wilde, Benjamin. What is most importantly specified is his pivotal class position between the respectable bourgeoisie and bohemia—a bohemia that, again, Thackeray in the Pendennis novels half invented for English literature and half merely housetrained.

Literally, it was Thackeray who introduced both the word and the concept of bohemia to England from Paris.[18] As a sort of reserve labor force and a semiporous, liminal space for vocational sorting and social rising and falling, bohemia could seemingly be entered from any social level; but, at least in these literary versions, it served best the cultural needs, the fantasy needs, and the needs for positive and negative self-definition of an anxious and conflicted bourgeoisie. Except to homosexual men, the idea of "bohemia" seems before the 1890s not to have had a distinctively gay coloration. In these bachelor novels the simple absence of an enforcing family structure was allowed to perform its enchantment in a more generalized way; and the most passionate male comradeship subsisted in an apparently loose relation to the erotic uses of a common pool of women. It might be more accurate, however, to see the flux of bohemia as the *temporal* space where the young, male bourgeois literary subject was required to navigate his way through his "homosexual panic"— seen here as a *developmental* stage—toward the more repressive, self-ignorant, and apparently consolidated status of the mature bourgeois paterfamilias.[19]

Among Thackeray's progeny in the exploration of bourgeois bachelors in bohemia, the most self-conscious and important are Du Maurier, Barrie, and—in, for example, *The Ambassadors*—James. The filiations of this tradition are multiple and heterogeneous. For instance, Du Maurier offered James the plot of *Trilby* years before he wrote the novel himself.[20]

18. Richard Miller, *Bohemia: The Protoculture Then and Now* (Chicago: Nelson-Hall, 1977), p. 58.

19. For some speculations on how and when this came to be represented as a specifically developmental narrative, see *Between Men*, pp. 176–79.

20. James, *Notebooks*, pp. 97–98.

For another, Little Bilham in *The Ambassadors* seems closely related to Little Billee, the hero of *Trilby*, a small, girlish-looking Left Bank art student. Little Billee shares a studio with two older, bigger, more virile English artists, whom he loves deeply—a bond that seems to give erotic point to Du Maurier's use of the Thackeray naval ballad from which Du Maurier, in turn, had taken Little Billee's name:

> There was gorging Jack and guzzling Jimmy,
> And the youngest he was little Billee.
> Now when they got as far as the Equator
> They's nothing left but one split pea.
>
> Says gorging Jack to guzzling Jimmy,
> "I am extremely hungaree."
> To gorging Jack says guzzling Jimmy,
> "We've nothing left, us must eat we."
>
> Says gorging Jack to guzzling Jimmy,
> "With one another we shouldn't agree!
> There's little Bill, he's young and tender,
> We're old and tough, so let's eat he.
>
> "Oh! Billy, we're going to kill and eat you,
> So undo the button of your chemie."[21]

As one moves past Thackeray toward the turn of the century, toward the ever greater visibility across class lines of a medicalized discourse of— and newly punitive assaults on—male homosexuality, however, the comfortably frigid campiness of Thackeray's bachelors gives way to something that sounds more inescapably like panic. Mr. Batchelor had played at falling in love with women, but felt no urgency about proving that he actually could. For the bachelor heroes of *Trilby* and *Tommy and Grizel*, though, even that renunciatory high ground of male sexlessness has been strewn with psychic land mines.

In fact, the most consistent keynote of this late literature is exactly the explicitly thematized sexual anesthesia of its heroes. In each of these fictions, moreover, the hero's agonistic and denied sexual anesthesia is treated as being *at the same time* an aspect of a particular, idiosyncratic personality type *and also* an expression of a great Universal. These (anti-) heroes offer, indeed, prototypes of the newly emerging incoherences between minoritizing and universalizing understandings of male sexual definition. Little Billee, for instance, the hero of *Trilby*, attributes his sudden inability to desire a woman to "a pimple" inside his "bump of"

21. "Ballads," in *Works of Thackeray*, 6: 337.

"fondness" — "for that's what's the matter with me — a pimple — just a little clot of blood at the root of a nerve, and no bigger than a pin's point!"[22] In the same long monologue, however, he attributes his lack of desire, not to the pimple, but on a far different scale to his status as Post-Darwinian Modern Man, unable any longer to believe in God. "Sentimental" Tommy, similarly, the hero of Barrie's eponymous novel and also of *Tommy and Grizel*, is treated throughout each of these astonishingly acute and self-hating novels both as a man with a specific, crippling moral and psychological defect and as the very type of the great creative artist.

Reading James Straight

James's "The Beast in the Jungle" (1902) is one of the bachelor fictions of this period that seems to make a strong implicit claim of "universal" applicability through heterosexual symmetries, but that is most movingly subject to a change of gestalt and of visible saliencies as soon as an assumed heterosexual male norm is at all interrogated. Like *Tommy and Grizel*, the story is of a man and a woman who have a decades-long intimacy. In both stories, the woman desires the man but the man fails to desire the woman. In fact, in each story the man simply fails to desire at all. Sentimental Tommy desperately desires to feel desire; confusingly counterfeits a desire for Grizel; and, with all the best intentions, finally drives her mad. John Marcher, in James's story, does not even know that desire is absent from his life, nor that May Bartram desires him, until after she has died from his obtuseness.

To judge from the biographies of Barrie and James, each author seems to have made erotic choices that were complicated enough, shifting enough in the gender of their objects, and, at least for long periods, kept distant enough from *éclaircissement* or physical expression, to make each an emboldening figure for a literary discussion of male homosexual panic.[23] Barrie had an almost unconsummated marriage, an unconsum-

---

22. George Du Maurier, *Trilby* (New York: Harper & Bros., 1922), p. 271.

23. The effect of emboldenment should be to some extent mistrusted — not, I think, because the attribution to these particular figures of an experience of male homosexual panic is likely to be wrong, but because it is so much easier to be so emboldened about men who are arguably homosexual in (if such a thing exists) "basic" sexual orientation; while what I am arguing is that panic is proportioned not to the homosexual but to the nonhomosexual-identified elements of these men's characters. Thus, if Barrie and James are obvious authors with whom to *begin* an analysis of male homosexual panic, the analysis I am offering here must be inadequate to the degree that it does not eventually work just as well — even better — for Joyce, Faulkner, Lawrence, Yeats, etc.

mated passion for a married woman (George Du Maurier's daughter!), and a lifelong, uncategorizable passion for her family of sons. James had—well, exactly that which we now all know that we know not. Oddly, however, it is simpler to read the psychological plot of *Tommy and Grizel*—the horribly thorough and conscientious ravages on a woman of the man's compulsion to pretend he desires her—into the cryptic and tragic story of James's involvement with Constance Fenimore Woolson than to read it directly into any incident of Barrie's life. It is hard to read Leon Edel's account of James's sustained (or repeated) and intense, but peculiarly furtive,[24] intimacies with this deaf, intelligent American woman author, who clearly loved him, without coming to a grinding sense that James felt he had with her above all something, sexually, to prove. And it is hard to read about what seems to have been her suicide without wondering whether the expense of James's heterosexual self-probation—an expense, one envisions if one has Barrie in mind, of sudden "generous," "yielding" impulses in him and equally sudden revulsions—was not charged most intimately to this secreted-away companion of so many of his travels and residencies. If this is true, the working-out of his denied homosexual panic must have been only the more grueling for the woman in proportion to James's outrageous gift and his moral magnetism.

If something like the doubly destructive interaction I am sketching here did in fact occur between James and Constance Fenimore Woolson, then its structure has been resolutely reproduced by virtually all the critical discussion of James's writing. James's mistake here, in life, seems to have been in moving blindly from a sense of the good, the desirability, of love and sexuality to the automatic imposition on himself of a specifically *hetero*sexual compulsion. (I say "imposition on himself," but of course he did not invent the heterosexual specificity of this compulsion; he merely failed, at this point in his life, to resist it actively.) The easy assumption (by James, the society, and the critics) that sexuality and heterosexuality are

24. Leon Edel, *Henry James: The Middle Years: 1882–1895*, vol. 3 of *The Life of Henry James* (New York: J. B. Lippincott, 1962; rpt. ed., New York: Avon Books, 1978), makes clear that these contacts—coinciding visits to some cities and shared trips to others (e.g., 3: 94), "a special rendezvous" in Geneva (3: 217), a period of actually living in the same house (3: 215–17)—were conducted with a consistent and most uncharacteristic extreme of secrecy. James also seems to have taken extraordinary pains to destroy every vestige of his correspondence with Woolson. Edel cannot, nevertheless, imagine the relationship except as "a continuing 'virtuous' attachment": "That this pleasant and *méticuleuse* old maid may have nourished fantasies of a closer tie does not seem to have occurred to him at this time. If it had, we might assume he would have speedily put distance between himself and her" (3: 217). Edel's hypothesis does nothing, of course, to explain the secrecy of these and other meetings.

always exactly translatable into one another is, obviously, homophobic. Importantly, too, it is deeply heterophobic: it denies the very possibility of *difference* in desires, in objects. One is no longer surprised, of course, at the repressive blankness most literary criticism shows on these issues; but for James, in whose life the pattern of homosexual desire was brave enough and resilient enough to be at last biographically inobliterable, one might have hoped that in criticism of his work the possible differences of different erotic paths would not be so ravenously subsumed under a compulsorily—and hence, never a truly "hetero"—heterosexual model. With strikingly few exceptions, however, the criticism has actively repelled any inquiry into the asymmetries of gendered desire.

It is possible that critics have been motivated in this active incuriosity by a desire to protect James from homophobic misreadings in a perennially repressive sexual climate. It is possible that they fear that, because of the asymmetrically marked structure of heterosexist discourse, *any* discussion of homosexual desires or literary content will marginalize him (or them?) as, simply, *homosexual.* It is possible that they desire to protect him from what they imagine as anachronistically gay readings, based on a late twentieth-century vision of men's desire for men that is more stabilized and culturally compact than James's own. It is possible that they read James himself as, in his work, positively refusing or evaporating this element of his eros, translating lived homosexual desires, where he had them, into written heterosexual ones so thoroughly and so successfully that the difference *makes* no difference, the transmutation leaves no residue. Or it is possible that, believing—as I do—that James often, though not always, attempted such a disguise or transmutation, but reliably left a residue both of material that he did not attempt to transmute and of material that could be transmuted only rather violently and messily, some critics are reluctant to undertake the "attack" on James's candor or artistic unity that could be a next step of that argument. Any of these critical motives would be understandable, but their net effect is the usual repressive one of elision and subsumption of supposedly embarrassing material. In dealing with the multiple valences of sexuality, critics' choices should not be limited to crudities of disruption or silences of orthodox enforcement.

Even Leon Edel, who traces out *both* James's history with Constance Fenimore Woolson *and* some of the narrative of his erotic desire for men, connects "The Beast in the Jungle" to the history of Woolson,[25] but

25. Edel, *Life of James*, vol. 4, *The Master: 1910–1916* (1972), pp. 132–40.

connects neither of these to the specificity of James's—or of any—sexuality. The result of this hammeringly tendentious blur in virtually all the James criticism is, for the interpretation of "The Beast in the Jungle," seemingly in the interests of showing it as universally applicable (e.g., about "the artist"), to assume without any space for doubt that the moral point of the story is not only that May Bartram desired John Marcher but that John Marcher *should have desired* May Bartram.

Tommy and Grizel is clearer-sighted on what is essentially the same point. "*Should have desired*," that novel graphically shows, not only is nonsensical as a moral judgment but is the very mechanism that enforces and perpetuates the mutilating charade of heterosexual exploitation (James's compulsive use of Woolson, for instance). Grizel's tragedy is not that the man she desires fails to desire her—which would be sad, but, the book makes clear, endurable—but that he pretends to desire her, and intermittently even convinces himself that he desires her, when he does not.

Impressively, too, the clarity with which *Tommy and Grizel* conveys this process and its ravages seems not to be dependent on a given, naive or monolithic idea of what it would mean for a man "really" to desire someone. On that issue the novel seems to remain agnostic, leaving open the possibility that there is some rather different quality that is "real" male desire or, alternatively, that it is only more and less intermittent infestations of the same murderous syndrome that fuel any male eros at all. That the worst violence of heterosexuality comes with the male *compulsion to desire* women and its attendant deceptions of self and other, however, Barrie says quite decisively.

Tommy and Grizel is an extraordinary, and an unjustly forgotten, novel. What has dated it and keeps it from being a great novel, in spite of the acuteness with which it treats male desire, is the—one can hardly help saying Victorian—mawkish opportunism with which it figures the desire of women. Permissibly, the novel's real imaginative and psychological energies focus entirely on the hero. Impermissibly—and here the structure of the novel itself exactly reproduces the depredations of its hero—there is a moralized pretense at an equal focus on a rounded, autonomous, imaginatively and psychologically invested female protagonist, who, however, far from being novelistically "desired" in herself, is really, transparently, created in the precise negative image of the hero—created to be the single creature in the world who is most perfectly fashioned to be caused the most exquisite pain and intimate destruction by him and him only. The fit is excruciatingly seamless. Grizel is the daughter of a mad prostitute, whose legacies to her—aside from vitality, intelligence, imagination—have been a strong sensuality and a terror (which the novel highly valorizes) of having that sensuality stirred. It was acute of Barrie to see that this is the exact woman—were such a woman possible—who, appearing strong and autonomous, would be most unresistingly annihilable precisely by Tommy's two-phase rhythm of sexual come-on followed by repressive frigidity, and his emotional geology of pliant sweetness fundamented by unyielding compulsion. But the prurient exactitude of the female fit, as of a creature bred for sexual sacrifice without resistance or leftovers, drains the authority of the novel to make an uncomplicit judgment on Tommy's representative value.

Read in this context, "The Beast in the Jungle" looks, from the point of view of female desire, potentially revolutionary. Whoever May Bartram is and whatever she wants, clearly at least the story has the Jamesian negative virtue of not pretending to present her rounded and whole. She is an imposing character, but—*and*—a bracketed one. James's bravura in manipulating point of view lets him dissociate himself critically from John Marcher's selfishness—from the sense that there is no *possibility* of a subjectivity other than Marcher's own—but lets him leave in place of that selfishness finally an *askesis*, a particular humility of point of view as being *limited* to Marcher's. Of May Bartram's history, of her emotional determinants, of her erotic structures the reader learns very little; we are permitted, if we pay attention at all, to *know* that we have learned very little. Just as in Proust it is always open to any minor or grotesque character to turn out at any time to have a major artistic talent with which, however, the novel does not happen to busy itself, so "The Beast in the Jungle" seems to give the reader permission to imagine some female needs and desires and gratifications that are not structured exactly in the image of Marcher's or of the story's own laws.

It is only the last scene of the story—Marcher's last visit to May Bartram's grave—that conceals or denies the humility, the incompleteness of the story's presentation of her subjectivity. This is the scene in which Marcher's sudden realization that *she* has felt and expressed desire for *him* is, as it seems, answered in an intensely symmetrical, "conclusive" rhetorical clinch by the narrative/authorial prescription: "The escape would have been to love her; then, *then* he would have lived."[26] The paragraph

---

26. "The Beast in the Jungle," in *The Complete Tales of Henry James*, ed. Leon Edel (London: Rupert Hart-Davis, 1964), 11: 401. All subsequent references to this work are to this edition and are cited parenthetically in the text by page number.

that follows, the last in the story, has the same climactic, authoritative (even authoritarian) rhythm of supplying Answers in the form of symmetrical supplementarities. For this single, this conclusive, this formally privileged moment in the story—this resolution over the dead body of May Bartram—James and Marcher are presented as coming together, Marcher's revelation underwritten by James's rhetorical authority, and James's epistemological *askesis* gorged, for once, beyond recognition, by Marcher's compulsive, ego-projective certainties. In the absence of May Bartram, the two men, author/narrator and hero, are reunited at last in the confident, shared, masculine knowledge of what she Really Wanted and what she Really Needed. And what she Really Wanted and Really Needed show, of course, an uncanny closeness to what Marcher Really (should have) Wanted and Needed, himself.

Imagine "The Beast in the Jungle" without this enforcing symmetry. Imagine (remember) the story with May Bartram alive.[27] Imagine a possible alterity. And the name of alterity is not *always* "woman." What if Marcher himself had other desires?

The Law of the Jungle

Names. . . Assingham—Padwick—Lutch—Marfle—Bross—
Crapp—Didcock—Wichells—*Putchin*—Brind—Coxeter—
Coxster. . . Dickwinter. . . Jakes. . . Marcher—
James, Notebook, 1901

There has so far seemed no reason, or little reason, why what I have been calling "male homosexual panic" could not just as descriptively have been called "male heterosexual panic"—or, simply, "male sexual panic." Although I began with a structural and historicizing narrative that emphasized the pre- and proscriptively defining importance of men's bonds with men, potentially including genital bonds, the books I have discussed have not, for the most part, seemed to center emotionally or thematically on such bonds. In fact, it is, explicitly, a male panic in the face of *hetero*sexuality that many of these books most describe. And no assumption could

---

27. Interestingly, in the 1895 germ of (what seems substantially to be) "The Beast in the Jungle," in James's *Notebooks*, p. 184, the woman outlives the man. "It's *the woman's sense of what might [have been] in him* that arrives at the intensity. . . . *She is his Dead Self: he is alive in her and dead in himself*—that is something like the little formula I seem to *entrevoir*. He himself, the man, must, *in* the tale, also materially die—die in the flesh as he has died long ago in the spirit, the *right* one. Then it is that his lost treasure revives most—no longer *contrarié* by his material existence, existence in his false self, his wrong one."

be more homophobic than the automatic association of same-sex object choice with a fear of heterosexuality or of the other sex. It is all very well to insist, as I have done, that homosexual panic is necessarily a problem only, but endemically, of nonhomosexual-identified men; nevertheless the lack in these books of an embodied male-homosexual thematics, however inevitable, has had a dissolutive effect on the structure and texture of such an argument. Part, although only part, of the reason for that lack was historical: it was only close to the end of the nineteenth century that a cross-class homosexual role and a consistent, ideologically full thematic discourse of male homosexuality became entirely visible, in developments that were publicly dramatized in—though far from confined to—the Wilde trials.

In "The Beast in the Jungle," written at the threshold of the new century, the possibility of an embodied male-homosexual thematics has, I would like to argue, a precisely liminal presence. It is present as a—as a very particular, historicized—thematics of absence, and specifically of the absence of speech. The first (in some ways the only) thing we learn about John Marcher is that he has a "secret" (358), a destiny, a something unknown in his future. "'You said,'" May Bartram reminds him, "'you had from your earliest time, as the deepest thing within you, the sense of being kept for something rare and strange, possibly prodigious and terrible, that was sooner or later to happen'" (359). I would argue that to the extent that Marcher's secret has *a* content, that content is homosexual.

Of course the extent to which Marcher's secret has anything that could be called a content is, not only dubious, but in the climactic last scene actively denied. "He had been the man of his time, *the* man, to whom nothing on earth was to have happened" (401). The denial that the secret has a content—the assertion that its content is precisely a lack—is a stylish and "satisfyingly" Jamesian formal gesture. The apparent gap of meaning that it points to is, however, far from being a genuinely empty one; it is no sooner asserted as a gap than filled to a plenitude with the most orthodox of ethical enforcements. To point rhetorically to the emptiness of the secret, "the nothing that is," is, in fact, oddly, *the same gesture* as the attribution to it of a compulsory content about heterosexuality—of the content specifically, "He should have desired her":

> *She* was what he had missed. . . . The fate he had been marked for he had met with a vengeance—he had emptied the cup to the lees; he had been the man of his time, *the* man, to whom nothing on earth was to have happened. That was the rare stroke—that was his visitation. . . . This the

companion of his vigil had at a given moment made out, and she had then offered him the chance to baffle his doom. One's doom, however, was never baffled, and on the day she told him his own had come down she had seen him but stupidly stare at the escape she offered him.

The escape would have been to love her; then, *then* he would have lived. (401)

The supposedly "empty" meaning of Marcher's unspeakable doom is thus necessarily, specifically heterosexual; it refers to the perfectly specific absence of a prescribed heterosexual desire. If critics, eager to help James moralize this ending, persist in claiming to be able to translate freely and without residue from that (absent) heterosexual desire to an abstraction of all possibilities of human love, there are, I think, good reasons for trying to slow them down. The totalizing, insidiously symmetrical view that the "nothing" that is Marcher's unspeakable fate is necessarily a mirror image of the "everything" he could and should have had is, specifically, in an *oblique* relation to a very different history of meanings for assertions of the erotic negative.

Let us attempt, then, a different strategy for its recovery. A more frankly "full" meaning for that unspeakable fate might come from the centuries-long historical chain of substantive uses of space-clearing negatives to void and at the same time to underline the possibility of male same-sex genitality. The rhetorical name for this figure is preterition. Unspeakable, Unmentionable, *nefandam libidinem*, "that sin which should be neither named nor committed,"[28] the "detestable and abominable sin, amongst Christians not to be named,"

> Whose vice in special, if I would declare,
> It were enough for to perturb the air,

"things fearful to name," "the obscene sound of the unbeseeming words,"

> A sin so odious that the fame of it
> Will fright the damned in the darksome pit,[29]

---

28. Quoted in Boswell, *Christianity*, p. 349 (from a legal document dated 533) and p. 380 (from a 1227 letter from Pope Honorius III).

29. Quoted in Bray, *Homosexuality*— the first two from p. 61 (from Edward Coke's *Institutes* and Sir David Lindsay's *Works*), the next two from p. 62 (from William Bradford's *Plimouth Plantation* and Guillaume Du Bartas's *Divine Weeks*), and the last from p. 22, also from Du Bartas.

"the love that dare not speak its name"[30] — such *were* the speakable nonmedical terms, in Christian tradition, for the homosexual possibility for men. The marginality of these terms' semantic and ontological status as substantive nouns reflected and shaped the exiguousness — but also the potentially enabling secrecy — of that "possibility." And the newly specifying, reifying medical and penal public discourse of the male homosexual role, in the years around the Wilde trials, far from retiring or obsolescing these preteritive names, seems instead to have packed them more firmly and distinctively with homosexual meaning.[31]

John Marcher's "secret," "his singularity" (366), "the thing she knew, which grew to be at last, with the consecration of the years, never mentioned between them save as 'the real truth' about him" (366), "the abyss" (375), "his queer consciousness" (378), "the great vagueness" (379), "the secret of the gods" (379), "what ignominy or what monstrosity" (379), "dreadful things . . . I couldn't name" (381): the ways the story refers to Marcher's secret fate have the same quasi-nominative, quasi-obliterative structure.

There are, as well, some "fuller," though still highly equivocal, lexical pointers to a homosexual meaning: "The rest of the world of course thought him *queer*, but she, she only, knew how, and above all why, queer; which was precisely what enabled her to dispose the concealing veil in the right folds. She took his *gaiety* from him — since it had to pass with them for gaiety — as she took everything else. . . . She traced his unhappy *perversion* through reaches of its course into which he could scarce follow it" (367; emphasis added). Still, it is mostly in the reifying grammar of periphrasis and preterition — "such a cataclysm" (360), "the great affair" (360), "the catastrophe" (361), "his predicament" (364), "their real truth" (368), "his inevitable topic" (371), "all that they had thought, first and last" (372), "horrors" (382), something "more monstrous than all the monstrosities we've named" (383), "all the loss and all the shame that are thinkable" (384) — that a homosexual meaning becomes, to the degree that it does become, legible. "I don't focus it. I can't name it. I only know I'm exposed" (372).

I am convinced, however, that part of the point of the story is that the reifying effect of periphrasis and preterition on this particular meaning is,

---

30. Douglas, "Two Loves."
31. For a striking anecdotal example of the mechanism of this, see Beverley Nichols, *Father Figure* (New York: Simon & Schuster, 1972), pp. 92–99.

if anything, *more* damaging than (though not separable from) its obliter-
ative effect. To have succeeded — which was not to be taken for granted —
in cracking the centuries-old code by which the-articulated-denial-of-
articulability always had the possibility of meaning two things, of meaning either (heterosexual) "nothing" or "homosexual meaning," would also
always have been to assume one's place in a discourse in which there was *a*
homosexual meaning, in which all homosexual meaning meant a single
thing. To crack a code and enjoy the reassuring exhilarations of knowingness is to buy into the specific formula "We Know What That Means."
(I assume it is this mechanism that makes even critics who think about the
male-erotic pathways of James's personal desires appear to be so un-
troubled about leaving them out of accounts of his writing.[32] As if this
form of desire were the most calculable, the simplest to add or subtract or
allow for in moving between life and art!) But if, as I suggested in the first
section of this chapter, men's accession to heterosexual entitlement has,
for these modern centuries, always been on the ground of a cultivated and
compulsory denial of the *un*knowability, of the arbitrariness and self-
contradictoriness, of homo/heterosexual definition, then the fearful or
triumphant interpretive formula "We Know What That Means" seems to
take on an odd centrality. First, it is a lie. But, second, it is the particular lie
that animates and perpetuates the mechanism of homophobic male self-
ignorance and violence and manipulability.

It is worth, accordingly, trying to discriminate the possible plurality of
meanings behind the unspeakables of "The Beast in the Jungle." To point,
as I argue that the narrative itself points and as we have so far pointed,
simply to *a* possibility of "homosexual meaning" is to say worse than
nothing: it is to pretend to say one thing. But even on the surface of the
story, the secret, "*the* thing," "the thing she knew," is discriminated, first of
all discriminated temporally. There are at least two secrets: Marcher feels
that he knows, but has never told anyone but May Bartram, (secret
number one) that he is reserved for some very particular, uniquely rending
fate in the future, whose nature is (secret number two) unknown to

32. Exceptions that I know of include Georges-Michel Sarotte's discussion of James in
*Like a Brother, Like a Lover: Male Homosexuality in the American Novel and Theater from
Herman Melville to James Baldwin*, trans. Richard Miller (New York: Doubleday/An-
chor, 1978); Richard Hall, "Henry James: Interpreting an Obsessive Memory," *Journal of
Homosexuality* 8, no. 3/4 (Spring–Summer 1983): 83–97; Robert K. Martin, "The 'High
Felicity' of Comradeship: A New Reading of *Roderick Hudson*," *American Literary
Realism* 11 (Spring 1978): 100–108; and Michael Moon, "Sexuality and Visual Terrorism
in *The Wings of the Dove*," *Criticism* 28 (Fall 1986): 427–43.

himself. Over the temporal extent of the story, both the balance, between the two characters, of cognitive mastery over the secrets' meanings, and the temporal placement, between future and past, of the second secret, shift; it is possible, in addition, that the actual content (if any) of the secrets changes with these temporal and cognitive changes, if time and intersubjectivity are of the essence of the secrets.

Let me, then, baldly spell out my hypothesis of what a series of "full" — that is, homosexually tinged — meanings for the Unspeakable might look like for this story, differing both over time and according to character.

For John Marcher, let us hypothesize, the future secret — the secret of his hidden fate — importantly includes, though it is not necessarily limited to, the possibility of something homosexual. *For Marcher*, the presence or possibility of a homosexual meaning attached to the inner, the future, secret has exactly the reifying, totalizing, and blinding effect we described earlier in regard to the phenomenon of the Unspeakable. Whatever (Marcher feels) may be to be discovered along those lines, it is, in the view of his panic, *one* thing, and the worst thing, "the superstition of the Beast" (394). His readiness to organize the whole course of his life around the preparation for it — the defense against it — remakes his life monolithically in the image of *its* monolith of, in his view, the inseparability of homosexual desire, yielding, discovery, scandal, shame, annihilation. Finally, he has "but one desire left": that *it* be "decently proportional to the posture he had kept, all his life, in the threatened presence of it" (379).

This is how it happens that the outer secret, the secret of having a secret, functions, in Marcher's life, precisely as *the closet*. It is not a closet in which there is a homosexual man, for Marcher is not a homosexual man. Instead, it is the closet of, simply, the homosexual secret — the closet of imagining *a* homosexual secret. Yet it is unmistakable that Marcher lives as one who is *in the closet*. His angle on daily existence and intercourse is that of the closeted person,

> the secret of the difference between the forms he went through — those of his little office under government, those of caring for his modest patrimony, for his library, for his garden in the country, for the people in London whose invitations he accepted and repaid — and the detachment that reigned beneath them and that made of all behaviour, all that could in the least be called behaviour, a long act of dissimulation. What it had come to was that he wore a mask painted with the social simper, out of the eye-holes of which there looked eyes of an expression not in the least matching the other features. This the stupid world, even after years, had never more than half-discovered. (367–78)

Whatever the content of the inner secret, too, it is one whose protection requires, for him, a playacting of heterosexuality that is conscious of being only window dressing. "You help me," he tells May Bartram, "to pass for a man like another" (375). And "what saves us, you know," she explains, "is that we answer so completely to so usual an appearance: that of the man and woman whose friendship has become such a daily habit — or almost — as to be at last indispensable" (368–69). Oddly, they not only appear to be but are such a man and woman. The element of deceiving the world, of window dressing, comes into their relationship *only* because of the compulsion he feels to invest it with the legitimating stamp of visible, institutionalized genitality: "The real form it should have taken on the basis that stood out large was the form of their marrying. But the devil in this was that the very basis itself put marrying out of the question. His conviction, his apprehension, his obsession, in short, wasn't a privilege he could invite a woman to share; and that consequence of it was precisely what was the matter with him" (365).

Because of the terrified stultification of his fantasy about the inner or future secret, Marcher has, until the story's very last scene, an essentially static relation to and sense of both these secrets. Even the discovery that the outer secret is already shared with someone else, and the admission of May Bartram to the community it creates, "the dim day constituted by their discretions and privacies" (363), does nothing to his closet but furnish it: camouflage it to the eyes of outsiders, and soften its inner cushioning for his own comfort. In fact the admission of May Bartram importantly *consolidates and fortifies* the closet for John Marcher.

In my hypothesis, however, May Bartram's view of Marcher's secrets is different from his and more fluid. I want to suggest that, while it is true that she feels desire for him, her involvement with him occurs originally on the ground of her understanding that he is imprisoned by homosexual panic; and her own interest in his closet is not at all in helping him fortify it but in helping him dissolve it.

In this reading, May Bartram from the first sees, correctly, that the possibility of Marcher's achieving a genuine ability to attend to a woman — sexually or in any other way — depends as an absolute precondition on the dispersion of his totalizing, basilisk fascination with and terror of homosexual possibility. It is only through his coming out of the closet — whether as *a homosexual man* or as a man with a less exclusively defined sexuality that nevertheless admits the possibility of desires for other men — that Marcher could even begin to perceive the attention of a

woman as anything other than a terrifying demand or a devaluing complicity. The truth of this is already evident at the beginning of the story, in
the surmises with which Marcher first meets May Bartram's allusion to
something (he cannot remember what) he said to her years before: "The
great thing was that he saw in this no vulgar reminder of any 'sweet'
speech. The vanity of women had long memories, but she was making no
claim on him of a compliment or a mistake. With another woman, a
totally different one, he might have feared the recall possibly even of some
imbecile 'offer'" (356). The alternative to this, however, in his eyes, is a
different kind of "sweetness," that of a willingly shared confinement: "her
knowledge . . . began, even if rather strangely, to taste sweet to him"
(358). "Somehow the whole question was a new luxury to him—that is
from the moment she was in possession. If she didn't take the sarcastic
view she clearly took the sympathetic, and that was what he had had, in
all the long time, from no one whomsoever. What he felt was that he
couldn't at present have begun to tell her, and yet could profit perhaps
exquisitely by the accident of having done so of old" (358). So begins the
imprisonment of May Bartram in John Marcher's closet—an imprisonment that, the story makes explicit, is founded on his inability to perceive
or value her as a person beyond her complicity in his view of his own
predicament.

The conventional view of the story, emphasizing May Bartram's
interest in liberating, unmediatedly, Marcher's heterosexual possibilities,
would see her as unsuccessful in doing so until too late—until the true
revelation that comes only after her death. If what needs to be liberated is
in the first place Marcher's potential for homosexual desire, however, the
trajectory of the story must be seen as far bleaker. I hypothesize that what
May Bartram would have liked for Marcher, the narrative she wished to
nurture for him, would have been a progress from a vexed and gaping self-
ignorance around his homosexual possibilities to a self-knowledge of
them that would have freed him to find and enjoy a sexuality of whatever
sort emerged. What she sees happen to Marcher, instead, is the "progress"
that the culture more insistently enforces: the progress from a vexed and
gaping self-ignorance around his homosexual possibilities to a completed
and rationalized and wholly concealed and accepted one. The moment of
Marcher's full incorporation of his erotic self-ignorance is the moment at
which the imperatives of the culture cease to enforce him, and he becomes
instead the enforcer of the culture.

Section 4 of the story marks the moment at which May Bartram realizes that, far from helping dissolve Marcher's closet, she has instead and irremediably been permitting him to reinforce it. It is in this section and the next, too, that it becomes explicit in the story that Marcher's fate, what was to have happened to him and did happen, involves a change in him from being the suffering object of a Law or judgment (of a doom in the original sense of the word) to being the embodiment of that Law.

If the transition I am describing is, in certain respects, familiarly oedipal, the structuring metaphor behind its description here seems to be peculiarly alimentative. The question that haunts Marcher in these sections is whether what he has thought of as the secret of his future may not be, after all, in the past; and the question of passing, of who is passing through what or what is passing through whom, of what residue remains to *be* passed, is the form in which he compulsively poses his riddle. Is the beast eating him, or is he eating the beast? "It hasn't passed you by," May Bartram tells him. "It has done its office. It has made you its own" (389). "It's past. It's behind," she finally tells him, to which he replies, "*Nothing*, for me, is past; nothing *will* pass till I pass myself, which I pray my stars may be as soon as possible. Say, however, . . . that I've eaten my cake, as you contend, to the last crumb—how can the thing I've never felt at all be the thing I was marked out to feel?" (391). What May Bartram sees and Marcher does not is that the process of incorporating—of embodying— the Law of masculine self-ignorance is the one that has the least in the world to do with feeling.[33] To gape at and, rebelliously, be forced to

---

33. A fascinating passage in James's *Notebooks*, p. 318, written in 1905 in California, shows how in James a greater self-knowledge and a greater acceptance and *specificity* of homosexual desire transform this half-conscious enforcing rhetoric of anality, numbness, and silence into a much richer, pregnant address to James's male muse, an invocation of fisting-as-*écriture*:

> I sit here, after long weeks, at any rate, in front of my arrears, with an inward accumulation of material of which I feel the wealth, and as to which I can only invoke my familiar demon of patience, who always comes, doesn't he?, when I call. He is here with me in front of this cool green Pacific—he sits close and I feel his soft breath, which cools and steadies and inspires, on my cheek. Everything sinks in: nothing is lost; everything abides and fertilizes and renews its golden promise, making me think with closed eyes of deep and grateful longing when, in the full summer days of L[amb] H[ouse], my long dusty adventure over, I shall be able to [plunge] my hand, my arm, *in*, deep and far, and up to the shoulder—into the heavy bag of remembrance—of suggestion—of imagination—of art—and fish out every little figure and felicity, every little fact and fancy that can be to my purpose. These things are all packed away, now, thicker than I can penetrate, deeper than I can fathom, and there let them rest for the present, in their sacred cool darkness, till I shall let in upon them the mild still light of dear old L[amb] H[ouse]—in which they will begin to gleam and glitter and take form like the gold and jewels of a mine.

swallow the Law is to feel; but to have it finally stick to one's ribs, become however incongruously a part of one's own organism, is then to perfect at the same moment a new hard-won insentience of it and an assumption of (or subsumption by) an identification with it. May Bartram answers Marcher's question, "You take your 'feelings' for granted. You were to suffer your fate. That was not necessarily to know it" (391). Marcher's fate is to cease to suffer fate and instead to become it. May Bartram's fate, with the "slow fine shudder" that climaxes her ultimate appeal to Marcher, is herself to swallow this huge, bitter bolus with which *she* can have *no* deep identification, and to die of it — of what is, to her, knowledge, not power. "So on her lips would the law itself have sounded" (389). Or, tasted.

To end a reading of May Bartram with her death, to end with her silenced forever in that ultimate closet, "her" tomb that represents (to Marcher) *his fate*, would be to do to her feminine desire the same thing I have already argued that Barrie, unforgivably, did to Grizel's. That is to say, it leaves us in danger of figuring May Bartram, or more generally the woman in heterosexuality, as only the exact, heroic supplement to the murderous enforcements of male homophobic/homosocial self-igno-rance. "The Fox," Emily Dickinson wrote, "fits the Hound."[34] It would be only too easy to describe May Bartram as the fox that most irreducibly fits this particular hound. She seems the woman (don't we all know them?) who has not only the most delicate nose for but the most potent attraction toward men who are at crises of homosexual panic... — Though, for that matter, won't most women admit that an arousing nimbus, an excessively refluent and dangerous maelstrom of eroticism, somehow attends men in general at such moments, even otherwise boring men?

If one is to avoid the Barrie-ism of describing May Bartram in terms that reduce her perfectly to the residueless sacrifice John Marcher makes to his Beast, it might be by inquiring into the difference of the paths of her own desire. What does she want, not for him, but for herself, from their relationship? What does she actually get? To speak less equivocally from my own eros and experience, there is a particular relation to truth and authority that a mapping of male homosexual panic offers to a woman in the emotional vicinity. The fact that male heterosexual entitlement in (at

34. *Collected Poems of Emily Dickinson*, ed. Thomas H. Johnson (Boston: Little, Brown, 1960), p. 406.

least modern Anglo-American) culture depends on a perfected but always friable self-ignorance in men as to the significance of their desire for other men means that it is always open to women to know something that it is much more dangerous for any nonhomosexual-identified man to know. The ground of May Bartram and John Marcher's relationship is from the first that she has the advantage of him, cognitively: she remembers, as he does not, where and when and with whom they have met before, and most of all she remembers his "secret" from a decade ago while he forgets having told it to her. This differential of knowledge affords her a "slight irony," an "advantage" (353) — but one that he can at the same time use to his own profit as "the buried treasure of her knowledge," "this little hoard" (363). As their relationship continues, the sense of power and of a marked, rather free-floating irony about May Bartram becomes stronger and stronger, even in proportion to Marcher's accelerating progress toward self-ignorance and toward a blindly selfish expropriation of her emotional labor. Both the care and the creativity of her investment in him, the imaginative reach of her fostering his homosexual potential as a route back to his truer perception of herself, are forms of gender-political resilience in her as well as of love. They are forms of excitement, too, of real though insufficient power, and of pleasure.

In the last scene of "The Beast in the Jungle" John Marcher becomes, in this reading, not the finally self-knowing man who is capable of heterosexual love, but the irredeemably self-ignorant man who embodies and enforces heterosexual compulsion. In this reading, that is to say, May Bartram's prophecy to Marcher that "You'll never know now" (390) is a true one.

Importantly for the homosexual plot, too, the final scene is also the only one in the entire story that reveals or tests the affective quality of Marcher's perception of another man. "The shock of the face" (399): this is, in the last scene, the beginning of what Marcher ultimately considers "the most extraordinary thing that had happened to him" (400). At the beginning of Marcher's confrontation with this male figure at the cemetery, the erotic possibilities of the connection between the men appear to be all open. The man, whose "mute assault" Marcher feels "so deep down that he winced at the steady thrust," is mourning profoundly over "a grave apparently fresh," but (perhaps only to Marcher's closet-sharpened suspicions?) a slightest potential of Whitmanian cruisiness seems at first to tinge the air, as well:

His pace was slow, so that—and all the more as there was a kind of hunger in his look—the two men were for a minute directly confronted. Marcher knew him at once for one of the deeply stricken . . . nothing lived but the deep ravage of the features he showed. He *showed* them—that was the point; he was moved, as he passed, by some impulse that was either a signal for sympathy or, more possibly, a challenge to an opposed sorrow. He might already have been aware of our friend. . . . What Marcher was at all events conscious of was in the first place that the image of scarred passion presented to him was conscious too—of something that profaned the air; and in the second that, roused, startled, shocked, he was yet the next moment looking after it, as it went, with envy. (400–401)

The path traveled by Marcher's desire in this brief and cryptic nonencounter reenacts a classic trajectory of male entitlement. Marcher begins with the possibility of *desire for* the man, in response to the man's open "hunger" ("which," afterward, "still flared for him like a smoky torch" [401]). Deflecting that desire under a fear of profanation, he then replaces it with envy, with an *identification with* the man in that man's (baffled) desire for some other, presumedly female, dead object. "The stranger passed, but the raw glare of his grief remained, making our friend wonder in pity what wrong, what wound it expressed, what injury not to be healed. What had the man *had*, to make him by the loss of it so bleed and yet live?" (401).

What had the man *had*? The loss by which a man *so bleeds and yet lives* is, is it not, supposed to be the castratory one of the phallus figured as mother, the inevitability of whose sacrifice ushers sons into the status of fathers and into the control (read both ways) of the Law. What is strikingly open in the ending of "The Beast in the Jungle" is how central to that process is man's desire for man—and the denial of that desire. The imperative that there *be* a male figure to take this place is the clearer in that, at an earlier climactic moment, in a female "shock of the face," May Bartram has presented to Marcher her own face, in a conscious revelation that was far more clearly of desire:

It had become suddenly, from her movement and attitude, beautiful and vivid to him that she had something more to give him; her wasted face delicately shone with it—it glittered almost as with the white lustre of silver in her expression. She was right, incontestably, for what he saw in her face was the truth, and strangely, without consequence, while their talk of it as dreadful was still in the air, she appeared to present it as inordinately soft. This, prompting bewilderment, made him but gape the

more gratefully for her revelation, so that they continued for some minutes silent, her face shining at him, her contact imponderably pressing,
and his stare all kind but all expectant. The end, none the less, was that
what he had expected failed to come to him. (386)

To the shock of the female face Marcher is not phobic but simply numb. It
is only by turning his desire for the male face into an envious identification
with male loss that Marcher finally comes into *any* relation to a woman—
and then it is a relation through one dead woman (the other man's) to
another dead woman of his own. That is to say, it is the relation of
compulsory heterosexuality.

When Lytton Strachey's claim to be a conscientious objector was being
examined, he was asked what he would do if a German were to try to rape
his sister. "I should," he is said to have replied, "try and interpose my own
body."[35] Not the joky gay self-knowledge but the heterosexual, self-
ignorant acting out of just this fantasy ends "The Beast in the Jungle." To
face the gaze of the Beast would have been, for Marcher, to dissolve it.[36]
To face the "kind of hunger in the look" of the grieving man—to explore at
all into the sharper lambencies of that encounter—would have been to
dissolve the closet, to recreate its hypostatized compulsions as desires.
Marcher, instead, to the very end, turns his back—recreating a double
scenario of homosexual compulsion and heterosexual compulsion. "He
saw the Jungle of his life and saw the lurking Beast; then, while he looked,
perceived it, as by a stir of the air, rise, huge and hideous, for the leap that
was to settle him. His eyes darkened—it was close; and, instinctively
turning, in his hallucination, to avoid it, he flung himself, face down, on
the tomb" (402).

35. Lytton Strachey, quoted in Michael Holroyd, *Lytton Strachey: A Critical Biography* (London: W. H. Heinemann, 1968), 2: 179.

36. Ruth Bernard Yeazell makes clear the oddity of having Marcher turn his back on
the Beast that is supposed, at this late moment, to represent his self-recognition (in
Language and Knowledge in the Late Novels of Henry James [Chicago: University of
Chicago Press, 1976], pp. 37–38).

5

Proust and the Spectacle of the Closet

"Vous devez vous y entendre mieux que moi, M. de Charlus, à faire marcher des petits marins. . . . Tenez, voici un livre que j'ai reçu, je pense qu'il vous intéressera. . . . Le titre est joli: *Parmi les hommes.*"

Proust, *A la recherche*

About the foundational impossibilities of modern homo/heterosexual definition, the questions we have been essaying so far have been, not how this incoherent dispensation can be rationalized away or set straight, not what it means or even how it means, but what it makes happen, and how. *A la recherche du temps perdu* demands to be a signalizing text of such an exploration. While the figure of Wilde may have been the most formative individual influence on turn-of-the-century Anglo-European homosexual definition and identity (including Proust's), *A la recherche* has remained into the present the most vital center of the energies of gay literary high culture, as well as of many manifestations of modern literary high culture in general. It offers what seems to have been the definitive performance of the presiding incoherences of modern gay (and hence nongay) sexual specification and gay (and hence nongay) gender: definitive, that is, in setting up positions and sight lines, not in foreclosing future performance, since it seems on the contrary that the closet drama of *A la recherche* is still *in* performance through its sustained and changing mobilizations of closural and disclosural rage, excitement, resistance, pleasure, need, projection, and exclusion.

Two recent, gay-affirmative critical ways of dealing with the incoherences around homosexuality in Proust, opposite in tone and methodology and in many ways opposite in intent, seem to find it necessary to make similar gestures of compartmentalizing Proust's treatment of sexual specification, disavowing one side of it and identifying with and nourishing the other. J. E. Rivers's 1980 book *Proust and the Art of Love*, a treatment of the centrality of the homosexual "theme" in Proust that is full of interesting scholarship and awful writing, undertakes essentially to set Proust straight on gay issues—and especially on his "negative stereotypes"—according to the latest in empirical research. The thrust of this research, as Rivers reproduces it, is to argue for the sheer *normality*—that is, ultimately, for the lack of heuristic interest—of homosexual orientation. The book is written with a flatness designed to discourage further textual production:

> The fact is that homosexuality is a perennial adjunct of mammalian sexuality, neither a pathological condition nor a biological perversion. It has always existed, both among humans and among animals.[1]

> [T]he two kinds of love [homosexual and heterosexual] can and often do involve comparable feelings of tenderness, comparable problems of adjustment, and a comparable potential for mutual respect and enrichment. (4)

Rivers quotes laboratory experiments demonstrating that homosexuals are *not* actually more creative than heterosexuals (pp. 181–82); he considers, on the subject of gay mutual recognition, that "it should be obvious to anyone who reflects for a moment . . . that homosexually oriented people do not organize or communicate with each other any more regularly or any more skillfully than other classes of people" (172);[2] and while he celebrates an ideal of androgyny, he dissociates it from homosexuality and indeed steadily denounces any resonance or cultural cathexis whatsoever between homosexuality and gender identification. In his zeal to correct "negative stereotypes" of homosexuality in Proust and to foster countervailing, normalizing positive (positivist) knowledge, Rivers repeatedly singles out one section of the book, the prefatory section of *Sodome et Gomorrhe*, the "Introduction to the Men-Women of Sodom"—the section often referred to as "La Race maudite"—and Proust's treatment of the Baron de Charlus who features so prominently there, as embodying Proust's "distortions, half-truths, outmoded ideas, and constant eruptions of . . . internalized homophobia" (205); while the later treatment of the sexually ambiguous Albertine is—apparently because it is *not* exactly about homosexuality—the object of Rivers's repeated praise.

---

1. J. E. Rivers, *Proust and the Art of Love: The Aesthetics of Sexuality in the Life, Times, & Art of Marcel Proust* (New York: Columbia University Press, 1980), p. 14. Further citations from this volume will be incorporated in the text.

2. Having reflected on this for more than a moment, I must say I still can't see why it should be obvious.

In a recent essay on Proust and Melanie Klein that is radically anti-positivist, and as deft with Proustian tones as Rivers's book is deaf to them, Leo Bersani nevertheless performs the same act of division on the later books of *A la recherche* and makes the same double valuation of them. Bersani, like Rivers, singles out for dispraise the "Introduction to the Men-Women," "the banal thematization of homosexuality . . . a thematization at once sentimental and reductive." Bersani deprecates in this section the very fact of its explicitly crystallizing "the secondary, and, in a sense, merely anecdotal question of 'sexual preference.'"[3] Like Rivers, Bersani concludes that this section of *A la recherche* should and can be "implicitly brushed aside" (416), once again by the effects of a later meditation associated with Albertine — a meditation on how desire may preserve its originary motility, its antisymbolic "appetitive metonymies" (414).

Bersani links this reading of Proust to an argument that the early work of Melanie Klein similarly suggests the possibility of an unanxious mobility of desire in the infant, a "primary pleasure" (407) prior and in opposition to the infant's fantasmatic, fetishizing symbolic violence of dismemberment and reparation upon the mother's body. Bersani attaches the highest value to this possibility of "primary pleasure" as against the aggression of definitional mutilation. This argument makes it, however, even more striking for Bersani than for Rivers that each of these two readers of Proust should be provoked to dramas of dismemberment and subsequent reparation of the textual body of *A la recherche* itself:[4] "The Men-Women of Sodom" as the poisonous breast to be excised, the geranium-cheeked and metamorphic Albertine as the nurturant breast to be, in its turn, plumped up with interpretive value.

It appears that Rivers in his almost heroically resolute banalization of the issue of sexual choice, and Bersani in his desire to envisage for Proust "a mode of excitement which . . . would enhance [the] specificity [of objects] and thereby fortify their resistance to the violence of symbolic intent" (420), may be motivated each by a differently produced resistance to the interpretation of homosexual identity. Rivers resists that interpreta-

---

3. Leo Bersani, "'The Culture of Redemption': Marcel Proust and Melanie Klein," *Critical Inquiry* 12, no. 2 (Winter 1986): 399–421; quoted from p. 416. Further citations from this essay will be incorporated in the text.

4. Bersani's gesture of dismemberment and restitution of this text has a near-rhyme, too, in Deleuze and Guattari's dichotomizing and double-valued treatment of the *race maudite*: "Proust . . . contrasts two kinds of homosexuality, or rather two regions only one of which is Oedipal, exclusive, and depressive, the other being anoedipal schizoid, included, and inclusive" (*Anti-Oedipus*, p. 70).

tion from the grounds of a normalizing minority politics of gay rights, Bersani out of the vision of an infinite "phenomenal diversity of the world" (419) and potentially of desire, too far dispersed to be done justice by the "sentimental and reductive thematization" of homosexual identity. I can see no reason to quarrel with this interpretive resistance in either Rivers's minoritizing or Bersani's universalizing framing (or refusal) of the issue of gay definition. Some form of such a resistance to interpretation is arguably the only nonvicious response to the historical fact of an extreme oppression that has, for most of a century, operated precisely through the hyperstimulation of one-directional capillaries of interpretation.[5] At the same time, the gesture by which each reader violently repulses one polarity of a text while grappling for the appropriation of its opposite — this double thrust of denunciation and reproximation — is one, signally effective, way of hurling into motion the vast enactment of the text. Imagine a Calder mobile on the monumental scale, and what it must take to get it into action. This powerful move, however, already takes its performative shape from the turn-of-the-century crisis of incoherence in homosexual definition.

Suppose we agree — as most readers, I among them, do — in perceiving Proust's chapter on *la race maudite*, in its direct thematization of gay identity, as sentimental and reductive. But suppose we also follow Rivers's scholarship which finds, like that of Maurice Bardèche, that it was Proust's conception in 1909, in response to a major homosexual scandal in Germany, of the beginnings of "La Race maudite" that quite suddenly catalyzed into a single vast fictional project of an entirely new sort what had been until then a collection of miscellaneous, generically unstable fragments and ideas. Until 1908, Bardèche argues, Proust had two main parallel projects, an abortive novel and the essay dealing with Sainte-Beuve:

> But suddenly we encounter, in the middle of Notebook 6 and the middle of Notebook 7 . . . two series of developments foreign at once to the novel of

5. It is instructive, for instance, that the sudden and virtually unanimous cultivation of a studied public agnosticism about the "causes of homosexuality" has turned out to be such an enabling crux in the development of civil rights–oriented gay politics. The rhetorical thrust of this unwavering agnosticism is typically double: to undo the historical alienation by certain explanatory disciplines and their experts of the propriodescriptive rights of gay individuals; and to press the question of causation, with its attendant mobilization of analytic visibilities and vulnerabilities, back in the direction of heterosexual object choice.

1908 and to the essay on Sainte-Beuve: the diverse fragments whose union will form the chapter entitled "La Race maudite". . . . and the first pieces devoted to the "little nucleus" of the Verdurins. Finally, as a decisive indication, in the middle of Notebook 7, we read about the entrance of the Baron de Charlus, presented here under the name of M. de Guercy; and at the same moment we rediscover the anonymous beach.

In Rivers's summary, "Bardèche argues that these experiments with homosexuality as a literary theme gave Proust's work a 'new orientation.' And he concludes that it was at about this time that Proust 'realized that he could produce a book from his fragments.'"[6]

If "La Race maudite" is reductive and sentimental on the one hand, and yet a—arguably, *the*—catalytic node, on the other, of a larger work to which these epithets are not habitually applied, then we can look at what substantively we are saying and doing by their use. "Reductive" suggests a relation of part to whole, in which the part seems to claim to offer an adequate representation of the whole through simple *quantitative* condensation (like a reduced gravy), but which the negative inflection on the adjective then seems to adjudge biased or *qualitatively* different. As a description of the "Introduction to the Men-Women" in relation to the whole of *A la recherche* it is notably responsive to what I have been describing as the indissoluble, incoherent yoking in this century of conceptual incongruities between minoritizing and universalizing views of homosexual definition. That is, the chapter that reifies and crystallizes as a principle of persons "the secondary, and, in a sense, merely anecdotal question of 'sexual preference'" necessarily misrepresents, in representing at all (any thematization here is "banal thematization"), what is elsewhere more universally and hence *differently* diffused as a narrative potential. But the bite, the tang and effectual animus of that diffusion depends unstably *on* the underlying potential for banal thematization; while the banal thematization itself (both in the form of the "Men-Women" chapter and in the body of M. de Charlus) displays, even as it uncontrollably *transmits*, the sheer representational anxiety of its reductive compaction.

After all, even though "La Race maudite" is almost universally thought of as distilling a certain minoritizing, gender-transitive paradigm of inversion in its purest form, it is even internally rife with versions of the same

6. Quoted (first part) and paraphrased (second part) in Rivers, *Proust*, pp. 150–51, from Maurice Bardèche, *Marcel Proust, romancier*, 2 vols. (Paris: Sept Couleurs, 1971), pp. 216–17.

contradictions that surround it. For instance, it is sensitive to a difference between aim and object: "Some [inverts] . . . are not greatly concerned with the kind of physical pleasure they receive, provided that they can associate it with a masculine face. Whereas others . . . feel an imperious need to localise their physical pleasure" (C 645).[7] Again, in the very same sentence in which he describes inverts as invested — albeit *by persecution* — "with the physical and moral characteristics of a race," the narrator also offers some elements of a historicizing constructivist view of homosexual identity. Inverts, he says, take

> pleasure in recalling that Socrates was one of themselves . . . without reflecting that there were no abnormal people when homosexuality was the norm . . . that the opprobrium alone makes the crime because it has allowed to survive only those who remained obdurate to every warning, to every example, to every punishment, by virtue of an innate disposition so peculiar [*tellement spéciale*] that it is more repugnant to other men . . . than . . . vices better understood . . . by the generality of men. (C 639)

Yet by the end of the chapter it is made explicit that far from being *tellement spéciale*, these "exceptional" creatures "are a vast crowd" — "If a man can number the dust of the earth, then shall th[eir] seed also be numbered" (C 654–55). Furthermore, the narrator all but dares the reader to discover that his minoritizing account also explains the "inso-lent" and self-protective motives and feelings with which a narrator (himself?) might offer a *falsely* minoritizing account of sexual inverts:

> a reprobate section of the human collectivity, but an important one, suspected where it does not exist, flaunting itself [*étalée*: spread out, displayed, disclosed], insolent and immune, where its existence is never guessed; numbering its adherents everywhere, among the people, in the army, in the church, in prison, on the throne; living, in short, at least to a great extent, in an affectionate and perilous intimacy with the men of the other race, provoking them, playing with them by speaking of the vice as of something alien to it — a game that is rendered easy by the blindness or duplicity of the others. (C 640)

7. Except where otherwise noted, Proust quotations are from *Remembrance of Things Past*, trans. C. K. Scott Moncrieff and Terence Kilmartin, 3 vols. (New York: Random House / Vintage, 1982). Citations within the text will refer by initial to individual books and give page numbers within the volume in which the book appears. Volume I contains *Swann's Way* (S) and *Within a Budding Grove* (W); Volume II, *The Guermantes Way* (G) and *Cities of the Plain* (C); and Volume III, *The Captive* (Cap), *The Fugitive* (F), and *Time Regained* (T).

One might think from such a passage that no one is finally imagined to be "of the other race" except the reader to whom it is addressed! But of course, its "affectionate and perilous" aggression involves, as well, the insinuation in its last five words that even that reader is likely to have his own, identical reasons for colluding in the definitional segregation of *la race maudite*.

In terms of gender, as well, this supposed locus classicus of the Ur-doctrine of sexual inversion, *anima muliebris in corpore virili inclusa*, actually presents a far more complex and conflicted cluster of metaphorical models. At the crudest level, the explanation that Charlus desires men because deep down he is a woman, an explanation that the chapter and indeed the whole book repeatedly proffers, is seriously undermined even in the short space between the narrator's first realization that Charlus reminds him of a woman (C 626) and the later epiphany that he had looked like one because "he was one!" (C 637). What the narrator has witnessed, however, in the interval is not at all a conquest of this female-gendered self by another self contrastively figured as male. Instead, the intervening pickup between Charlus and Jupien has been presented in two other guises. Primarily it is seen as a mirror-dance of two counterparts "in perfect symmetry" (C 626), tacitly undermining the narrator's decision to reject the term "homosexuality" on account of its reliance on a model of similarity. At the same time—startlingly indeed, and not the less so because the aporia goes unmarked—the transaction is figured as the courtship by a *male*-figured Charlus of a *female*-figured Jupien. "One might have thought of them as a pair of birds, the male and the female, the male seeking to make advances, the female—Jupien—no longer giving any sign of response to these overtures, but regarding her new friend without surprise" (C 628).

The gender figuration is even further destabilized by an overarching botanical metaphor in which sex/gender difference and species difference keep almost-representing and hence occluding one another. The framing of "La Race maudite" involves the display, in the Guermantes's courtyard window, of a rare orchid ("they're all ladies") that can be fertilized only through the providential intervention of exactly the right bee. As the duchess explains, "It's a kind of plant where the ladies and the gentlemen don't both grow on the same stalk. . . . [T]here are certain insects whose duty it is to bring about the marriage, as with sovereigns, by proxy, without the bride and bridegroom ever having set eyes on one another. . . . But the odds are so enormous! Just think, he would have to have just been to see a person of the same species and the opposite sex, and he must then have taken it into his head to come and leave cards at the house. He hasn't appeared so far" (G 535–36). And in the last sentence of "La Race maudite" the narrator is "distressed to find that, by my engrossment in the Jupien-Charlus conjunction, I had missed perhaps an opportunity of witnessing the fertilisation of the blossom by the bumble-bee" (C 656).

The point continually emphasized in the analogy between Charlus's situation and that of the orchid is simply the pathos of how unlikely fulfillment is, of how absurdly, impossibly specialized and difficult is the need of each. This point is explicitly undone by the universalizing move at the end of the chapter ("I greatly exaggerated at the time . . . the elective character of so carefully selected a combination" [C 654]). Furthermore, it is silently undone by the entire remaining stretch of *A la recherche*, in which the love relationship entered into on this occasion between Charlus and Jupien is demonstrated—though it is never stated—to be the single exception to every Proustian law of desire, jealousy, triangulation, and radical epistemological instability; without any comment or rationalization, Jupien's love of Charlus is shown to be steadfast over decades and grounded in a completely secure knowledge of a fellow-creature who is neither his opposite nor his simulacrum.

Even while the pathos of the rarity and fragility of orchid-mating is let stand, however, the analogy opens gaping conceptual abysses when one tries—as the chapter repeatedly does—to compare any model of same-sex desire with the plight of the virginal orchid. After all, the difference between the situation of the non-proximal orchids and that of any normative heterosexual human pair is not that the orchid partners are both of the same sex, nor that either or both have a misassignment or misattribution of sex: one orchid is still just plain male, the other just plain female. Rather, the peculiarity of their situation is that, being immobilized, they must employ a third party—of a different species, sex unspecified—as a go-between. No mapping of Jupien or Charlus as either the bee or the other orchid does anything to clarify or deepen a model of sexual inversion; and the narrator's introduction of the red herring of botanical hermaphrodism (to indulge another cross-species conjunction) makes the possible decoding of the metaphor all the more dizzyingly impossible. So much so, indeed, that this layering of images from "nature," each with its own cluster of contradictory, moralizing-cum-scientific appeals to what is finally "natural," may have most the effect of denaturing nature itself as a resort of the explanatory, leaving it, instead, only as the name of a space or even a principle of high-handed definitional flux. To give only one, not atypical example:

> The laws of the vegetable kingdom are themselves governed by increasingly higher laws. If the visit of an insect, that is to say the transportation of the seed from another flower, is generally necessary for the fertilisation of a flower, that is because self-fertilisation, the insemination of a flower by itself, would lead, like a succession of intermarriages in the same family, to degeneracy and sterility, whereas the crossing effected by insects gives to the subsequent generations of the same species a vigour unknown to their forebears. This invigoration may, however, prove excessive, and the species develop out of all proportion; then, as an anti-toxin protects us against disease, as the thyroid gland regulates our adiposity, as defeat comes to punish pride, as fatigue follows indulgence, and as sleep in turn brings rest from fatigue, so an exceptional act of self-fertilisation comes at the crucial moment to apply its turn of the screw, its pull on the curb, brings back within the norm the flower that had exaggeratedly overstepped it. (C 624–25)

Whether nature operates at the level of the survival of the individual, the species, or some overarching "norm" of "proportion"; whether, on the other hand, punishment for moral failings or, alternatively, the mitigation of their punishment is the telos of nature; whether "the crossing effected by insects" may best be understood as a crossing of boundaries of the individual, of genders, or of forms of life; why nature may have chosen to exempt M. de Charlus from her regime of thyroid homeostasis: these are among the questions the narrative provokes at the same time as overrides.

One thing the triangle of orchid-bee-orchid does suggest, however, as a persistently foregrounded analogy to the encounter in the courtyard, is a possible dependence of that apparently two-sided eros on the highly invested busy-ness of some mobile, officious, vibrant, identification-prone third figure who both is and isn't a transactor in it. On, in short, the narrator and / or the variously indeterminate, acrobatic spying boy he represents to us; and perhaps as well a dependence on us insofar as we are invited at once to scrutinize and to occupy his vicariated positionings. As we discussed in Chapter 3, this foregrounding of voyeuristic reader relations of the tacitly vicarious may well be part of the claim on our attention here, also, of the other damning category adduced by Bersani about this chapter of Proust: the category "sentimental."

About the phenomenon of "sentimentality," we have said, as more specifically about such subcategories of vicarious knowledge-relation as prurience, morbidity, knowingness, and snobbism, two things can be said. First, and crucially: *It takes one to know one*. But the apparent symmetry of that epistemological catchphrase, in which the One who Knows and the One who is Taken appear interchangeable, belies the extreme asymmetry of rhetorical positioning implicit in the projectile efficacy of these attributions. The ballistics of "the sentimental" requires the freeze-framing of one targeted embodiment of sentimentality, its presentation *as spectacle* to a further sentimentality whose own privileged disembodiment and invisibility are preserved and reenabled by that highly differential act of staging. Thus, in the second place, it must be said that sentimentality *as spectacle* is structured very differently from sentimentality *as viewpoint* or habitation; that this difference is rhetorical; and that it is most powerfully charged for textual performance.

It takes one to know one: Need I make explicit that the first resort of such a structure in Proust is the epistemology of the closet? "For," Proust announces in the "Introduction to the Men-Women,"

> the two angels who were posted at the gates of Sodom to learn whether its inhabitants (according to Genesis) had indeed done all the things the report of which had ascended to the Eternal Throne must have been, and of this one can only be glad, exceedingly ill chosen by the Lord, Who ought to have entrusted the task to a Sodomite. Such an one would never have been persuaded by such excuses as "I'm the father of six and I've two mistresses," to lower his flaming sword benevolently and mitigate the punishment. . . . These descendants of the Sodomites . . . have established themselves throughout the entire world; they have had access to every profession and are so readily admitted into the most exclusive clubs that, whenever a Sodomite fails to secure election, the black balls are for the most part cast by other Sodomites, who make a point of condemning sodomy, having inherited the mendacity that enabled their ancestors to escape from the accursed city. (C 655)

This important passage, of course, enacts exactly the process it describes: both Proust's biography and, more important, the passage itself tell us that the authoritative worldliness that alone can underwrite such sweeping attributions is available only to an observer who both is himself a "descendant of the Sodomites" and at the same time has himself "inherited the mendacity" of homophobic denial and projection. This suggests, however, as a corollary, that an ability to articulate the world as a whole, as a universe that includes (while it may transcend) "the worldly," may well be oriented around the tensely attributive specular axis between two closets: in the first place the closet viewed, the *spectacle of the closet*; and in the second its hidden framer and consumer, the closet inhabited, the *viewpoint of the closet*.

If this is true—or, at a minimum, true of "the world" as we have it in Proust—then it makes all the sense *in* the world that it was exactly the invention, for the story's purposes, of the Baron de Charlus, in the sentimental matrix of "La Race maudite" in 1909, that should conversely have had the power to constitute for the first time as a speaker of more than fragmentary and more than sentimental narrative the thereby disembodied interlocutor whose name is probably not Marcel. "La Race maudite" may be the least appetizing neighborhood of *A la recherche*, but its genius loci M. de Charlus is nonetheless the novel's most ravishingly consumable product. And the endless, endlessly lavish production of M. de Charlus—as spectacle; as, to be specific, the spectacle of the closet—enables the world of the novel to take shape and turn around the steely beam of his distance from the differently structured closet of the narrative and its narrator.

Reassure yourself here: the by now authentically banal exposure of Proust's narrator as a closeted homosexual will not be the structuring gesture made by the reading ahead. Yet I don't see how that banality, either, can be excluded from the text or even so much as rendered optional to it. The novel seems both to prohibit and to extort from its readers such a violence of interpretive uncovery against the narrator, the violence of rendering his closet, in turn, as spectacle. The least bathetic question would seem to be how the reader, in turn, gets constituted in this relation: how, among the incoherent constructions of sexuality, gender, privacy, and minoritization, a dangerously enabling poetics and politics of exemption may construct themselves in and through her.

◆   ◆   ◆

The irresistibleness of the Baron de Charlus: subject as inexhaustible, and as difficult of approach, as is, Proust remarks, that of the profanation of the mother—to which, we must add, it is anything but irrelevant. Charlus is the prodigal gift that keeps *opening itself* to the wonder and pleasure of the reader. At least, that is the experience of the reader, who is invited not to concentrate too much on the mechanics of this miraculous proffer. Like the faithful on the little train, readers of certain long stretches of *A la recherche* may feel that

> if M. de Charlus did not appear, they were almost disappointed to be travelling only with people who were just like everybody else, and not to

have with them this painted, paunchy, tightly-buttoned personage, reminiscent of a box of exotic and dubious origin exhaling a curious odour of fruits the mere thought of tasting which *soulèverait le coeur*. (C 1074)[8]

(I give the last phrase in French because Scott Moncrieff renders it so attractively as "stirs the heart";[9] Kilmartin doughily corrects it to "would turn the stomach.") Infatuated with Charlus—ostensibly in spite of his homosexuality, but in fact "quite unconsciously" because of it (C 1075)— the Verdurin circle nonetheless generates a ceaseless spume of homophobic wit about him, uttered beyond the reach of his appreciation but delicately reproduced for ours. The cautious or daring tracery of the involuted perimeters of Charlus's "secret" lends his presence an endlessly renewed vibrancy, for the faithful as for their readers. The entire magnetism of every element of instability in the twentieth-century epistemology of the closet radiates toward and from, if it cannot ever be said to belong to, the Baron.

To begin with, he is alienated from the authority to describe his own sexuality. This appears most symptomatically in the tropism by which the narrator's presentations of Charlus persist in reaching out toward an appeal to, and identification with, the medical expert:

> A skilled physician need not even make his patient unbutton his shirt, nor listen to his breathing—the sound of his voice is enough. How often, in time to come, was my ear to be caught in a drawing-room by the intonation or laughter of some man whose artificial voice . . . was enough to indicate: "He is a Charlus" to my trained ear . . . ! (C 688)

When the previously hypervirile Charlus grows more effeminate with the passage of time, the narrator diagnoses:

> he would now utter involuntarily almost the same little squeaks (involuntary in his case and all the more deep-rooted) as are uttered voluntarily by those inverts who hail one another as "my dear!"—as though this deliberate "camping," against which M. de Charlus had for so long set his face, were after all merely a brilliant and faithful imitation of the manner that men of the Charlus type, whatever they may say, are compelled to adopt when they have reached a certain stage in their malady, just as sufferers

8. The French is from the Pléiade edition, 3 vols. (Paris: Gallimard, 1954), 2: 1043. Further citations from this edition will be given in the text.

9. Marcel Proust, *Cities of the Plain*, trans. C. K. Scott Moncrieff (New York: Random House/Vintage, 1970), p. 314. Further citations from this translation will be given in the text as *Cities* and the page number.

from general paralysis or locomotor ataxia inevitably end by displaying certain symptoms. As a matter of fact — and this is what this purely unconscious "camping" revealed — the difference between the stern, black-clad Charlus with his hair *en brosse* whom I had known, and the painted and bejewelled young men, was no more than the purely apparent difference that exists between an excited person who talks fast and keeps fidgeting all the time, and a neurotic who talks slowly, preserves a perpetual phlegm, but is tainted with the same neurasthenia in the eyes of the physician who knows that each of the two is devoured by the same anxieties and marred by the same defects. (Cap 209)

The narrator scarcely says that medicine is the discursive system under which M. de Charlus can be most adequately considered. The physicians enter these passages only metaphorically, yet they roll up to the door, over and over, with all the regularity of the bygone time of house calls.[10] Their function here is not themselves to assume jurisdiction over Charlus and his confrères. But the fact that since the late nineteenth century it was by medicine that the work of taxonomy, etiology, diagnosis, *certification* of the phenomenon of sexual inversion was most credibly accomplished means that even the vestibular attendance of the medical consultant ratifies a startling, irreversible expropriation. For, once there is known to exist a system by which the authority of the classified invert to say what in him is voluntary and what compelled, what authentic and what imitative, what conscious and what unconscious, can be not only abstracted from himself but placed in an ironclad epistemological receivership, the result is that not only the medical expert but *anyone* who witnesses and identifies the invert feels assured of knowing more about him than he knows about himself. The very existence of expertise, to whomever it belongs, guarantees everyone who is not its designated object an empowering and exciting specular differential of knowledge that seems momentarily insulated from the edginess of "It takes one to know one."

Thus, if Charlus's being in the closet means that he possesses a secret knowledge, it means all the more that everyone around him does; their incessant reading of the plot of his preserving his secret from them

---

10. When Charlus and some other guests are exchanging gay gossip at a party, for instance: "There is no social function that does not, if one takes a cross-section of it and cuts sufficiently deep, resemble those parties to which doctors invite their patients, who utter the most intelligent remarks, have perfect manners, and would never show that they were mad if they did not whisper in your ear, pointing to some old gentleman going past: 'That's Joan of Arc'" (Cap 245). More examples: C 1083; T 868–69.

provides an all the more eventful plot for them to keep secret from him.[11] Undoubtedly the insistence of this drama is a sign of how predatory and wasting is the conscious imaginative life of the Verdurin circle. Still, the narrator circulates it as his and hence our imaginative life as well. "Oh!" whispers unhilariously the sculptor Ski on the train, "If the Baron begins making eyes at the conductor, we shall never get there, the train will start going backwards" (C 1075); but it is in the narrator's own voice that Charlus's "proud erectness, his eagerness to be admired, his conversational verve" are offered to us so thickly plastered to the ritually desubordinated corporeal ground of, faced away from himself and thus exposed to everyone's interpretive espial but his own, "*un derrière presque symbolique*" (C 890, Pléiade II: 861).

Of course, it is hardly unheard-of in Proust — in fact, it is the law — that characters in general take on vitality and momentum to the degree that they are mystified about their own involuntary, inauthentic, or unconscious motivations. Charlus is not an exception to the law but its blazing sacrificial embodiment, the burning bush, very flesh of that word. The pressure of the *presque* in the *presque symbolique*, the resistance to Charlus's conclusive subsumption under some *adequately* intelligible interpretive system, suggests that the scandalizing materiality of this fat man is too crucially productive at the enabling nexuses of incoherence in the text to be allowed to be fully sublimated. Those enabling incoherences include the unstable dichotomies that we have discussed as contested sites that have been most ineffaceably marked by the turn-of-the-century crisis of homo/heterosexual definition. Most obvious of these are secrecy/disclosure and private/public; masculine/feminine, as well, for Charlus, is too all-pervasive a definitional and descriptive problematic to require or permit any précis.[12] The transfer, effected by the taxonomic gaze, of the

---

11. The passage C 1075–88 offers a good concentration of instances of this effect.
12. If one had to choose one passage, however, it might be this:

Mme Verdurin asked him: "Did you try some of my orangeade?" Whereupon M. de Charlus, with a gracious smile, in a crystalline tone which he rarely adopted, and with endless simperings and wrigglings of the hips, replied: "No, I preferred its neighbour, which is strawberry-juice, I think. It's delicious." It is curious that a certain category of secret impulses has as an external consequence a way of speaking or gesticulating which reveals them. If a man believes or disbelieves in the Immaculate Conception, or in the innocence of Dreyfus, or in a plurality of worlds, and wishes to keep his opinion to himself, you will find nothing in his voice or in his gait that will betray his thoughts. But on hearing M. de Charlus say, in that shrill voice and with that smile and those gestures, "No, I preferred its neighbour, the strawberry-juice," one could say: "Ah, he likes the stronger sex," with the same

authority to designate what is natural/artificial, healthy/decadent, and new/old (or young/old), is clear in the sentence from which I have already quoted a phrase:

> Now, in a light travelling suit which made him appear stouter, as he waddled along with his swaying paunch and almost symbolic behind, the cruel light of day decomposed, into paint on his lips, into face-powder fixed by cold cream on the tip of his nose, into mascara on his dyed moustache whose ebony hue contrasted with his grizzled hair, everything that in artificial light would have seemed the healthy complexion of a man who was still young. (C 890)

The decadence of mien (in the Swiftian literalness of its decomposition into separate pieces), which seems to be the same thing as the self-exposure as artifice of each of those pieces, is revealed through a chiasmic relation between the object and the circumstance of its viewing (since what looks natural in artificial light looks artificial in natural light) by which the viewer is perceptually exempted from the representational fissures framed in the description.

Not only is Charlus not alone in his self-mystification on each of these points, but he is written, of course, into a text in which each of them is quite pivotally problematized. Whatever one may want to say about modern Western culture at large, Proust is hardly Exhibit A if one wants to demonstrate—even if only for immediate deconstruction—the normative privileging of, for instance, masculine over feminine, majority over minority, innocence over initiation, nature over artifice, growth over decadence, health over illness, cognition over paranoia, or will over involuntarity. But again, it seems to be the very ambience of destabilization that renders so focal and so (for the process of reading) precious the *un*inter-

---

certainty as enables a judge to sentence a criminal who has not confessed, or a doctor a patient suffering from general paralysis who himself is perhaps unaware of his malady but has made some mistake in pronunciation from which it can be deduced that he will be dead in three years. Perhaps the people who deduce, from a man's way of saying: "No, I preferred its neighbour, the strawberry-juice," a love of the kind called unnatural, have no need of any such scientific knowledge. But that is because here there is a more direct relation between the revealing sign and the secret. Without saying so to oneself in so many words, one feels that it is a gentle, smiling lady who is answering and who appears affected because she is pretending to be a man and one is not accustomed to seeing men put on such airs. And it is perhaps more gracious to think that a certain number of angelic women have long been included by mistake in the masculine sex where, feeling exiled, ineffectually flapping their wings towards men in whom they inspire a physical repulsion, they know how to arrange a drawing-room, to compose "interiors." (C 999)

mitted frontal glee with which the vision of Charlus's glass closet is presented to the hungry window-shopping eye. Every ethical valuation, every analytic assignment has its own volatile barometric career, and not least in their interimplications with the figure of Charlus. But the relations of who views whom — who, that is, describes and who consumes whom — guaranteed by Charlus's unkeepable secret enable him to dazzle and dazzle from his unfluctuating, almost immobilized eminence of unrationalized representational office.

Take the famous moment from "La Race maudite" when the narrator, from his place of concealment, witnesses a sudden secret eye-lock between Charlus and Jupien in the courtyard.

> I was about to change my position again, so that he should not catch sight of me; I had neither the time nor the need to do so. For what did I see! Face to face, in that courtyard where they had certainly never met before . . . the Baron, having suddenly opened wide his half-shut eyes, was gazing with extraordinary attentiveness at the ex-tailor poised on the threshold of his shop, while the latter, rooted suddenly to the spot in front of M. de Charlus, implanted there like a tree, contemplated with a look of wonderment the plump form of the aging baron. But, more astounding still, M. de Charlus's pose having altered, Jupien's, as though in obedience to the laws of an occult art, at once brought itself into harmony with it. The Baron, who now sought to disguise the impression that had been made on him, and yet, in spite of his affectation of indifference, seemed unable to move away without regret, came and went, looked vaguely into the distance in the way which he felt would most enhance the beauty of his eyes, assumed a smug, nonchalant, ridiculous air.[13] Meanwhile Jupien, shedding at once the humble, kindly expression which I had always associated with him, had — in perfect symmetry with the Baron — thrown back his head, given a becoming tilt to his body, placed his hand with grotesque effrontery on his hip, stuck out his behind, struck poses with the coquetry that the orchid might have adopted on the providential arrival of the bee. I had not supposed that he could appear so repellent. . . .
>
> This scene was not, however, positively comic; it was stamped with a strangeness, or if you like a naturalness, the beauty of which steadily increased. (*Cities* 626–27)

"More *astounding* still," "*ridiculous* air," "*becoming*," "*grotesque* effrontery," "so *repellent*," "not positively *comic*." The almost epidermal-level

---

13. Kilmartin translates "*ridicule*" as "fatuous," which supplements the impact of "*fat*" = "smug," but doesn't reproduce the particular adjectival effect I want to point to in the French.

zephyrs of responsiveness and stimulation in this passage are wafted along on the confidence—that is to say, the apparent *arbitrariness*, verging on self-contradiction—with which these adjectives are assigned, adjectives each alluding to an assumed audience relation ("astounding," "ridiculous," "becoming," "grotesque," "repellent," "comic," each *to* someone else) which the spying narrator in turn is airily, astringently prepared to indulge, parlay, or supersede. To the extent that any child's ability to survive in the world can be plotted through her wavering command of a succession of predicate adjectives (important milestones might include the ability to formulate "I must be tired," "X is violent," "Y is dying," "Z must be stupid," "A and B are quarrelling," "C is beautiful," "D is drunk," "E is pregnant"), so that the assignment of adjectives and the creation of reliable adjectival communities become ached-for badges of the worldly, the framing of the homosexual scene by Proust's young-old narrator must both disorient and reassure the reader, disorient almost in proportion as she already finds the scene familiar; the stripping away of the consistencies by which she would normally find her way through it seems also a kind of reassurance of the narrator's high descriptive hand.[14]

But the reader partakes of the narrator's arbitrary descriptive power only by acquiescing and sharing in his self-concealment, his unexplained, unpredictable gusts of desire and contempt toward the tense interrogative staging of the scene of gay recognition. It is from the borrowed shelter of that adjectival closet that the three abstract nouns ("empreinte d'*une étrangeté*, ou si l'on veut d'*un naturel*, dont *la beauté* allait croissant" [Pléiade II: 605]) can then issue with their almost operatic definitiveness. The adjudication of *un naturel* being to all appearances the assigned task of this most "homosexual" chapter of Proust (framed as it is by the Question of the Orchid), the marked intensification, with these nouns, of the narrator's Zenlike highhandedness of attribution discloses at the same time an affection and a contempt for the terms in which the question of homosexual desire can from a distance be so much as posed. To let *l'étrangeté* equal *le naturel*, after all, is not simply to equate opposites but to collapse a domino chain of pairings, each with its different, historical gay involvements: natural/unnatural, natural/artificial, habitual/de-familiarized, common/rare, native/foreign. The *bouleversement* here of

14. Some Proustian assertions and examples of the power of the predicate adjective: "mad" (G 394), "pregnant" (C 636).

the various systematics by which homosexual desire was, in this chapter, supposed to be analyzed and measured has, however, less than no power to interrupt the outpouring of this aria, which is to continue in exactly the same key at the same pitch for another two pages.[15] It would be an understatement to say that the coherence of the analytic categories is subordinated to the continuity of their enunciation; rather, the authoritative positioning of enunciation itself is borne along by just the imperiousness with which the categories are seen to be overridden. "*Dont la beauté allait croissant*": what after all grows and grows, in these sentences, and therefore what one is compelled to consume (and does consume) *as beauty*, is no indwelling quality of Charlus or Jupien or their encounter but the swelling, sustained, inexhaustibly affecting verve and assurance of the narrator's descriptive entitlement at their expense. In fact, every analytic or ethical category applied throughout *A la recherche* to the homosexuality of M. de Charlus can easily be shown to be subverted or directly contradicted elsewhere. What these proliferating categories and especially their indissoluble contradictions do unflaggingly sustain, however, is the establishment of *the spectacle of the homosexual closet* as a presiding guarantor of rhetorical community, of authority — someone else's authority — over world-making discursive terrain that extends vastly beyond the ostensible question of the homosexual.

15. To try to explain what is meant by this key, this pitch: e.g., we are told in the long paragraph that the men are speaking to each other, but we are given none of the language they exchange; instead we receive the narrator's language about *what kind of* thing they would be saying, which makes it increasingly impossible to imagine what they could actually be saying. The real effect is that one is convinced that the men are quite mute (augmenting the sense of magic, beauty, eerie atemporality, but also of theatrical pantomime about the scene), while the whole is suffused by the voice of the hidden narrator. Again, language that is ostensibly about the two men keeps seeming to describe even better the sustained tour de force of the descriptive staging, the uncannily dilated silence itself: "that feeling of the brevity of all things which . . . renders so moving the spectacle of every kind of love":

> Thus, every other minute, the same question seemed to be put . . . like those questioning phrases of Beethoven's, indefinitely repeated at regular intervals and intended — with an exaggerated lavishness of preparation — to introduce a new theme, a change of key, a "re-entry." On the other hand, the beauty of the reciprocal glances of M. de Charlus and Jupien arose precisely from the fact that they did not, for the moment at least, seem to be intended to lead to anything further. It was the first time I had seen the manifestation of this beauty in the Baron and Jupien.

The repeated touching of the same string, "beauty," has just the effect described, a suspension between stasis and initiation, organized around the rights of ocular consumption.

◆　　◆　　◆

The efficacy of M. de Charlus for the novel as a whole depends so much on Proust's presenting *the spectacle of the closet* as *the truth of the homosexual*, and that is accomplished with such apparent fullness, that it becomes one of the most difficult problems of Proust-reading to find a space in this Charlus-oriented world in which the other homosexual desires in the book can at all be made visible. Especially, to try to pull the eros surrounding the narrator and Albertine into any binocular focus with the novel's presentation of Charlus is a wrenchingly difficult task. There is a simple explanation for this difficulty: it is exactly in their *relation to visibility* that the two erotic loci are so violently incommensurable. Seemingly, Charlus's closet is spectacularized *so that* the erotics around Albertine (which is to say, around the narrator) may continue to resist visualization; it is from the inchoate space that will include Albertine, and to guarantee its privileged exemption from sight, that the narrator stages the presentation of Charlus; it is around the perceptual axis between a closet viewed and a closet inhabited that a discourse of the world takes shape.

That is the simple way to formulate the difficulty, and I think the crucial one; but if it were just that simple the difficulty would be easy to master analytically. Instead, the difference of visibility accomplishes itself through all the channels of those major, intractable incoherences of homo/heterosexual definition and gender definition established in the crisis of sexual discourse around the turn of the century.

To begin with: while the spectacle of M. de Charlus is ostentatiously that of *a closet* with *a homosexual* concealed, with riveting inefficiency, in its supposed interior, it is on the other hand notoriously hard to locate *a homosexual* anywhere in the fluctuous privacy surrounding Albertine. With all their plurality of interpretive paths, there is no way to read the Albertine volumes without finding same-sex desire *somewhere*; at the same time, that specificity of desire, in the Albertine plot, notoriously refuses to remain fixed to a single character type, to a single character, or even to a single ontological level of the text. Given a male narrator fixated on the interpretation of a female Albertine who in turn has, or has had, or may have had, sexual connections with numerous other women, one would expect that narrator to mobilize in the service of "explaining" and "understanding" her all the *idées reçues* on the exotic subject of inversion in general, and Gomorrah in particular, laboriously assembled by him in "La Race maudite." But it almost never happens. The awful dilation of interpretive pressure on Albertine is overwhelmingly brought to bear on her, not under the category of "the invert," but under the category of "the beloved object" or, as if this were synonymous, simply of "woman."[16] And, of course, while "the invert" is defined in Proust as that person over whom everyone else in the world has, potentially, an absolute epistemological privilege, "the beloved object" and "woman" are defined on the contrary by the complete eclipse of the power to know them of the one person, the lover, who most needs to do so. Charlus, *the* "invert," is scarcely presented as a love object in the Proustian sense — though, as we have noted, he is *loved*, by Jupien, whose anomalously perfect understanding of his beloved may indeed owe something to the very hyperlegibility of Charlus-as-The-Invert. Morel, who *is* Charlus's object in the Proustian sense, isn't presented as an invert (and therefore can be genuinely inscrutable). Only for the Princesse de Guermantes is Charlus a classic object, i.e., someone to whom she can be, in the important respects, blind. But it is not to his homosexuality that she is blind; exceptionally, however, she does not treat his relation to his sexuality as a demeaning spectacle, and so she is rendered mortally vulnerable to him. (Note, however, that "mortally vulnerable" just means, in Proust, "in love"; her vulnerability isn't exceptional except in its choice of object.)

Thus, while the Charlus who loves men is described as typical of "the invert" as a species, the Albertine who loves women seems scarcely to come under a particular taxonomic heading on that account; it is as if the two successive stages of homosexual definition, the premedicalization one of same-sex *acts* and the postmedicalization one of homosexual *types*, coexisted in Albertine and Charlus in an anachronistic mutual blindness. Or, alternatively, Albertine can seem to some readers to embody the utopian fulfillment of a universalizing view of homo/heterosexual definition, even as the incomparable Charlus (incomparable, that is, to Albertine) dystopically embodies the minoritizing view.

But perhaps it is not to Albertine "her"self or to her girlfriends that one should, in the nest of relationships surrounding her, look first for the figure of the homosexual. As J. E. Rivers points out, the flurry of rereadings that surfaced after 1949 based on the supposition that Albertine "was

16. Examples: Cap 74, F 512.

really" a man—i.e., was based, as Proust had suggested to Gide and others, on a portrait of Proust's chauffeur, Alfred Agostinelli, or on some other man—however vulgarizing, confused, and homophobic, however illegitimate as literary criticism or inadmissible in their assumptions about writing and loving, did nevertheless respond so strongly to a variety of unmistakable provocations in the text that the possibility of reading Albertine "as," in some radically to-be-negotiated sense, a man, is by now at least inalienably grafted onto the affordances of the text.[17] To the degree that Albertine is a man, however, the question left unanswered is less why *he* isn't brought under the taxonomic rubric of "the invert" than why the male narrator who covets him isn't, as he isn't. But with this possibility of "transposition" a lot of other contradictions also rise to the surface. For instance, if Albertine and the narrator are of the same gender, should the supposed outside loves of Albertine, which the narrator obsessively imagines as imaginatively inaccessible to himself, then, maintaining the female *gender* of their love object, be transposed in *orientation* into heterosexual desires? Or, maintaining the transgressive same-sex *orientation*, would they have to change the *gender* of their love object and be transposed into male homosexual desires? Or, in a homosexual framework, would the heterosexual orientation after all be more transgressive? Or—as the Valley folk say—what?

Thus, both the range of contradictions around homo/heterosexual definition, and the intersection *of* that with the range of contradictions around gender definition, are mobilized—to the extent that they fail to be interrogated—in the Albertine plot, and in its incommensurability with the presentation of Charlus. In addition, the gender question itself is tied up in contradiction here. Nothing is of course more insisted upon in the drawing of Charlus than that his desire for men is necessarily the result of sexual *inversion*, of the captivity and occultation of a true female self within his deceptively, even defensively masculine exterior. As we have discussed, this model requires the assignment to each person of a "true" inner gender, and the pairing off of people in heterogendered pairs according to these "true" genders. We have shown how the narrative insistence on this "inversion" reading of homosexual desire overrides even notable instances of dizzying confusion and apparent contravention in the sections that, oriented around Charlus, claim to be definitive presenta-

17. Rivers, *Proust*, pp. 2–9, 247–54 (where he insists on a reading of Albertine as fully androgynous).

tions of homosexuality as a phenomenon. So much the odder, then, that in the Albertine volumes, in the swollen meditations on what this woman may have felt about or acted out with other women (or, in a transposed reading, on what this man may have felt about or acted out with the male narrator or with other men), *that* chain of inferences, or of potential clues, is virtually dropped. Is it because, in some ontologically other sense, "Albertine" "*is*" "deep down" "really" a man that we are so seldom presented with language that tries to explain Albertine's sexuality by positing that she is, deep down, really a man? But nor are such transsexual explanations broached about the narrator, nor often about Andrée, Esther, Léa, the laundresses or shop girls with whom Albertine has or is thought to have connections. Wherever it is that same-sex sexuality is to be looked for in the involvements around Albertine, assignments of "true" "inner" heterogender are not an important part of that perceptual process. Or perhaps better said, the sweeping blur or erasure of those involvements *as objects of perception* requires as well the eclipse of the "inversion" trope whose maintenance had been all along a matter of careful and rather costly framing. In its place, although incompatible with it, there seems to occur a gender-separatist emphasis on Albertine's female connections with women as being, not transitive across gender or liminal between genders, not virilizing, but, rather, in their very lesbianism, of the essence of the female — centrally and definingly located within femininity. Indeed, all that the two versions of homosexual desire seem to have in common may be said to be a sort of asymmetrical list toward the feminine: Charlus is feminized by his homosexual desire, but so, to the extent that gender is an active term in her sexuality at all, is Albertine most often feminized by hers.[18]

If the homosexuality attached to the figure of Charlus and the homo-

---

18. This formulation was suggested to me by Steven Shaviro. I don't, of course, mean by "femininity" here an adherence to stereotypical gender roles (weakness, passivity, prettiness, etc.), but rather *femaleness* figured as a form of power — in particular, however, the power of what is other than the (male-figured) subject itself. This attribution goes back to Proust's specifically epistemological, and specifically male, definition of *the female* as *that which cannot be known* (through the heterosexist detour of defining the female as, definitionally, *the object of love* and hence of unknowledge). How far "femininity" or "femaleness" in Proust can be seen as a syntactic positioning (notably, the accusative as opposed to the nominative) and how far it reaches out toward an anchoring in the semantic, in particular loci and meanings, remains to be discussed, perhaps in relation, not only to Barthes, but to the fascinating paragraph in Bersani's essay about "the ontological necessity of homosexuality [in the other sex] in a kind of universal *hetero*sexual relation of all human subjects to their own desires" (416).

sexuality dispersed in the vicinity of Albertine can't be brought into focus with each other through any consistent reading of either *sexual orientation* or *gender*, there remains the possibility that the practice of the same sexual *acts* could provide a way of describing the two of them in some congruence with each other. After all, it was through *acts*—and acts not defined by either the personality structure or, necessarily, the gender of the persons who performed them—that the category "sodomy" was defined in premodern Europe, and still is in premodern Georgia. Even under the heading of sexual acts, however, Charlus and Albertine seem to persist in remaining mutually incommensurable, although it is perhaps only under this heading that an intelligible *narrative of change* may be legible. We have already noted the "*derrière presque symbolique*" sported by Charlus. Ski, who fantasizes that Charlus's preoccupations will make the train run backward, and Jupien, who sets out (successfully) to woo him with "various remarks lacking in refinement such as '*Vous avez un gros pétard*'" [C 632; Pléiade II: 610], seem to agree with the narrator in confidently attributing to Charlus a receptive anal sexuality that makes all too neat a rhyme with the "truth" of his deep-down femininity, and with the later treatment of his sexuality as degenerating into a masochism that had been, in this rendering, from the start its hidden essence. (Let me pause for an instant to bring fellow Anglophones up to date: if you are one of those to whom French is Greek, and if you've depended for decades on Scott Moncrieff for your Proust, you may not recognize "*Vous avez un gros pétard*," oddly translated there as "Aren't you naughty!" [*Cities*, 9]. Further surprises of the same kind await.)

For Albertine, as usual, the same conceptual gridwork will not suffice to provide a map. If a particular erotic localization is to be associated with her it must be the oral: "As for ices," she says,

> "whenever I eat them, temples, churches, obelisks, rocks, a sort of picturesque geography is what I see at first before converting its raspberry or vanilla monuments into coolness in my gullet. . . . They make raspberry obelisks too, which will rise up here and there in the burning desert of my thirst, and I shall make their pink granite crumble and melt deep down in my throat which they will refresh better than any oasis" (and here the deep laugh broke out, whether from satisfaction at talking so well, or in self-mockery for using such carefully contrived images, or, alas, from physical pleasure at feeling inside herself something so good, so cool, which was tantamount to sexual pleasure). (Cap 125–26)

She is also associated with edibles consumed by the narrator, with that torrid period of the year when sensuality, evaporating, is more readily inclined to visit the organs of taste, seeking above all things coolness. More than for the kiss of a girl, it thirsts for orangeade, for a bath, or even to gaze at that peeled and juicy moon that was quenching the thirst of heaven. (C 669)

But as even these brief citations suggest, if a grainy blowup of Albertine's sexuality might begin with a vista of tonsils, still that erotic localization has most the effect of voiding — of voiding by so exceeding it — the very possibility of erotic localization. Certainly the neat dichotomy of "active" and "passive" (never mind their respective association with "masculine" and "feminine") seemingly attached to Charlus's anal sexuality is obviated in this muscular cave where the pleasures of sucking, eating, uttering, and chuckling pulse so freely together; but the emphasis on "coolness," for instance, further renders as an organ of this sexuality the whole cutaneous envelope of the body, inside and out, which seems further prolonged by the elastic integument of vision itself, extending to crush against its palate fine the peeled and juicy moon.

> I could see Albertine now, seated at her pianola, pink-faced beneath her dark hair; I could feel against my lips, which she would try to part, her tongue, her maternal, incomestible, nutritious, hallowed tongue, whose strange moist warmth, even when she merely ran it over the surface of my neck or my stomach, gave to those caresses of hers, superficial but somehow administered by the inside of her flesh, externalised like a piece of material reversed to show its lining, as it were the mysterious sweetness of a penetration. (F 507-8)

Little wonder that Albertine and the narrator evince some confusion over whether they should be considered lovers "in the full sense of the word" (Cap 91): although it is, at least for the narrator, orgasmic, this sexuality of which French is only the metonym is almost not exclusive enough to figure as sexuality in the same register as Charlus's constricted, "pursy"[19] Greek.

At the same time, it is in this arena of (roughly speaking) sexual acts that it is easiest to construct a value-charged, utopian narrative around the comparison of Charlus to Albertine. Not only can Albertine's sexuality be seen as representing infinity, indeterminacy, contingency, play, etc. etc.

---

19. Scott Moncrieff's translation of the adjective "bedonnant" so frequently applied to Charlus; e.g., *Cities*, 4.

etc., in contrast to that of Charlus, whose circumscription can then be made to look like work, but there is even an evolutionary narrative to which these attributions may be attachable: it is beginning to look as though historians of sexuality will have to learn to think about something like a world-historical popularization of oral sex, sometime in the later nineteenth century.[20] This would suggest, in turn, that the relatively fixed equation by which anal sex had been the main publicly signifying act of male-male intercourse was supplemented around the turn of the century by an increased signifying visibility of oral sex between men. (The Wilde trials, in which publicity was given to insinuations concerning acts of anal sex that in the event turned out not to characterize Wilde's sexuality at all, would offer a convenient milestone in this transformation.)[21] The relative difficulty with which oral sex, as opposed to anal, can be schematized in the bipolar terms of active/passive or analogically male/female, would also seem congruent with the process by which the trope of gender inversion was giving way to the *homo-* trope of gender sameness. And from this point of view the backward-looking sexuality of the Baron de Charlus could be seen to have as emblematic and discrediting a link to his reactionary politics as it ostentatiously has to his demeaned femininity; Albertine, correspondingly, could be seen to embody a modern, less mutilating and hierarchical sexuality even as she (or he) represented the more empowered "New Woman."[22]

This utopian reading of Albertine is attractive, not only because it seems to offer a certain relatively consistent footing for a visionary politics, but because it seems to suggest a conceptual frequency band (the range of Hz between "constricted" and "expansive," between "backward" and "modern") at which the apparently incommensurable wavelengths of Charlus and Albertine could be, as it were, received on the same radio. Under this view the radio must be acknowledged, however, to have periods of going on the fritz, the frequencies to drift and interfere. Albertine, for instance: gifted as she obviously is in the use of her native tongue, there are disruptive suggestions that, at bottom, French is Greek to her too. At a climactic moment in the tensions and pretenses between

---

20. This was suggested to me by two historians of sexuality, Henry Abelove and Kent Gerard.

21. Richard Ellmann, *Oscar Wilde* (New York: Random House/Vintage, 1988), pp. 460–61.

22. Mme Verdurin finally relegates Charlus to the damning category "pre-war" (T 787).

her and the narrator, he offers to make a grand dinner-party for her: "'Thank you for nothing!'" she responds, "with an air of disgust":

> "I'd a great deal rather you left me free for once in a way to go and get myself (*me faire casser*). . ."
> At once her face flushed crimson, she looked appalled, and she put her hand over her mouth as though she could have thrust back the words which she had just uttered and which I had quite failed to catch. (Cap 343)

Obsessive paragraphs later, the narrator figures out what was truncated from Albertine's sentence: the phrase had been *me faire casser le pot*, glossed by Kilmartin as "an obscene slang expression meaning to have anal intercourse (passive)" (Cap 1110). The point here isn't just that Albertine's sexuality includes an anal component; there is no obvious reason why such a component could not figure under the protean and polymorphous sign of the raspberry obelisk: as just another, densely populated nerve center in the expansive inside-and-out glove of an epidermal responsiveness still best symbolized as oral. (Scott Moncrieff, for instance, recuperates this moment for the culinary by offering the unglossed translation "break my pot";[23] and Albertine herself keeps trying to insist, afterwards, that what she had been asking for really was to be allowed to give a dinner-party [Cap 343].) But neither Albertine nor the narrator finds this subsumption under the contingent, the metonymic, a plausible or stable one. Albertine's desperation to eat her words— "crimson with shame," as the narrator repeats, "pushing back into her mouth what she was about to say, desperately ashamed" (Cap 346)— registers not the pleasure of browsing on edibles but the need to undo the evidence of another kind of accident. It is the mouth here that is conscripted into the service of the anal—and the anal *not* as just another site of desire but as a defining breakage in the continuity of desire, under whose excitement and demand any more protean or diffuse sensuality turns back into an architecture of icy vanilla.

"Demand": the one way in which the narrator, in his broodings over it, does *not* (explicitly) interpret Albertine's remark is as a requisition of a specific sexual act, something they could actually do together. Instead, it occasions in him only "horror!" "despair," "rage," "tears" (Cap 345–46);

23. Marcel Proust, *The Captive*, trans. C. K. Scott Moncrieff (New York: Random House/Vintage, 1970), 238–39.

his level of paranoid charade and anticipatory rejection is catapulted to a critical, indeed terminal, height by Albertine's seemingly far from cryptic ejaculation. This is rather unaccountable. He remarkably manages to interpret her expressed desire to get buggered as a sign of her essential *lesbianism*, hence of her inaccessibility to himself:

> Twofold horror! For even the vilest of prostitutes, who consents to such a thing, or even desires it, does not use that hideous expression to the man who indulges in it. She would feel it too degrading. To a woman alone, if she loves women, she might say it, to excuse herself for giving herself to another man. Albertine had not been lying when she told me that she was half dreaming. Her mind elsewhere, forgetting that she was with me, impulsively she had shrugged her shoulders and begun to speak as she would have spoken to one of those women, perhaps to one of my budding girls. (Cap 345–46)

What these farfetched despondencies seem to suggest is that the narrator may really hear Albertine's desire as terrifying, not because it isn't directed toward him, but because it is, her desire registering on him as demand for a performance he fears he cannot give.[24] As so often in the Albertine-associated plot of *A la recherche*, however, the crossing of an axis of sexual desire by an axis of gender definition has most the effect of guaranteeing, in the incoherence of the conceptual space thereby articulated, the infinite availability of hidden bolt-holes for the coverture of meaning, intention, regard. If one cannot say with the utopian readers that either within or around Albertine there are erotic possibilities that mark a potentially regenerative *difference from* the spectacularized Charlus plot, neither, in this fearful, shadowy blur of desiring too much, desiring too little, desiring the always wrong thing from the always wrong kind of person, can an intelligible *similarity to* Charlus be allowed to become visible. The chalky rag of gender pulled across the blackboard of sexuality, the chalky rag of sexuality across the blackboard of gender: these most create a cloudy space from which a hidden voice can be heard to insist, in the

---

24. At the same time, this signal of Albertine's extreme impatience with the diffuse sexuality they had so far practiced makes audible in retrospect how fully the narrator's demand, and her own captivity, had shaped her articulation of that lambent orality. By that articulation at the time, indeed, he had said:

> I was, in spite of everything, deeply touched, for I thought to myself: True, I myself wouldn't speak like that, and yet, all the same, but for me *she* wouldn't be speaking like that. She has been profoundly influenced by me, and cannot therefore help but love me, since she is my creation. (Cap 125)

words of a contemporaneous manifesto of male homosexual panic,[25] "That is not what I meant at all. That is not it, at all."

◆   ◆   ◆

I wonder if other novel-critics who set out to write about Proust feel that if the task is more irresistible than others it is also, not more difficult in degree, but almost prohibitively distinctive in kind: the problem being, not that *Remembrance of Things Past* is so hard and so good, but that "it's all true." I can only report here on my own reading life, but with Proust and my word processor in front of me what I most feel are Talmudic desires, to reproduce or unfold the text and to giggle. Who hasn't dreamt that *A la recherche* remained untranslated, simply so that one could (at least if one knew French) by undertaking the job justify spending one's own productive life afloat within that blissful and hilarious atmosphere of truth-telling.

Nor, for that matter, is the truth-effect of Proust confined to an ethereal space of privacy. To the contrary: fully competitive, in the genre of wisdom literature, with modern embodiments that offer less good advice on interiors, "success" haberdashery, or "power" entertainments, *The Sixty-Year Manager* puts its sociological acuity humbly at the reader's service in the most inglorious, the least customarily acknowledged of our projects. I was reading Proust for the first time during just the short stretch of years during which it occurred to me to have ambitions that were not exclusively under the aspect of eternity: to want to publish visibly, know people, make a go of it, get a run for my money.[26] Oddly, of course, it was reading Proust that made me want these adventures and think I could find them. The interminable meditation on the vanity of human wishes was a galvanizing failure for at least one reader: it was, if anything, the very sense of the transparency and predictability of worldly ambitions that gave me the nerve and skill to have worldly ambitions of my own. Like, I

25. T. S. Eliot, "The Love Song of J. Alfred Prufrock," in *The Complete Poems and Plays 1909–1950* (New York: Harcourt, Brace & World, 1952), p. 6. I am using the phrase "male homosexual panic" in the sense explained in Chapter 4: to denote the panicky response to a blackmailability over homo/heterosexual definition that affects all *but* homosexual-identified men.

26. The cheering equestrian devil-may-care of the very word *career*, which I could only associate with *careen*, let me imagine mine as one of those long-stemmed precarious carriages whose speed over bad roads reliably culminates, in the eighteenth-century novel, in a splintering upset out of whose wreckage only the romantic lead is, in attractive dilapidation, picked.

believe, most young women, I never had a shred of identification with Julien Sorel or the nineteenth-century French male plot of conquering the capital—until after the years of Proust-reading; then both the hero's airy ambition and his concomitant uncritical adoption of a master text became intelligible and engaging traits. I am now able to prescribe "Proust" to my friends in erotic or professional crisis or in, for that matter, personal grief with the same bland confidence as I do a teaspoon of sugar (must be swallowed quickly) to those suffering from hiccups.

But it is harder to say in what this truth-effect of Proust consists. All the paradoxes of a more traditionally conceived *vraisemblance* are especially active here: molecularly, there are relatively few individual propositions in or arising from the book that it would make sense to consider true; and even at the molar level, propositions or "values" or "attitudes" (erotic or political pessimism, for instance) that could be extracted from Proust do not necessarily seem true to me, to whom, nonetheless, "Proust" seems so "true." Plainly, classically, it can be said that the coherence and credibility of the work, its *vraisemblance* in the usual senses, depend on an internal structuration of materials and codes that can only *as* relation, *as* structure, be interdigitated with or tested against the relational structures of a "reality" that surrounds and interleaves and thus mutually constitutes it. The truth-effect I am describing goes beyond questions of the work's coherence and credibility, however. It has to do with the *use* of the literary work, its (to sound censorious) expropriability by its readers, its (to sound, in a different vocabulary, celebratory) potential for empowering them.

For, unmistakably, the autobiographical parable I have just encapsulated as "the years of Proust-reading" represents both a prolonged instance of textual abuse and a story of empowerment.[27] The value, to return to this example, of the book's practical wisdom in the conduct of affairs of the heart ought seemingly to depend on some subscription to its unswerving erotic pessimism. That sensible "ought" concealed from me for years the simplest fact about myself: the most buoyant temperamental, cognitive, all but theoretical erotic optimism. Yet neither before nor after this optimism was finally acknowledged has it seemed, as it "ought"

---

27. Specifically in this case, of course, female empowerment—i.e., of someone who can choose, in her twenties, *whether or not* an investment of vital energies will be made in a career. And empowerment more specifically of a professional-class female: i.e., of someone for whom the cathexis that is there to be chosen *is*, not trade or job, but career.

to have done, to go at all against the grain of the Proustianizing adoptions. Instead, what have become visible are a variety of techniques of "bad faith" or creative mislabeling by which pessimistic heuristics of desire are tacitly yoked into the service of sanguine manipulative projects, or discouraging erotic formulas are powerfully reproduced with only the tiny modification of a single, secret exemption, always in the first person. (The reader, by the way, who does not have a native endowment of these techniques can go for lessons in them to the infinitely discreditable main character in *Remembrance of Things Past*.) If its textual abusiveness and ethical equivocalness do not prevent this relation to Proust from being, at the same time, an authentic instance of empowerment, still less does the admitted double meaning by which the "empowerment" of an individual within a social system necessarily also involves her subjection to a circulatory symbolic economy of power; to be shot into this circulation with the force of some extra quanta of borrowed energy ("Proust") and with a disposition to travel always offers the chance, for long enough, of feeling like mastery. And there is no certainty that the effects of this illusion, or of its decomposition, will not be persistent or corrosive enough to alter in fact, however unpredictably, the itineraries of flow and distribution.

I don't think I am the only reader on whom Proust has an almost coarsely energizing effect that is difficult to account for on any grounds of the purely kosher. I am constrained to wonder what is happening when we, as Proust readers, frame for our own use an account of the world (signalized by this novelistic world) structured around the theatricization of a closet-figured-as-spectacle to preserve the privacy of someone else's closet-occluded-as-viewpoint. We have already seen how great a sense of creativity and mastery are involved in the readerly identification with the narrator's hidden, accusative framing of the closet of the other. But can our own empowering effort to reconfront the two closets with each other as symmetrical objects of our own analysis have less the force of accusation? How far, in adopting such an account, are we drawing our own surplus value of interpretive energies from the homophobic commonplace that attributes the enforcement of heterosexist norms to, precisely and double-damningly, the closeted homosexual himself?

It is, after all, as we have mentioned, entirely within the experience of gay people to find that a homophobic figure in power has, if anything, a disproportionate likelihood of being gay and closeted. This fact, if fact it be, or this appearance, is too important and too easily misused to be discussed briefly. Both the strength of the appearance and its aptitude for complicated misuse were evident in the poisonous coverage of the recent death of the poisonous Roy Cohn.[28] Cohn's death caused to resurface recurrent speculation that many of the main figures behind the homophobic depredations of 1950s McCarthyite red-baiting (Cohn, McCarthy, G. David Schine, J. Edgar Hoover) may have been actively homosexual. The *New York Times* remarked in Cohn's long obituary:

> As they plowed through investigations of the State Department and the Voice of America, relentlessly trying to sniff out Communists or their sympathizers, Mr. Cohn, Mr. Schine and Senator McCarthy, all bachelors at the time, were themselves the targets of what some called "reverse McCarthyism." There were sniggering suggestions that the three men were homosexuals, and attacks such as that by the playwright Lillian Hellman who called them "Bonnie, Bonnie and Clyde."[29]

It is a nice question where the sniggering is located in an obituary whose subject is "Fiery Lawyer" in the front-page headline and then "Flamboyant Lawyer" in the inside one—why not say "flaming" and be done with it?—; whose prose explains that "his parents, particularly his mother, doted on their only child" and that "his office contained an extensive collection of stuffed animals"; whose pace makes a leisurely meal of his repeated denials that he had AIDS and of the lovingly pieced together revelation that he died of it, without any mention of the issues of government confidentiality, crucial to tens of thousands of gay people and others, raised by the semiofficial leakage of such reports during his lifetime; and whose homophobic punchline is allowed to be delivered, not in the voice of the *Times* which chooses to reproduce it, but in that of a leftist and female victim of McCarthyism with whom Cohn can then be presented by the magisterial *Times* as engaged in a symmetrically ("'reverse McCarthyism'") bitchy hair-pulling squabble. Just as Black anti-Semitism and Jewish racism are favored objects of media highlighting and exacerbation because they contribute to the obscurity from which white, Prot-

---

28. Andy Rooney in his nationally syndicated column of August 9, 1986, for instance, gave the list of the "detestable" things that Cohn had denied doing but nonetheless been guilty of: Cohn "denied he participated in [the] witch hunt that unfairly damaged the careers of hundreds [!] of good Americans"; he "denied he owed millions of dollars in back taxes"; he "denied he conned an elderly multimillionaire on his deathbed"; and, of course climactically, he "denied he was a homosexual suffering from AIDS. Death was an effective rebuttal to that last denial."

29. Albin Krebs, "Roy Cohn, Aide to McCarthy and Fiery Lawyer, Dies at 59," *New York Times*, August 3, 1986, pp. 1, 33.

estant privilege is allowed to operate as usual, so revelation of the homophobic enforcement performed by closeted gay people yields an astonishingly sweet taste to the mouths of the presumedly straight public.

It is not only straight-identified or certifiably homophobic people whom such revelation can invigorate, however. What Magnus Hirschfeld's Scientific-Humanitarian Committee referred to in 1903 as "the frequently suggested 'path over corpses'"—"denunciations of homosexuals of high standing," James Steakley explains—is a tactic whose potential, and sometimes execution, have fascinated the gay movement from its inception.[30] From Hirschfeld's and Adolf Brand's willingness to testify that a prince and a chancellor were persons of "homosexual orientation," in the 1907–9 Eulenburg affair that so galvanized Proust,[31] through Hirschfeld's appearance as an expert witness at the 1924 trial of the police informer and mass murderer Fritz Haarmann,[32] to the traditional gay epithet "Alice Blue Gown" for cops and especially vice cops, to the recent relish for information about the cause of death of New Right wunderkind Terry Dolan, to the restorative animus with which, for instance, gay journalist Boyd McDonald sets out after the sexuality of vicious men like William F. Buckley, Jr.,[33] it has at various times and for various reasons

30. Discussed in Steakley, *The Homosexual Emancipation Movement in Germany*, pp. 32–40; quotation is from p. 33.

31. On the discursive complications of this case see James Steakley, "Iconography of a Scandal: Political Cartoons and the Eulenburg Affair," *Studies in Visual Communication* 9, no. 2 (Spring 1983): 20–49; on the motives and consequences of Hirschfeld's participation, see esp. pp. 30, 32, 42–44; on *Brand v. Bulow*, pp. 30–32. Charlus follows the case closely and, while admiring the discretion of Eulenberg and the other accused noblemen in not implicating the emperor (C 979), is obviously not interested in reproducing it.

32. On this see Richard Plant, *The Pink Triangle: The Nazi War against Homosexuals* (New York: Henry Holt, 1986), pp. 45–49.

33. A characteristic paragraph from McDonald, who has written regular columns for *Christopher Street* and the *Native*, as well as movie books and invigorating collections of sex anecdotes:

Those Lips, Those Hips

Homosexuals demonstrating against Justice Burger's August 11 visit looked good on the Channel 5 news. The only outrageous gay stereotype in the segment was, as sometimes happens, a putative heterosexual, and an anti-homosexual one to boot: Justice Burger himself. He didn't go near the demonstrators, but he was shown mincing along a corridor in a limp-wristed, swivel-hipped waddle. He looked like an arrogant old queen. He was surrounded by four bodyguards. I recommend that he always be, as protection against fag-bashers who may not know who he is. (*New York Native*, no. 175 [August 25, 1986]: 17)

McDonald's explanation, in an earlier column, of his preferred assignment of epithets:

The word "bitch" is so radioactive and contagious that it boomerangs and

seemed to gay people that there was some liberatory potential in articulating the supposed homosexual secrets of men in power, often homophobic men. This selective utterance of the open secrets whose tacitness structures hierarchical enforcement can be a tragically wrong move for gay politics, as it was in the Eulenberg and Haarmann interventions. It is always an intensely volatile move, depending as it does for its special surge of polemical force on the culture's (though not on the speaker's) underlying phobic valuation of homosexual choice (and acquiescence in heterosexual exemption). And yet, where that ambient homophobia seems, as it can rightly seem, the very warp and woof of meaning itself at the most important nexuses of the culture, the composing of any intervention whose force would *not* depend on it may seem an impossible or an impossibly isolating task; while the energy and community that seem to be available from the knitting of those homophobia-rinsed threads into one's own discursive fabric are almost impossible to choose to forego, if their use can even at all be said to be optional.

Charlus gets an addictive charge out of the naming of names:

> "I knew Constantine of Greece very well indeed when he was Diadoch, he is a really splendid man. I have always thought that the Emperor Nicholas had a great affection for him. Of course I mean to imply nothing dishonourable. Princess Christian used to talk openly about it, but she is a terrible scandalmonger. As for the Tsar of the Bulgars, he is an out-and-out nancy and a monstrous liar, but very intelligent, a remarkable man. He likes me very much."

M. de Charlus, who could be so delightful, became horrid when he

---

contaminates all who use it. . . . In extreme cases, I would call someone a name associated with the opposite sex; such fag-baiters as Eddy Murphy, Cardinal O'Connor, and William F. Buckley, Jr., who have no masculinity to spare, might actually enjoy being called pricks, but I doubt that they want to be called bitches. That, therefore, is what I'd call *them*.

If there is such a thing as an authentic fag-baiter, I don't think I'd mind it; but all of the fag-baiters I read about seem to have personal reasons for their attacks— reasons which are secret, debasing, and litigious, having to do with their real attitudes toward, and in some cases experiences with, men.

I don't always live up to my high ideal of not using feminine names for women. I have called Babs Bush an old bag, when that name would be more appropriate for Bob Hope, and Nancy Reagan an old hag, when that would be more suitable for Dick Cavett. (*New York Native*, no. 163 [June 2, 1986]: 18)

Not surprisingly, McDonald picked up early and gleefully on the medical leaks about Roy Cohn ("Fag-Baiter Has AIDS," his story in the *Native* was headed [*New York Native*, no. 173 (August 11, 1986): 16]), echoing the *Times's* unconcern about confidentiality of AIDS records, though with the difference made by publication in a gay-affirmative paper with a gay audience.

touched on these subjects. He brought to them that same sort of compla-
cency which we find so exasperating in the invalid who keeps drawing
attention to his good health. I have often thought that in the "twister" of
Balbec the faithful who so longed to hear the admission which he was too
secretive to make, would in fact have been unable to endure any real
display of his mania; ill at ease, breathing with difficulty as one does in a
sick-room or in the presence of a morphine addict who takes out his
syringe in public, they would themselves have put a stop to the confidences
which they imagined they desired. . . . Thus it was that this dignified and
noble man put on the most imbecile smile to complete the following little
speech: "As there are strong presumptions of the same kind as for Ferdinand of Coburg in the case of the Emperor William, this may well be the
reason why Tsar Ferdinand has joined the side of the "Empires of Prey."
After all, it is very understandable, one is indulgent to a *sister*, one refuses
her nothing." (T 813–14)

But it is not only Charlus who names names. Nothing can be more
obvious than that the narrator, compulsively diagnosing this addiction
and others in him, has access to an inexhaustible, indeed an increasing,
plenitude of energy and artistic motive in naming Charlus's name along
with those of many, many others. Finally, openly and, decade after
decade, less openly gay readers have formed a loose, conflictual, phe-
nomenally buoyant community with straight and with openly homophobic readers to partake in both the several levels of homophobic
blackmail-cum-homosexual identification in the novel, and the even more
potent homophobic blackmail-cum-homosexual identification *of* the
novel. We must know by now, in the wracking jointure of minoritizing and
universalizing tropes of male sexual definition, better than to assume that
there is *a homosexual man* waiting to be uncovered in each of the closets
constituting and constituted by the modern regime of the closet; yet it is by
the homosexual question, which has never so far been emptied of its
homophobic impulsions, that the energy of their construction and exploitation continues to be marked.

◆   ◆   ◆

If an extension outward in concentric ripples of what is, after all, essentially Charlus's understanding of a world constituted by homophobic
homosexual recognition were the only enactment of *A la recherche*, it
would be a powerful book but not the one it is. So many other, in some
ways even more electrified filaments of meaning are knotted around that
signalizing thread of the sexual subject. In particular, the pattern of

exception and exemption, the projective poetics by which the viewer's mastery is constituted through a highly volatile categorization of what are unstably framed as objects of view, structures the book's performance of class and of artistic vocation (as it more obviously does of Jewish definition). Let me tell you why I have waited until so late to broach this pluralizing of the novel's subject, and even now barely mention it, and only with serious misgivings. I know from some experience of interacting with people about this and related material how well lubricated, in contemporary critical practice and especially that of heterosexual readers, is the one-way chute from a certain specificity of discourse around gay issues and homophobia, by way of a momentarily specific pluralizing of those issues, to—with a whoosh of relief—the terminus of a magnetic, almost religiously numinous insistence on a notional "undecidability" or "infinite plurality" of "difference" into whose vast and shadowy spaces the machinery of heterosexist presumption and homophobic projection will already, undetected, have had ample time to creep. A nominally pluralistic reading will often be a quiet way of performing for Proust the ritual of hiding the copies of *Gay Community News* and sending the lover off to the library before Mom arrives for brunch: it can de-gay the novel. So I need to emphasize that, for instance, even the extreme privileging in *A la recherche* of a certain version of authorial vocation, which is surely one of the things that let the novel's thrilling poetics of exemption work its way so deeply into the consciousness system of a young female writer for whom male homosexual panic was not in any obvious sense an item on the agenda of self-constitution—even that version of authorial vocation (rich as it is in the vibrativeness of modern instabilities of secrecy/disclosure, private/public, masculine/feminine, majority/minority, innocence/initiation, natural/artificial, growth/decadence, urbane/provincial, health/illness, same/different, cognition/paranoia, sincerity/sentimentality, voluntarity/addiction) has its terms and structure so intimately marked by the specificity of turn-of-the-century sexual crisis that to imagine a floating-free of those terms, or an infinity of non-homosexmarked alternatives to them, is already a phobic form of understanding.

Perhaps I can, though, gesture at the outline of one different, though not an alternative, angle of reading to bring to the novel.[34] That would have to do with bringing the specificity of the male homo/heterosexual

34. I was indebted, in working on this train of thought, to a valuable discussion with Jack Cameron.

crisis that so animates the book into some more direct relation to the specificity of, not a male or male-identified reader who may consume it through a direct, mimetic chain of quasi-phobic self-constitution, but a female or female-identified reader whose status as a consumer of it must be marked by a particular difference. I would want to argue that, in some ways, a woman reader is precisely the intended consumer of *A la recherche*: not just any woman reader, but specifically someone in the position of a mother, that of the narrator or of the author. If *A la recherche* is a charter text in that most intriguing of all genres, the coming-out story that doesn't come out, what is preserved by that obdurate transparency, or transparent obduracy, are after all two different effects. The first, as we have seen, is the unexhausted freshness of the highly contagious energies of a male paranoid theatricization of the male closet. The second thing preserved, however, through the incomplete address to the figure of the mother, is the attribution of an extreme or even ultimate power to an auditor who is defined, at the same time, as the person who *can't know*.

Is it not the mother to whom both the coming-out testament and its continued refusal to come out are addressed? And isn't some scene like that behind the persistent force of the novel's trope, "the profanation of the mother"? That that woman who lovingly and fearfully scrutinizes narrator and narrative *can't know* is both an analytic inference (she never acts as if she knows, and anyway how could she know?) and a blank imperative: she *mustn't* know. Imaginably, as two of Proust's earlier stories suggest, either a homosexual confession would kill the person making it (as in "Avant la Nuit") or discovery of the hidden sexuality would kill the mother herself (as in "La Confession d'une jeune fille").[35] The hint of a contradictory analysis or imperative — "She *must* know" — seemingly lends a narrative momentum to the *mustn't* of *A la recherche*; but the most striking counterweight, if it *is* a counterweight, to the absolute ignorance continually ascribed to (or prescribed for) the mother is the ascriptive absoluteness of her power over the putatively inscrutable son. The result is that the mother has a *power* over whose uses she has, however, no cognitive *control*.

This topos of the omnipotent, unknowing mother is profoundly

---

35. "Before Nightfall," translated as an appendix to Rivers, *Proust*, pp. 267–71; "A Young Girl's Confession," *Pleasures and Regrets*, trans. Louise Varèse (New York: Ecco Press, 1984), pp. 31–47. Although the latter of these stories concerns a young *woman's* relationship with a man, it is most often and most plausibly read as an account of Proust's fear that his mother would discover his early homosexual affairs.

rooted in twentieth-century gay male high culture, along the whole spectrum from Pasolini to David Leavitt, by way of, for instance, James Merrill, whose mother figures in *Divine Comedies* as the all-powerful blank space in the Ouija-board alphabet, "the breath drawn after every line, / Essential to its making as to mine."[36] In E. M. Forster's story, "The Other Boat," similarly, the homosexual panic of the main character is inflamed literally to madness by the vision of "his mother, blind-eyed in the midst of the enormous web she had spun — filaments drifting everywhere, strands catching. There was no reasoning with her or about her, she understood nothing and controlled everything."[37] If this topos hasn't been a feature of gay male criticism and theory, as it richly has of literary production, that is for an all too persuasive reason: the reinforcement it might seem to offer to unthinking linkages between (homo)sexuality and (feminine) gender, and its apparent high congruence with the homophobic insistence, popularized from Freudian sources with astonishing effect by Irving Bieber and others in the fifties and sixties, that mothers are to be "blamed" for — always unknowingly — causing their sons' homosexuality.

Only one more, spectacular example in a chain of examples of the homophobic construction, by men, of the figure of *the woman who can't know*, as the supposed ultimate consumer for presentations of male sexuality, was a flagrantly inflammatory front-page article from the *Times* of April 3, 1987: "AIDS Specter for Women: The Bisexual Man." Writing at a moment when AIDS discourse was shifting with a startling rapidity from its previous exclusive and complacent (minoritizing) focus on dangers to distinct "risk groups" to a much broader, less confident (universalizing) focus on dangers to "the general public," the *Times* journalist, Jon Nordheimer, responded to the implicit crisis of definition by attempting to interpolate the rather amorphous category of bisexual men as a new minority risk group — one that had, however, the potential of providing the deadly "bridge" by which the disease could cross over from affecting minorities to affecting the so-called general public.

This male-authored article mobilizes and ferments the anxiety and uncertainty, as it appropriates the actual voices, of women who sup-

36. James Merrill, "The Book of Ephraim," *Divine Comedies* (New York: Atheneum, 1976), p. 128.

37. E. M. Forster, *The Life to Come and Other Short Stories* (New York: Avon / Bard, 1976), p. 206.

posedly *have to know* all the secrets of men's sexuality — so that, apparently, they can avoid having any sex with bisexual men and have unprotected sex with certifiably heterosexual men. This *having to know* is artificially constructed in the article, which is carefully framed to omit the obvious, epistemologically relaxing option that these women might choose to use care and condoms in all their sexual contacts at this point. But the hyped-up imperative to know is only a foil or pretext: *must know* inevitably generates *can't know*, and *can't know* just as surely generates, in the article's main performative act, its intended object: The Shadowy Bisexual himself. For an imagined middle-class woman, the article says, "experts say"

> the figure of the male bisexual, cloaked in myth and his own secretiveness, has become the bogy-man of the late 1980's, casting a chill on past sexual encounters and prospective ones.
>
> She might also be distressed to learn that bisexuals are often secretive and complex men who, experts say, probably would not acknowledge homosexual activity even if questioned about it. Indeed, some cannot even admit such behavior to themselves.

In the unknowing, unconsenting name of the woman who can't know, and under the picture of a woman expert who says she *doesn't* know, the whole discursive machinery by which new sexual identities get constructed is trundled, for our edification, out onto the field. We learn what to say to a bisexual man ("'You're not a man!'" a woman tells her husband when she discovers "the truth" — or so we are informed by "one therapist"). We learn that their attentions impart to women "a deep sense of humiliation." We learn that bisexuals (such as "Stuart"), unlike the experts on them (such as "Dr. Alfred C. Kinsey," "Dr. Bruce Voeller," "Dr. Theresa Crenshaw"), don't have last names. We learn that there is a history of their study. We learn most crucially that bisexuals fit into five categories: "married men . . . who lead clandestine homosexual lives and rarely if ever have sexual relations with women other than their wives"; "openly bisexual men who are promiscuous only in their homosexual orientation and interact with women in a sporadic, serial manner, returning to the company of men when a relationship with a woman ends"; "those men, unsettled by identity confusion who, in the words of one expert, 'jump here and there and back again'"; "a fourth group, young men who experiment with homosexuality in college or some other environment where it is tolerated or easy to hide"; and finally, "'ambisexuals,' a small but 'dangerous' group of men who have very frequent sexual contact with both men and women." Each of these categories is more sociopathic-sounding than the last, although they seem very difficult to tell apart. No matter, however: it is the mere existence of multiple categories that guarantees the legitimacy of the classifying process. By this certifying process we, as women, learn yet another way in which we are powerless, unless we can finally master the unmasterable map of male sexuality.

And we, as historically alert readers, note that this confident proffer of "new" expertise doesn't signal any movement at all on two analytic blockages as old as the century: the transitive/separatist question about gender identity, and the minoritizing/universalizing question about sexual definition. Are these men characterized by "'their little effeminate ways,'" or are they, to the contrary, "very masculine"? Further, are they a tiny self-contained minority, as Dr. Richard A. Isay of Cornell Medical Center suggests? Or do they, rather, represent, as Dr. Fritz Klein, "a California authority on bisexuality," asserts, a vast potential among the "many men" "out there" to be "very active with both men and women"?

"The numbers on bisexuals," Dr. June Reinisch is twice quoted as saying, "have always been a problem." The problem of "the numbers on bisexuals" is only barely not the problem of the number *of* bisexuals. This article works at converting Dr. Reinisch's acknowledgment of a conceptual deadlock into a rationale for a final solution, projecting its own intractable unknowing onto women with the same gesture as it projects the entirety of male mendacity and threat onto a newly framable and themselves very endangered group of men.

In short, I would want to say, the way figures of women seem to preside, dumbly or pseudo-dumbly, over both gay and homophobic constructions of male gender identity and secrecy is among the fateful relations dramatized in and around *A la recherche*. I don't assume (and I want to emphasize this) that for women to reach in and try to occupy with more of our own cognitive and desiring animation this cynosural space which we already occupy passively, fantasmically, but none the less oppressively (all around), would be a more innocuous process, either on the part of the female reader or on that of the Proustian text, than the dangerously energizing male-directed reading relations we have been discussing so far. Willy-nilly, however, I have of course been enacting that occupation as well, all along; the wrestling into motion *that* way of this propulsive textual world cannot perhaps in the present text be my subject, as it has been my project.

Index